Zsuzsa Polgar
Hoainhan "Paul" Truong
Leslie Alan Horvitz

Alpha
Teach Yourself

Chess

in 24 hours

ALPHA

A Pearson Education Company

Alpha Teach Yourself Chess in 24 Hours

International Standard Book Number: 0-02-864408-5
Library of Congress Catalog Card Number: 2002111665

Printed in the United States of America

First printing: 2002

04   03   02   4   3   2   1

Note: This publication contains the opinions and ideas of its authors. It is intended to provide helpful and informative material on the subject matter covered. It is sold with the understanding that the authors and publisher are not engaged in rendering professional services in the book. If the reader requires personal assistance or advice, a competent professional should be consulted.

The authors and publisher specifically disclaim any responsibility for any liability, loss, or risk, personal or otherwise, which is incurred as a consequence, directly or indirectly, of the use and application of any of the contents of this book.

Trademarks

All terms mentioned in this book that are known to be or are suspected of being trademarks or service marks have been appropriately capitalized. Alpha Books and Pearson Education, Inc., cannot attest to the accuracy of this information. Use of a term in this book should not be regarded as affecting the validity of any trademark or service mark.

For marketing and publicity, please call: 317-581-3722

The publisher offers discounts on this book when ordered in quantity for bulk purchases and special sales.

For sales within the United States, please contact: Corporate and Government Sales, 1-800-382-3419 or corpsales@pearsontechgroup.com

Outside the United States, please contact: International Sales, 317-581-3793 or international@pearsontechgroup.com

ACQUISITIONS EDITOR
Gary Goldstein

DEVELOPMENT EDITOR
Tom Stevens

PRODUCTION EDITOR
Katherin Bidwell

INDEXER
Heather McNeill

PRODUCTION
Angela Calvert
Megan Douglass
Rebecca Harmon

COVER DESIGNER
Charis Santillie
Douglas Wilkins

BOOK DESIGNER
Gary Adair

MANAGING EDITOR
Jennifer Chisholm

PRODUCT MANAGER
Phil Kitchel

PUBLISHER
Marie Butler-Knight

To my parents Klara and Laszlo, my sisters Zsofia and Judit,
and my children Tommy and Leeam.
—Zsuzsa (Susan) Polgar

To my parents Martha and Michel, my brother Anthony,
and my heart and soul: my daughter Brittany and my son PJ.
—Hoainhan (Paul) Truong

Overview

Contents

APPENDIXES

Introduction

"Chess is life," said Bobby Fischer, former chess World Champion and arguably the best known (and most controversial) player in the history of the game. Boris Spassky, another former World Champion, agrees: "Chess," he said, "is everything—art, science, and sport."

You might think that both Fischer and Spassky are exaggerating—just a little. But if you are reading these words, chances are that you might have a suspicion that they are onto something. Chess isn't just a game; it's a whole world. In fact, it is now a recognized Olympic sport! But for people who are outside that world, who may know little or nothing about the game—and you might be one of those people—chess too often seems like a rarefied pastime, impossibly complicated and difficult to learn. That's why we wrote this book—to dispel that notion. Chess is actually accessible to just about anybody who is willing to put in the time and effort to learn it. Think of *Alpha Teach Yourself Chess in 24 Hours* as your guidebook to this new world.

Did you know where chess originated—or when? Or why we play with standard chess pieces on a board of sixty-four squares? You can find out the answers in the first hour where we take a look back at how chess evolved into the game we play today. Then we introduce you to the basics of the game: the significance and role of each piece, how each piece moves and captures an opponent's pieces. You'll find out how to keep score and distinguish between ranks, files, and diagonals on a chessboard. You'll discover the difference between a positional and material advantage and learn why sometimes neither player can win—or lose—a game.

In Part 2, "Now That I Know the Basics, What Is the Next Step?" you'll learn how to play an actual game. One of the features of this book is seldom found in other introductory chess books: an abundance of easy-to-read diagrams. These diagrams—and there are hundreds of them throughout—allow you to follow the course of various games, learn tactics, and avoid stumbling into traps or making critical mistakes. In Part 3, "Okay, I Know How a Game Is Played, So How Do I Get Started?" you learn about the three phases of the chess game: the opening, middlegame, and endgame. As you'll see, each phase has its own demands and challenges. A strategy that works well for one phase might turn out to be disastrous for another, and we'll take a closer look at each of these phases.

xvi | Alpha Teach Yourself Chess in 24 Hours

Did you know that there are thousands of openings and opening variations? We don't expect you to know them all—not even the most brilliant chess player could make that boast—but we do hope to show you various opening choices that may suit your style. By the same token, you will have a chance to learn how to develop a strategy for the middle- and endgames. You'll learn about pawn promotion, castling, and developing your pieces. Throughout this book, we will not only teach you what to do but what not to do.

"Chess is a fairy tale of 1001 blunders," observed Grandmaster Savielly Tartakower. One of our objectives is to help you avoid making blunders or falling into traps laid for you by your opponents. Everybody makes mistakes—even the best players once in a while—but if you pay careful attention to our lessons, and with a little practice, you won't be kicking yourself after every game wondering why you didn't see the threat from your opponent's rook until it was too late. (And to make sure that you've retained the lesson you've just read, we've added a brief quiz at the end of every hour. It won't be too tough, we promise.)

If you think of the chessboard as a battlefield, then you'll appreciate the idea that controlling as much territory as possible and keeping your enemy on the defensive are among the most important goals in playing the game. To do that, you need to gain a mastery of tactics. And it's the subject of tactics that we'll be discussing in Part 4, "I Am Confident Now. How Do I Get Better?" "Chess is 99 percent tactics," declared Richard Teichmann, a German grandmaster. You'll learn how to skewer, fork, pin, and make a discovery attack. We'll even teach you how to create a zugzwang. (No, it's not a German dance.) You'll find out that these tactical maneuvers (as well as some others) can tip a game in your favor and leave your opponent gasping in bafflement.

"Chess is ruthless," said Grandmaster Nigel Short. But chess should also be enjoyable—and it's a great way of making friends as well! So we'll be talking about other aspects of the game—beyond the chessboard. There are certain standards of behavior that are generally accepted when you play chess—what we call chess etiquette—and we'll clue you in on what they are. That way you can rest assured that win, lose, or draw, you'll be invited back to play another day.

Once you've reached the last part of our guide, you should have gained enough knowledge—and with practice, enough experience—to consider the next step: playing chess competitively. If you would like to play in a tournament, we'll give you all the information you need to enter one. If, on the other hand, you can't get to a tournament or feel that you need more time to develop your skills, you can still compete—whether against others who are at your level or even professionals—without leaving home.

In the last few years, a number of exceptional chess websites have sprung up on the Internet. These sites allow you to play games—around the clock if you so choose—with opponents who could be next door or in Ireland or Madagascar. Even if you don't play the game, you could simply chat with likeminded enthusiasts. You won't need to look any further than the appendixes for a description of the best chess sites on the Web, types of chess software appropriate for beginners and more advanced players, and a listing of chess organizations and clubs throughout the United States.

"Chess," states an old Indian proverb, "is a sea in which a gnat may drink and an elephant may bathe," which is just another way of saying that chess is a world that is open to everyone, whatever your age, sex, or background. Maybe you won't necessarily conclude that chess *is* life exactly, as Bobby Fischer maintained, but you may very well come away from reading this book thinking that chess is very much like life.

To smooth the way through the book, we've added some sidebars in each hour, where appropriate, that offer tips and information to enhance your learning experience.

GO TO ▶
Looking for more information on a subject—this will direct you to the relevant hour.

STRICTLY DEFINED
This is where you'll find brief definitions of terms used in the text.

PROCEED WITH CAUTION
This sidebar alerts you to problems or misconceptions that you need to look out for.

JUST A MINUTE
Here you'll find practical advice or reminders about how to get things done more simply and quickly.

FYI Here you'll find related information to the subject at hand.

About the Authors

Women's World Champion **Zsuzsa (Susan) Polgar**, considered by many the pioneer in women's chess and the oldest of the legendary Polgar sisters, has played chess for almost 30 years. She has spent more than 20 years as a professional chess competitor, trainer, and writer.

Zsuzsa started to play chess at the age of four. In the same year, she won the Budapest Chess Championship (for girls under 11) with a perfect 10–0 score! In 1981, at the age of 12, Zsuzsa won the World Championship for girls under 16. In 1984, she achieved the International Master title, and in that same year, at the age of 15, Zsuzsa became the highest rated woman player in the world. Zsuzsa led the Hungarian National Team (with her sisters Sophia and Judit) to win the Olympiad Gold for Hungary in 1988, ending the Soviet domination in women's chess. Between 1988 and 1994, Zsuzsa won six Olympic medals: three gold, two silver, and one bronze.

In 1991, Zsuzsa became the first woman ever to earn the grandmaster title, the highest achievement in chess. The following year in 1992, she won two World Championships: the Women's Rapid World Championship and the Women's World Blitz Championship.

Zsuzsa soundly defeated the legendary former World Champion Maia Chiburdanidze in 1994 by the score of 5.5 to 1.5, earning her a spot in the final for her fourth world championship title. In 1996, she defeated the reigning World Champion Jun Xie by the score of 8.5–4.5 to capture her fourth World Championship. In recognition of her triumph, she received the elite chess "Oscar" award for the best player of the year.

During her illustrious career, Zsuzsa has broken through every barrier to bring women's chess to a new level throughout the world. She and her sisters, Judit and Zsofia, have been the subject of countless articles and books. Today, Zsuzsa, a mother of two children (Tommy and Leeam), is concentrating on promoting chess for women and youth.

Hoainhan "Paul" Truong has played and taught chess for more than 32 years. A chess prodigy and one of the most promising juniors in Asia back in the 1970s, Paul played his first tournament at the age of five, only two weeks after he learned the rules of chess from his father. Facing other juniors four times his age, he stunned the entire country by winning the National Junior (under 21) Championship. He followed up his victory by winning the next three Junior Championships, going undefeated along the way.

In 1974, he once again achieved a startling victory, winning the overall National Championship of Vietnam at the age of eight. Paul successfully defended his title for the next four years. Unfortunately, after the fall of South Vietnam in 1975, the Communist regime did not allow Paul to compete internationally.

On April 30, 1979, Paul and his father escaped Vietnam, finally arriving in the United States on December 1, 1979. Renewing his chess career in the United States, Paul achieved the USCF (United States Chess Federation) Master Title and went on to acquire his Life Master title as well as FIDE (Federation International Des Echecs) Master title a few years later. Paul's last serious tournament took place in 1986. For the next 15 years, Paul established an incredibly successful business career. In the summer of 2001, he decided to join forces with his friend of 16 years, World Champion Zsuzsa Polgar, to work on a number of chess projects to promote chess for juniors and women in the United States.

After almost 15 years of being inactive in competitive chess, Paul entered and won his first serious tournament, the U.S. Open Blitz Championship in August 2001. Paul currently dedicates his time working on several ideas to bring youth chess and chess for women in America to a new level.

Leslie Alan Horvitz is an author and journalist with over 20 books of fiction and nonfiction to his credit. His most recent books include *Eureka: Stories of Scientific Discovery*, *Understanding Depression* (with Dr. Raymond DePaulo) and *The Complete Idiot's Guide to Evolution*.

Acknowledgments

I would like to thank my parents, Laszlo and Klara Polgar, for introducing me to this beautiful game of chess and for supporting me throughout my entire career. Special thanks also to my two sisters, all my coaches, training partners, supporters, sponsors, fans, and friends for encouraging and helping me through the years, during good and bad times.

A warm and special thanks to everyone at the Polgar Chess Center for their unconditional support and encouragement.

I wish to thank Mark Donlan for all the technical assistance. The diagrams in this book were produced with the Chessbase software.

—Zsuzsa (Susan) Polgar

I would like to thank Kathy for always believing in my ability. Special thanks to my dearest friend CK for all her support, encouragement, and loyalty. My thanks also go to my friends John Snoddy, Dr. Larry Roberman and Dr. ZZ for all their support.

My sincere appreciation to NM K. Clayton, GM A. Lein, the late NM John W. Collins, and GM S. Reshevsky, and, of course, GM Susan Polgar for assisting me in various ways during my chess career. My gratitude also goes to all my chess friends and supporters, especially the ones in Bergen County and NJ where I started chess in America—you are all great.

A warm thank you to my business partners, Bob Weissman and Dr. Mitch Felder. Thank you, Mark Donlan for your technical help. Last but not least, without Leslie Horvitz, this project would not have happened. Thank you Leslie.

—Hoainhan "Paul" Truong

PART I

Introduction to the Wonderful World of Chess

HOUR 1
The World of Chess

CHAPTER SUMMARY

LESSON PLAN:

Chess is a popular game played by more than 150 million people throughout the world. For all its mystique, though, chess is actually a very accessible game, open to people of all ages and of all socioeconomic levels.

In this hour you learn ...

- How chess began as a war game.
- How chess spread throughout the world.
- What chess and baseball have in common.
- How chess tournaments are organized nationally and internationally.
- Why a chess player is a commander-in-chief.

Chess is different from other board games in that it is a more challenging game, and it has a rich and venerable history filled with colorful legends, a lot of eccentric characters, and a surprising amount of controversy—even maiming and assassination! At one time in India, players waged their fingers on the outcome of the game, and during the Ottoman Empire, a caliph actually ordered a chess opponent put to death because he suspected him of deliberately losing a game. At various times in history, the game has been banned by governments or forbidden as sinful by religious leaders, but attempts to ban the game proved futile. Chess fired the imagination of too many people to be suppressed for long. Moreover, chess crosses all boundaries and transcends all cultural, ethnic, religious, and socioeconomic differences.

Chess is more popular than it has ever been. To appreciate why, we need to take a look back through time to its invention, evolution, and spread, and why chess remains what it began as in ancient India—a game of war.

EXPLORING CHESS HISTORY

Chess is one of the oldest and most popular board games ever played. It was created some time prior to 600 C.E. in northern India at a time when the military enjoyed a prominent position in society. In the military aristocracy—called the *Ksatriyan*—a challenge to a board game was like being challenged to a duel, so to play a board game like chess or one of its predecessors was equivalent to going to battle.

Chess seems to have emerged from much simpler games, one of which was called asthapada. It's difficult to know exactly how these simpler board games evolved into chess, but what is known is that asthapada served as the basis for a new board game called chaturanga, whose invention is attributed to an Indian philosopher. This new board game was based on the four corps of the Indian army: infantry, cavalry, elephants, and boatmen. In the game, four armies, each commanded by a Rajah (King), compete for power with two players being loosely allied against the other two. The board for chaturanga, like the board we know today, consisted of 64 squares. Most of the pieces are also familiar: the infantry, for instance, was symbolized by pawns, the cavalry by a knight, the elephant by a rook, and the rajah was represented by a human figure. Only the ship, representing the boatmen, has vanished from the modern game. In addition to the requirement of four players, the main difference between modern chess and chaturanga was that players threw dice to determine which piece moved each turn.

Over time chaturanga was transformed so that only two competitors were needed to play the game; however, the objective—overthrowing the ruler of the rival kingdom—stayed the same. Once the ruler was toppled, the game was lost. The most revolutionary change of this early board game came about when the Hindus, who dominated India, banned gambling. As a consequence, dice were eliminated from the game. The elimination of dice from the game was a radical step. These early board games were designed to imitate life; winning or losing was determined by whether or not luck (or the gods) favored you. When you throw dice you are gambling on fate. Fate (or karma) plays a significant role in Indian beliefs and culture. By eliminating dice from the game victory or defeat no longer depended on chance or karma. Henceforth, the player became master of his or her own destiny. Although luck still had a part to play, skill and experience, not fate, became the key to victory.

In another change to the game, the rajahs diminished in power, and the resulting game was called Shatranj. The first reference to Shatranj is found in a Persian book written about 600 C.E.

FYI Chess is known as the royal game or the game of kings not only because kings are crucial pieces in the game but because so many royal families over the centuries have enjoyed chess.

From India chess gradually began to spread around the world. In the late sixth century it reached Persia (present-day Iran), where the game was called chatrang (later shatranj after the Arabs conquered Persia).

Historians believe that by the late eighth or early ninth centuries, traders traveling across central Asia over the famous Silk Road brought chess to China, where the game was called xiangqi.

Over the years, chess pieces were changed to reflect medieval Europe: The king remained unchanged; foot soldiers became pawns; elephants became bishops; horses became knights; and chariots became rooks. Subsequently, the vizier was transformed into the queen, the most powerful piece in the game of chess.

JUST A MINUTE

It's easy to identify chess pieces:

Pawns are the smallest pieces.

Rooks look like tiny castles.

Knights resemble diminutive horse heads.

Bishops have little balls on the top.

The queen is the second tallest piece.

The king is the tallest with a cross on top.

There are at least three different accounts of how Shatranj reached Europe, but according to the most popular theory, European Crusaders of the eighth century brought the game back with them from Arab lands. However it got to Europe, the game remained much the same for the next four centuries. From time to time exotic variations were introduced, including one known as circular chess and another called the courier game, a form of extended chess played on a board consisting of 12×8 checkered squares. In 1485 the first known modern chess game was recorded, and less than a century later, the first documented chess competition took place in Madrid.

Chess was by no means always welcomed as it moved from place to place. In the eighth century, for instance, it was banned in Japan by the emperor, and a few centuries later, it was condemned by some Eastern Orthodox churches. The great Jewish philosopher Maimonides included it in a list of games he believed should be forbidden. (Later however, Jewish authorities recognized chess as a legitimate pastime observant Jews could enjoy on the Sabbath.) Nonetheless, chess continued to spread.

The following are important dates in chess history (all dates are C.E.):

- 550   Chaturanga, the earliest chess precursor, was created in the Punjab.
- 570   A form of chess was being played in China with dice.
- 900   Chess was introduced to Europe.
- 1641   The first mention of chess in America was recorded in a Dutch history of settlers.
- 1786   Benjamin Franklin published his essay "Morals of Chess."
- 1857   The first American chess association was founded.

MODERNIZING CHESS

Modern chess was developed about 500 years ago. Before that, the queen and bishop were relatively weak. In the Middle Ages, both the queen and the bishop were considered little more important than the pawn and were much more constrained in their freedom to move. These constrictions slowed the pace of the game considerably. In some way, the position of the queen in chess reflected the precarious position of flesh-and-blood queens in the Middle Ages. While the king often relied on his queen's advice, there was no guarantee that he wouldn't discard her, imprison her, or in the worst case, have her executed. Many queens schemed and intrigued to maintain their power, and in some instances actually wielded more power than the king.

In the fifteenth century, the queen and the bishop gained new prominence. The queen was given far more power and freedom of movement than the king. The bishop also acquired more power. As a result of these changes, the pace of the game picked up enormously. A good case can be made that modern chess was the product of the same historical forces responsible for the Renaissance, an unparalleled period of innovation that saw the creation of transcendent works of art, the invention of the printing press, and the discovery of America.

It didn't take long after Columbus for chess to reach the New World. Spanish settlers brought the game with them in the early fifteenth century—the Spanish were the most enthusiastic chess players in Europe at the time—and some evidence suggests that they taught the game to the Indians. We can only speculate about the early history of chess in the United States, though, because the first documented references to chess don't appear until the late 1600s and early 1700s.

Despite the absence of historical evidence, some chess historians contend that the first chess game in what is now the United States took place in St. Augustine, Florida (settled in 1565). They base their theory on the fact that the founder of St. Augustine, Pedro Menendez, was a favorite of King Philip II of Spain, who was a patron of Ruy Lopez, a famous chess-playing priest.

The best source of information about chess in early America comes from Benjamin Franklin who, along with his other remarkable accomplishments, wrote the first known account of chess, *The Morals of Chess,* which was published in 1786. Franklin was an avid player, and he regularly played with two friends, one of whom was studying Italian. Whoever lost a game, according to Franklin's rules, had to memorize a particular passage in Italian as a penalty. "As we played pretty equally," Franklin wrote, "we thus beat each other into that language." Alas, so few people knew chess that Franklin ran out of people to play with. In a letter to a friend he wrote, "Honest David Martin, Rector of our Academy, my principal antagonist at chess, is dead, and the few remaining players here are very indifferent …."

STIRRING AMERICAN ENTHUSIASM FOR CHESS

Chess didn't really catch on in the United States until the early nineteenth century. One sign of the rising interest in chess at that time was the publication in 1805 of the first chess book by an American author. We don't know the author's name, but we do know that he proposed to change the names of the pieces that he thought were "better adapted to our feelings as citizens of a free republic." In place of king, queen, rook, bishop, knight, and pawn he suggested "governor, general, colonel, major, captain, and pioneer." Needless to say, his suggestion didn't get anywhere.

PROCEED WITH CAUTION

You're not supposed to refer to the rows and columns on a chessboard as a "row" and a "column," but rather as a "rank" and a "file."

In the late 1820s and early 1830s, chess gained new popularity because of the "great chess automaton"—a kind of nineteenth-century precursor of a chess playing computer. This automaton was designed to resemble a large "mechanical brain" capable of playing masterful games of chess. In actuality, the games were played by a human being hidden inside the machine. The deception was so cleverly done, however, that the audiences invited to peer inside the machine before the exhibition began were none the wiser. That the automaton turned out to be a fraud did nothing to dampen the surging enthusiasm for the game. By the middle of the nineteenth century, chess had come into its own in America.

Between 1857 and 1860, there were only two major sports "crazes" in the United States: baseball and chess. In 1857, both chess and baseball were among the first sports to form national organizations. That was also the year that the American Chess Association was founded. Chess and baseball were so closely linked in the public's mind that Amherst College hosted a "double header," which featured both the first intercollegiate baseball game and the first intercollegiate chess match. A local newspaper called the matches, between Amherst and neighboring Williams College, a "trial of mind as well as muscle ...." The reporter added that both chess and baseball "serve as a relaxation from study, strengthen and develop body and mind."

DESIGNING THE CHESS PIECES

Until the middle of the nineteenth century, chess pieces tended to be very ornate and elegantly made or else roughly hewn wooden lumps, whose purposes were distinguished only by their height. The former were often so large that they were top-heavy and impractical (and could only be afforded by the wealthiest players), whereas the latter were simply ugly. In 1847, an English craftsman named John Jacques created chess pieces that had the advantage of being both practical, elegant, and affordable. The pieces were also easily identifiable: the king had a crown, the queen had a coronet, and the bishop had a miter. The pawn was designed to represent the Masonic symbol for square and compasses. By the end of the century, the John Jacques design had only changed slightly, mainly so that the pieces were sturdier and easier to mass-produce.

These pieces have remained the standard for chess sets since that time. Now, of course, if you want to play chess, you don't need pieces. Computer programs capable of playing chess were first written in the 1960s. The early programs were easily beaten and many chess experts were convinced that computers could never defeat human players. But chess programs have gotten increasingly more powerful and in 1997, an IBM program called Deep Blue 2 succeeded in beating Gary Kasparov, the best player in the world at the time.

TIME SAVER

When you set up your pieces, it's useful to remember that the pieces get taller as you move inward, and the queen is always placed on her own color facing your opponent's queen.

THE WORLD OF CHESS TODAY

Today, according to recent polls, 25–30 million people play chess in the United States alone. Worldwide, chess is played in more than 150 countries, and it is estimated that hundreds of millions of people know how to play chess.

What accounts for the popularity of chess? Well, for one thing, chess is one of the fairest games of all. Men, women, and children of all ages start out in chess at the same level. Children with little experience can beat adults who have played for years. There is no advantage due to height, weight, sex, age, skin color, nationality, or social class. To play, you don't have to have money or belong to a club; all you need is a chess set and a place to play (or you can play on a computer over the Internet).

Unlike other board games, chess is considered a combination of art, sport, and science. Certainly chess can be fun and can be played by everyone. But to be a competitive or professional chess player requires skill, knowledge, strategy, experience, wit, logic, focus, patience, discipline, fitness, good memory, strong nerves, mental toughness, and yes, sometimes even luck.

Chess wasn't always thought of as an equal opportunity game. At one time, chess was considered something of a rarefied pastime, competitively dominated by men who were generally wealthy and well connected. But in the last few decades, the world of competitive chess has broken wide open. For instance, the Polgar sisters from Hungary—Susan (Zsuzsa), Sophia (Zsofia), and Judit—proved to the world that women can play chess as well as men, competing with and beating their male counterparts. Nor is age a barrier to achievement: young teenagers such as Ruslan Ponomariov from Ukraine (the current World Chess Federation Champion), Teimour Radjabov from Azerbaijan, Xiangzhi Bu from China, and Andrei Volokitin from Russia are all world-class grandmasters.

FYI   Competitive chess players train as vigorously as Olympic athletes, spending up to 8 to 10 hours a day analyzing games of opponents.

In the United States, there are several noteworthy young female stars, such as the talented 18-year-old teenager International Master Irina Krush, a former U.S. Women's Chess Champion, followed by the charismatic 22-year-old Woman International Master Jennifer Shahade, the reigning U.S. Women's Champion. The future of men's chess in the U.S. will be in the hands of the sensational Hikaru Nakamura (14 years old and the youngest International

Master in the country and reigning U.S. Junior Champion), the dynamic International Master Dmitry Schneider (17 years old), and International Master Vinay Bhat (17 years old).

PROCEED WITH CAUTION

Chess is not just about skill, it's also about psychology. The more you know about your opponent, the more advantage you will most likely have when you play against him or her.

ORGANIZING CHESS PLAY

National and international chess competition is governed by several chess organizations that regularly hold tournaments and award rankings based on players' performance. The most important chess organization is the World Chess Federation, which is also known by its French acronym FIDE (Fédération Internationale des échecs) and was founded on July 20, 1924, in Paris, France. With its headquarters in Switzerland, FIDE is the umbrella organization for hundreds of national chess federations, as reflected by its motto: *Gens Una Sumus* (we are one family). National chess federations, such as USCF (United States Chess Federation), which have been admitted to FIDE, have principal authority over chess activities in their respective countries. With 156 member countries and more than 5 million registered chess players worldwide, FIDE is one of the largest organizations recognized by the IOC (International Olympic Committee).

FYI The U.S. Chess Federation boasts 88,000 members and publishes two magazines, *Chess Life* and *Schoolmates* (for scholastic and novice players).

FIDE awards the following international chess titles:

- Grandmaster (GM)
- International Master (IM)
- FIDE Master (FM)
- Woman Grandmaster (WGM)
- Woman International Master (WIM)
- Woman FIDE Master (WFM)
- International Arbiter (IA)

LEARNING THE BASICS

To the average person, chess may seem like a very difficult and complicated game. It is certainly a lot easier to follow other games such as golf or tennis, where you can tell who is winning or losing based on the score. Chess, on the other hand, is more complex. Different people observing the exact same chess game in progress can come up with different evaluations for whom they believe has the best chance of winning. But the mystique of the game, which can sometimes prove so puzzling to novices, also makes it more interesting and challenging.

Does that mean that you can only enjoy the game of chess after years of studying and playing? Absolutely not! While playing chess at the highest professional level may be difficult, learning, playing, and enjoying the game are actually quite simple. You can teach yourself chess with the help of this book in 24 hours or less, and once you have mastered its lessons, you can enjoy chess for a lifetime.

GO TO ▷
To learn about the basic moves of chess, please go to Hour 3.

Think of chess the way the Indians did centuries ago, as a war game—a Battle of the Minds—that is played on a 64-square chessboard. The two players ultimately act as opposing commanders-in-chief, controlling their own armed forces represented by chess pieces. To win, they employ various strategies; by anticipating their opponent's next move, they can then determine the best way to maneuver their own armed forces.

One opponent plays the white pieces and the other plays the black pieces. In a friendly game, who plays white and who plays black can be decided by a coin toss. In a tournament, however, it is the tournament director who decides which color a player is given based on tournament guidelines.

The player with the white pieces always makes the first move. After that, the players move alternately. Only one move can be made at a time and the game is played until one player resigns, is *checkmated*, or the game is drawn. To ensure the game does not go on indefinitely, most serious chess games are played by the clock. The players are given a certain amount of time to complete the game. The time control can be varied from game to game or tournament to tournament.

STRICTLY DEFINED

Checkmate means to prevent or thwart any movement of an opponent's king, leading to the opponent's defeat.

The 64 squares of the chessboard are arranged in eight rows of eight. Each player starts with 16 pieces: one king, one queen, two rooks (or castles), two bishops, two knights, and eight pawns. In our next hour, we learn more about these pieces and gain some insights to their capabilities and their limitations.

HOUR'S UP!

1. True or False: Chess was invented in Northern India.

2. True or False: The earliest precursor of chess was called shatranj.

3. True or False: The modern game of chess came about because of the new importance given to the queen and the knight.

4. True or False: Chess didn't become popular in the United States until the middle of the nineteenth century.

5. True or False: Over 150 million people in over 150 countries play chess.

6. True or False: An international master has a higher rank than a grandmaster.

7. True or False: FIDE is the French acronym for the International Chess Federation.

8. True or False: Each player in a chess game has 14 pieces.

9. True or False: The player who begins with white plays first.

10. True or False: Time constraints are imposed on chess games to make certain that the games don't last indefinitely.

HOUR 2

How to Set Up the Board and Pieces

CHAPTER SUMMARY

LESSON PLAN:

Learning the pieces is a must, but learning the chessboard is important, too.

In this hour you learn …

- How the chessboard is arranged.
- What are ranks and files.
- How to set up black and white pieces.
- Why kings are fragile and queens have more power and freedom.
- How to move the pieces.

Each chess piece has advantages and limitations. Some pieces can move diagonally, for instance, while others must move in a straight line. Some pieces are capable of moving several squares while others are can only move one square at a time. Where any piece is moved can be designated by latitude and longitude.

GETTING TO KNOW THE CHESSBOARD

Before a game of chess can be started, one must know how to set up the board. To do that, and to begin playing, one must know the parts of the board. Let's go through this step by step together.

A chessboard consists of 64 squares on an 8×8 board, with alternate colors (light and dark). The chessboard must be set up with a lighter square in the right corner. (See the following figure.)

When setting up your chessboard, be sure to place it so that a lighter corner is to your right as you face it.

LEARNING ABOUT FILES

The eight vertical columns on a chessboard are referred to as files, designated by the letters a, b, c, d, e, f, g, h. (See the following figure.)

The dots are on those squares that make up the e file.

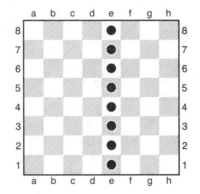

LEARNING ABOUT RANKS

On a chessboard there are also eight ranks. Ranks are the rows that extend horizontally across the board (see the following figure). White sets up the pieces on the first and second ranks while black sets up the pieces on the seventh and eighth ranks.

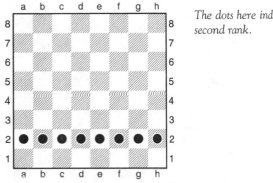

The dots here indicate the second rank.

LEARNING ABOUT DIAGONALS

Diagonals are rows of squares of the same color slanting across the board. There are many diagonals on the chessboard (see the following figures).

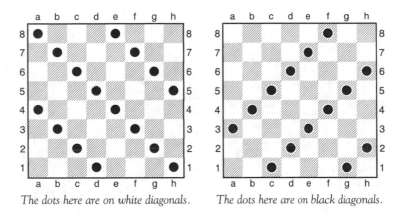

The dots here are on white diagonals.   *The dots here are on black diagonals.*

LEARNING NOTATION

To designate a location on a map, geographers refer to longitude and latitude coordinates. Chess players use coordinates, too, so that they can record the progress of their games by indicating the location of their pieces after every move. This system of coordinates is based on a combination of letters (from a–h) and numbers (from 1–8) and is called *algebraic notation* (see diagram below). The files are designated by letters, and the ranks are designated by numbers. Letters are always used to pinpoint the files, and numbers are always used to pinpoint the ranks.

Algebraic notation is the term used to refer to the combination of letters and numbers that designate the coordinates of the chessboard.

The files are indicated by letters, and the ranks are indicated by numbers.

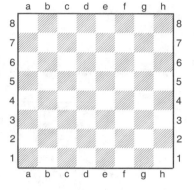

When referring to coordinates, the letter will always precede the number. See the following figures for examples.

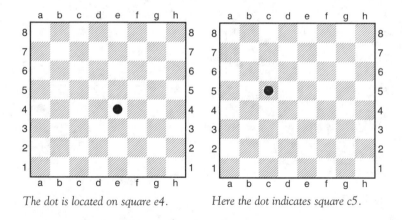

The dot is located on square e4.   *Here the dot indicates square c5.*

PUTTING THE PIECES IN PLACE

Each player has 16 pieces (of 6 types) as shown in the following table and figure.

Piece	Symbol	Piece	Symbol
king	K	bishop	B
queen	Q	knight	N
rook	R	pawn	P

The symbols shown in the preceding table are important for notation, which is discussed further in the next hour and used throughout this book.

Although chess pieces come in a variety of designs, those pictured here are fairly typical. From left to right: king, queen, bishop, knight, rook, and pawn.

Both white and black have eight pawns each. White's eight pawns always start the game on the second rank and black's eight pawns always start on the seventh rank. Ranks, remember, are the lines running across the board.

White's other pieces always start on the first rank, and black's other pieces always start on the eighth rank:

- Rooks are placed on the a and h files. Files are the lines running up and down the board.
- Knights are placed on the b and g files.
- Bishops are placed on the c and f files.
- Queens are placed on the d file.
- Kings are placed on the e file.

Sound complicated? It really isn't. Take a look at the following figure, and you can see how all the pieces are set up for both sides.

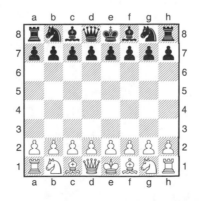

Here are all the pieces set and ready for a game.

INTRODUCING THE CHESS PIECES

Now that you know how to position the board and the pieces, let's look at the movement and power of each piece.

THE KING

The king is the most vital piece in chess. If you lose your king, you lose the game. Therefore, you must protect the king from being *captured* at all cost.

STRICTLY DEFINED

When a piece is captured it is removed from the board and replaced on its square by the capturing piece.

JUST A MINUTE

The object of chess is to checkmate your opponent's king, which means putting the king in a position in which capture cannot be avoided on the next move.

The following figure shows the starting position for the king on both sides.

The white king always starts on the e1 square and the black king on the e8 square.

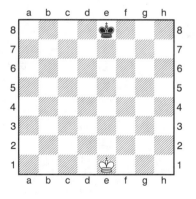

The king can move any direction on the board (horizontally, vertically, or diagonally), but even though he is important, he can only move one square at a time. See the following figure.

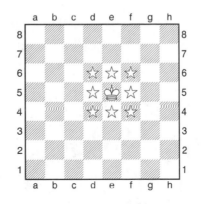

Here the stars indicate all the king's possible moves.

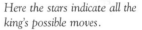

Looking at the preceding figure, notice that the king can move to eight different squares: d6, e6, f6, d5, f5, d4, e4, or f4.

Now take a look at the following two figures. In the left figure, the king can move to five possible squares: h5, g5, g4, g3, h3. But sometimes the king's moves are very limited, as shown in the following figure on the right. Here the king can only move to three possible squares: h2, g2, and g1.

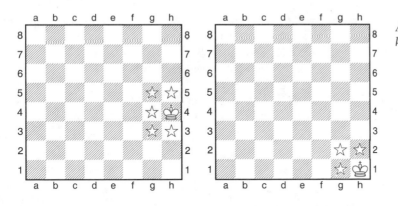

Again, the stars indicate the king's possible moves.

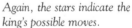

FYI The king can capture any of the opponent's pawns or pieces that are in a square where the king can move (unless the opponent's pawns or pieces are protected by other pieces or pawns).

The Queen

Each player has only one queen, and the following figure shows the starting position for the queen on both sides.

Queen takes her color is an easy way to remember the queen's starting position. The white queen always starts on the d1 square, which is a white square, and the black queen on the d8 square, which is a black square.

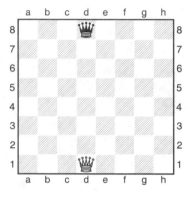

Although the king is the most vital piece on the board, his mobility, as we've seen, is pretty limited. The queen, on the other hand, is the most powerful and versatile piece in chess. The queen moves the same way the king does—that's to say, in all directions; however, whereas the king can move only one square at a time, the queen has a much longer range (see the following three figures). We say that the queen is versatile because she is able to move like both a rook and bishop combined—pieces we talk about shortly.

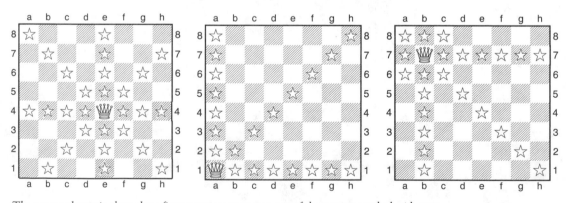

The queens shown in these three figures can move to any one of the squares marked with stars.

FYI   The queen can capture any of the opponent's pawns or pieces that are in a square where the queen can move (except the king).

THE ROOK

The rook is the second most powerful piece in chess. Each player has two rooks, as shown in the following figure.

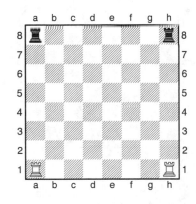

Here each of the two players' rooks are shown in their starting positions.

The rook can move horizontally or vertically to any vacant square. (See the following figure.)

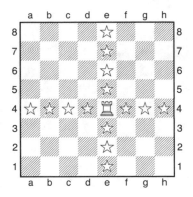

The rook can move to any vacant square located in the same rank and file.

FYI The rook can capture any of the opponent's pawns or pieces that occupies a square to which the rook can move (except the king).

THE BISHOP

The bishop moves diagonally on squares of the color it begins on. That is to say, if the bishop begins on a white square it can only move to another white square and vice versa. Additionally, the bishop can move in any diagonal direction.

Each side has two bishops, one on a white square and one on a black square, as shown in the following figure.

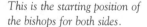

This is the starting position of the bishops for both sides.

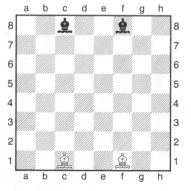

In the following figure on the left, the bishop is located on a white square; therefore, this bishop can only move to the diagonal white squares. The bishop shown in the following figure on the right moves only to the diagonal black squares.

Again, the stars indicate the possible moves for the bishop.

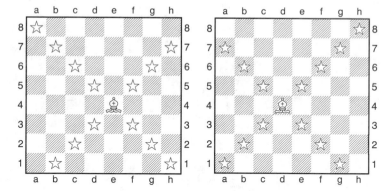

FYI   The bishop can capture any of the opponent's pawns or pieces that are in a square to which the bishop can move (except the king).

THE KNIGHT

The knight is the most unique piece in chess. Each player has two knights, as shown in the following figure.

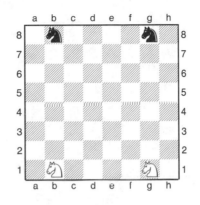

Here the knights are shown in the starting positions for both sides.

The knight's move resembles a capital L. Note that the knight must move to a square of a different color. (See the following figures.)

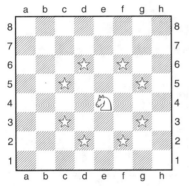

Here the knight can move to eight different squares. However, the knight must move from the light color square to a dark color square.

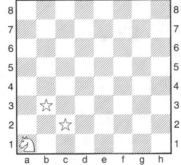

The knight shown here can move only to squares b3 and c2.

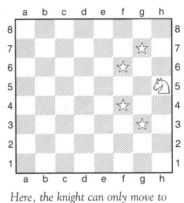

Here, the knight can only move to squares g3, g7, f4, and f6.

FYI The knight can capture any of the opponent's pawns or pieces that are in a square in which the knight can move (except the king).

THE PAWN

Pawns are basically foot soldiers. The pawn has considerably less power and mobility than all other pieces. Each side has eight pawns, as shown in the following figure.

GO TO ▶
To learn more about the pawn's unique capabilities, see Hour 3.

This is the starting position for the pawns of both sides.

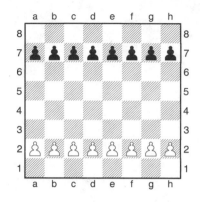

The pawn can only move in a straightforward direction one square at a time with one important exception: When you move a pawn for the first time, you have the choice of moving one or two squares, as shown in the following two figures.

As shown here, the pawn may move two squares on its first move, but thereafter moves only one square each move.

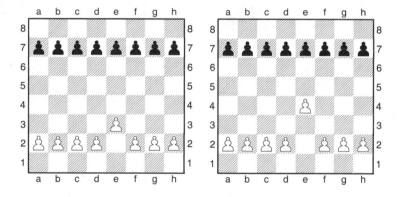

Even though the pawn can only move straight ahead, one square at a time, the pawn captures diagonally, one square ahead. The pawn cannot move or capture backward. In the following figure, the white pawn can capture either the black knight or black rook.

The pawn can take the knight on d5 or the rook on f5.

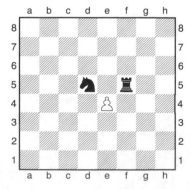

However, the pawn cannot move forward if there is an opponent's piece in front of it. (Note, however, that the pawn attacks diagonally, so even if it cannot move forward, it can still attack.) In the following figure, none of the white pawns can move forward because there are black pieces blocking them.

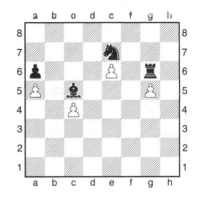

The pawn is the only piece that moves differently from how it captures. The pawn proceeds forward one square at a time, and unlike the other pieces, the pawn can never go back.

Learning the Queenside and Kingside

Now that you know about the pieces and where they're placed, we can return to the chessboard to learn the queenside and kingside. See the following figure.

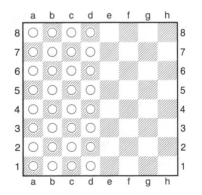

In this figure, the queenside appears on the left and the kingside on the right. All the squares with circles, starting from the a file through the d file, are the queenside. All the squares from the e file through the h file are kingside.

This concept is important for castling, which is discussed in the next hour.

HOUR'S UP!

1. True or False: A chessboard consists of 64 squares of alternating light and dark colors.

2. The vertical lines on a chessboard are referred to as:

   a. Ranks

   b. Files

   c. Diagonals

   d. Circles

3. True or False: The king can move in any direction.

4. True or False: The queen can move in any direction.

5. White's pawns always start the game on which rank?

   a. Second

   b. Seventh

   c. Sixth

   d. Eighth

6. White's pieces always start the game on which rank?

   a. First

   b. Eight

   c. Seventh

   d. Sixth

7. Black's pieces always start on which rank?

   a. First

   b. Seventh

   c. Eighth

   d. Sixth

8. True or False: A pawn can only move in one direction.

9. Bishops are placed on which files?

   a. c and f

   b. c and d

   c. f and e

   d. c and h

10. True or False: The bishop's move resembles a capital L shape.

Hour 3
Basic Rules of Chess

Chapter Summary

LESSON PLAN:

Before tackling basic chess strategy, there's more to learn about piece movement.

In this hour you learn ...

- What it means for the king to be checked—and checkmated.
- How castling can protect the king from check.
- What happens when a stalemate occurs.
- How pawns can be promoted.
- How a pawn can capture in a special way.

The pieces have some surprising capabilities, even the lowly pawn. However, let's first look at a move to keep the king safe.

Knowing How to Castle

Castling is one of the special moves or exceptions, the purpose of which is to move the king to a safer place. A player can move the king to the kingside or to the queenside. When castling is played, the king and the rook move simultaneously (counting together as one move) along the back rank. (See the following figures.)

GO TO ▶
For an explanation of queenside and kingside, see Hour 2.

STRICTLY DEFINED

Castling is a tactic to save the king from check. When castling, a player moves the king two squares toward the rook, and the rook is moved immediately to the other side of the king.

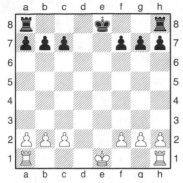

The king and rooks are shown in their original positions.

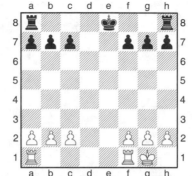

White is castling on the kingside. To do this, the king moves two squares to kingside, and the rook moves two squares toward queenside.

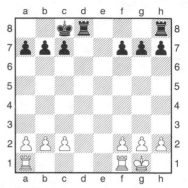

Black is castling on the queenside. To do this, the king moves two squares to the queenside, and the rook moves three squares toward the kingside.

When castling, keep the following basic rules in mind:

- The king always moves over two squares, whether it is on the kingside or queenside.
- The rook moves over two squares if it is castling to the kingside and three squares if castling to the queenside.
- The king and the rook must be on their original squares and not have been moved. Once either the rook or the king has moved, castling is no longer allowed.
- Castling is not allowed while the king is in check.
- The king cannot castle into a check.
- The king cannot castle across a check.

JUST A MINUTE

Before you think of castling, be sure that all the squares between the king and the rook are vacant.

FYI

If the rook on the queenside moved, castling into the queenside is no longer allowed. However, if the rook on the kingside has not moved yet, it is still okay to castle to the kingside.

A NOTE ON READING NOTATION

Before we go any further, we need to talk just a little about notation so that you'll understand the moves that are discussed in the following section.

A hyphen (-) is used in chess notation to indicate a move. So, for example, e8-d8 would indicate that a piece was moved from the e file on the eighth rank to the d file on the eighth rank.

To indicate exactly which piece was moved, the piece symbol is used. So, for example, were the piece being moved the king, that would be written as Ke8-d8.

Castling, however, is noted differently. The notation is 0-0 when castling on the kingside and 0-0-0 when castling on the queenside.

If a piece captures another piece, an "x" is used. So, for example, if a knight on c3 were capturing a pawn on e4, that move would be noted as Nc3xe4.

And finally, for now anyway, if the move results in a check—discussed in the following section—that is noted with a plus sign (+). So, for example, Qh6-g6+ indicates that when the queen moved from square h6 to square g6, the opposing king was placed in check.

GO TO ▶
For a more complete list of notation symbols, see Hour 9.

KNOWING HOW TO CHECK

A check occurs when the king is directly attacked by an enemy piece, as in the following figure. In other words, if the king were not moved, the enemy piece would take him and put an end to the game. When this happens, the person with the threatening piece announces "check." When the king is in check, the player of that king must remove it from check on the next move.

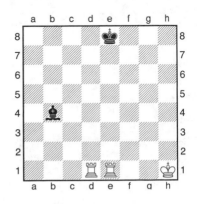

White's rook on e1 is checking black's king on e8.

MOVING OUT OF CHECK

Because a check threatens the king (and if you lose the king, you lose the game), you cannot move the king into another square that would place him in check again. So if, for example, your king were placed in the situation illustrated in the preceding figure in which the black king is being attacked by the white rook, you would need to get the king out of check. (See the following figures.)

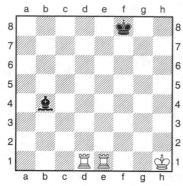

One way to get out of the check presented in the previous figure would be to move the black king to square f8, as shown here.

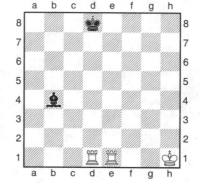

The move Ke8-d8, shown here, is not allowed because the king is moved into another check from white's rook on d1.

BLOCKING THE CHECK

Another way of defending the king against a check is to put a piece between the attacking piece and the king, as shown in the following figure.

Continuing with the preceding example, the move Be7 protects the king from white's rook.

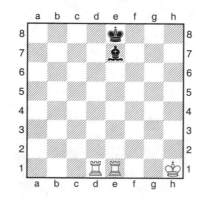

There are two exceptions to blocking a check: When a knight or a pawn check a king, the king must move or the attacking knight or pawn must be captured. There is no possible way to block a check by a knight or pawn.

JUST A MINUTE

If the king is under attack—that is to say, if the king is in check—the next move the player makes must ensure that the attack is thwarted.

CAPTURING THE ATTACKER

Another way to thwart a check is by capturing the piece attacking the king. (See the following figure.)

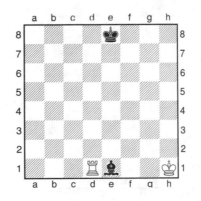

Again, continuing with the preceding example, you can see how using the bishop on b4 to capture white's rook on e1 eliminates the rook checking the king.

KNOWING HOW TO CHECKMATE

A *checkmate* occurs when there is no defense against a check. What does that mean? It means all of the following:

- The king has no safe square to move to.
- It is not possible to block the check.
- It is not possible to capture the piece that is checking the king.

STRICTLY DEFINED

A checkmate (or mate) occurs when a king is attacked and is unable to avoid capture on the next move.

In the following figure, the white rook on e8 is checking black's king on a8. Black's king cannot move; there is no piece to block the check, and black cannot capture white's rook. Therefore, it is a mate.

The three moves the black king might otherwise make—a7, b7, and b8—would leave the king remaining in check.

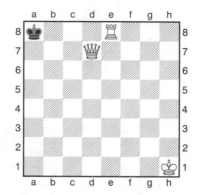

CONFRONTING A STALEMATE

A stalemate occurs when it is a player's move, his or her king is not in check, yet no legal move can be made. Should a stalemate occur, the game is considered a draw. (See the following figure.)

GO TO ▷
To learn how a stalemate can lead to a draw, see Hour 4.

It is black's turn to move, but black has no legal move. Black is stalemated.

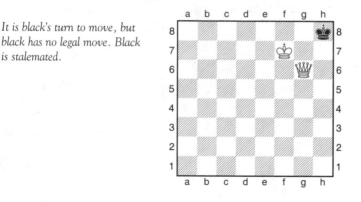

The following figures illustrate how a stalemate can occur and what you should do to avoid it.

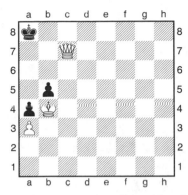

If white captures the pawn on b5 with the king, white will create a stalemate. However, if the white king makes any other move to clear the b4 square for the black pawn to move, white would avoid a stalemate.

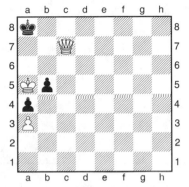

If the white king moves Kb4-a5, as shown here, no stalemate occurs because the black pawn on b5 can move to b4.

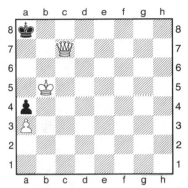

If instead the king plays Kb4xb5, it is a stalemate because black has no legal move.

A stalemate can occur when both players have few pieces left, as in the preceding figure, but it can also occur when players have many pieces, as shown in the following figure.

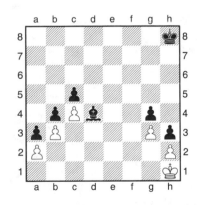

It is white's turn to move, but white has no legal move. Therefore, a stalemate results.

BENEFITING FROM PAWN PROMOTION

If an employee is competent and works hard, he or she will often be promoted to a better position. It turns out that pawns can be "promoted," too. Even though pawns have the least value of all the chess pieces, they have a unique ability to become promoted to any other piece except the king. This remarkable transformation occurs when a pawn reaches the last rank of the opponent's side. The player whose pawn it is has the right to immediately promote the pawn to a queen, rook, bishop, or knight. This is done by removing the pawn from the chessboard and replacing it with another piece, shown in the following figures.

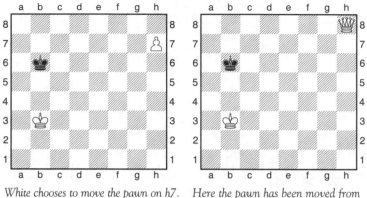

White chooses to move the pawn on h7.

Here the pawn has been moved from h7 to h8 and promoted to a queen.

In the following two figures, white decides to promote the pawn into a rook rather than a queen because promotion to a queen would result in a stalemate.

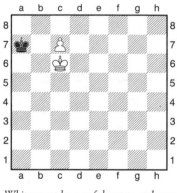

White must be careful not to stalemate black.

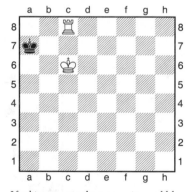

If white queens the pawn, it would be a stalemate. Promoting the pawn to a rook avoids that.

CAPTURING PAWNS BY *EN PASSANT*

En passant is another special move the pawn can make. This special move occurs when a pawn moves up two squares from the starting position and finds itself adjacent to an opponent's pawn. If this situation should arise, the opponent has the option to capture this pawn just as if it had only moved one square, which would have put it under attack. However, the opponent must make the capture immediately or the opportunity for en passant is gone forever. (See the following figures.)

STRICTLY DEFINED

En passant is French for "in passing."

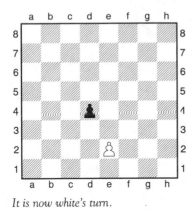

It is now white's turn.

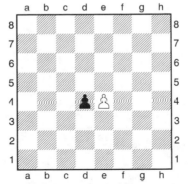

White moves the pawn from e2 to e4, and now black has the option to capture en passant.

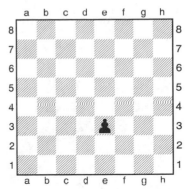

Black captures en passant by moving to e3.

HOUR'S UP!

1. Castling is a move intended to protect the
   a. King
   b. Queen
   c. Rook
   d. Bishop

2. A pawn can be promoted to any piece except for the
   a. Queen
   b. Rook
   c. King
   d. Bishop

3. True or False: En passant refers to a situation on the board in which opposing pawns occupy adjacent squares.

4. True or False: Castling can never occur if either the king or the rooks have been moved from their original positions.

5. True or False: Stalemate usually happens at the latter part of the game.

6. True or False: A stalemate occurs when one player cannot make any legal move.

7. How many different potential options are available to a player to save the king from check?
   a. 1
   b. 2
   c. 3
   d. 5

8. Which of the following chess pieces can move in a diagonal direction?

   a. Bishop

   b. Knight

   c. Rook

   d. Cardinal

9. True or False: A stalemate results in a draw.

10. True or False: The king can castle into check.

Hour 4

Piece Values, Winning, Losing, and Drawing

CHAPTER SUMMARY

LESSON PLAN:

There are a number of ways to win, lose, or draw at chess, and they relate to piece value.

In this hour you learn ...

- How to calculate the value of your chess pieces.
- How acquiring a material advantage can lead to a win.
- How you can win a game.
- How you can draw a game.
- How you can lose a game.
- How to record chess moves.

Not all games are won by checkmating your opponent's king, and likewise, you can lose a game without losing your king. How could that be? The answer lies in the specific value of each piece, except for the king. It is possible for a player to gain an advantage in value (a material advantage) over his or her opponent.

CALCULATING THE VALUES OF YOUR CHESS PIECES

In the game of chess, the goal is to capture your opponent's king. This, however, is not an easy thing to do. So as an alternative, players try to win by gaining an advantage based on the *point value* of their pieces. The player can exploit this material advantage by slowly converting it into a victory.

STRICTLY DEFINED

Point value refers to the system in chess in which values are assigned to pieces depending upon how valuable they are.

Imagine yourself in a real war situation in which you could launch an attack directly against the enemy's headquarters, but only if you wished to see your troops decimated. You would be better advised to wage a war of attrition—picking off the enemy's forces one battalion at a time, eliminating his source of supplies, and cutting off lines of retreat. That same kind of strategy can be successfully employed in a chess game as well.

In order to evaluate a chess position, the players add the values of the chess pieces remaining on the board. Usually, the player with the higher point value has the advantage. The following table shows the point values for each piece and the total point values for all the pieces combined.

Piece	Abbreviation	Value	Number Per Side	Total Values
pawn	P	1	8	8
knight	N	3	2	6
bishop	B	3	2	6
rook	R	5	2	10
queen	Q	9	1	9
king	K	priceless		
				Total: 39

By using the points, the players' positions can be evaluated. So how do we evaluate the position? Let's take a look at the following example, in which each player has already lost some pieces.

White has the following pieces remaining, and the points are calculated:

6 pawns (6 pawns × 1 point) = 6 points

2 rooks (2 rooks × 5 points) = 10 points

1 bishop (1 bishop × 3 points) = 3 points

1 queen (1 queen × 9 points) = 9 points

White's total = 28 points

Black has the following pieces remaining:

6 pawns (6 pawns × 1 point) = 6 points

2 rooks (2 rooks × 5 points) = 10 points

1 bishop (1 bishop × 3 points) = 3 points

1 queen (1 queen × 9 points) = 9 points

Black's total = 28 points

The values for both sides are the same and the game is considered equal. (See the following figure.)

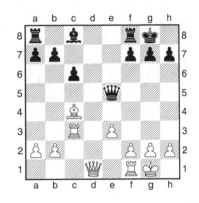

Black and white have equal material value.

Let's examine another example.

White has the following pieces remaining, and again the points are calculated:

4 pawns (4 pawns × 1 point) = 4 points

2 rooks (2 rooks × 5 points) = 10 points

1 bishop (1 bishop × 3 points) = 3 points

1 queen (1 queen × 9 points) = 9 points

White's total points = 26 points

Black has the following pieces remaining:

6 pawns (6 pawns × 1 point) = 6 points

2 rooks (2 rooks × 5 points) = 10 points

1 bishop (1 bishop × 3 points) = 3 points

1 queen (1 queen × 9 points) = 9 points

Black's total = 28 points

Black has two more points than white; therefore, black has the advantage and thus is in a better position. (See the following figure.)

In this diagram, black has material advantage.

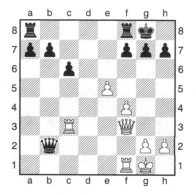

How a Game Is Won

A chess game can end several ways. One of those ways is by winning, and a chess game can be won by any of the following:

- A player checkmates the opponent.
- A player acquires such a superior material advantage that the opponent chooses to resign.
- A player wins on time (when the game is timed).

Win by Checkmate

In the following figure, it is white's turn to move, and white has two ways of checkmating black.

As will become clear in the following figures, white has two ways of checkmating black with this setup.

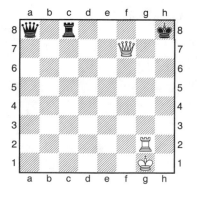

PROCEED WITH CAUTION

Even when a player is more skillful and makes mostly the best moves, a win is not guaranteed. Players have been known to play awful games and still win sometimes. In chess, even after making a series of very good moves, it is enough to make one really bad move and lose the game. Luck figures into victories as well as skill.

The first way white can checkmate black in this match is by moving his queen from f7 to g7. Black is then in check and cannot move his king, nor can he capture the threatening piece. Therefore, it is a checkmate and white wins, as shown in the following figure.

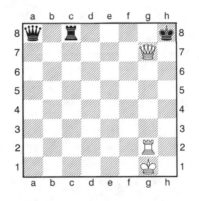

The white queen is moved from f7 to g7, putting black in checkmate.

The second way that white can checkmate black is by moving his rook from g2 to h2, as shown in the following figure. Black is then in check and cannot move his king. Therefore, it is also a checkmate and white wins.

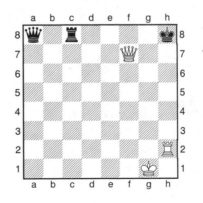

The white rook is moved from g2 to h2.

WIN BY RESIGNATION

A game can also be won if your opponent gives up or resigns. When resigning, the player gently tips his or her king over to its side. This is the gesture of resignation.

Why would a player resign if he or she hasn't been checkmated? In many cases, the player simply feels that his or her position is hopeless and that it makes more sense to resign and save time rather than playing until checkmate inevitably occurs.

In the following figure, black has two pawns and two rooks (12 points total). White has two pawns, two rooks, and a queen (21 points total). Since white's material advantage is overwhelming, black might choose to resign when confronting a position like this.

Confronting this position, black might choose to resign.

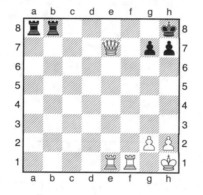

WIN BY TIME

Any chess game that is played with a chess clock can also be won on time. Each player is allotted a certain amount of time per game, or the game is based on a specified number of moves. If a player exceeds the allotted time or the maximum allotted moves, that player will lose on time, and the opponent is declared the winner.

TIME SAVER

Chess clocks are used in competitive chess. Each clock has two sides, to keep track of time used by each player.

GO TO ▷
For more on chess clocks, see Hour 18.

How a Game Is Drawn

A game can be drawn in any of the following ways:

- Both players agree to a draw.
- Neither player has mating material to checkmate.
- Perpetual check occurs.
- Repetition occurs.
- Stalemate occurs.
- The 50-move rule comes into play.

Draw by Agreement

Usually, players agree to draw because their positions are even and both have the same material. That means that neither player has a serious chance to win. Rather than wasting more time, one player may offer the other player a draw.

PROCEED WITH CAUTION

Don't agree to a draw too soon. Just because you might be low on material doesn't mean that you won't be capable of mating your opponent's king.

The following figure illustrates an even position in which neither player has a serious chance to win, a typical position for a draw.

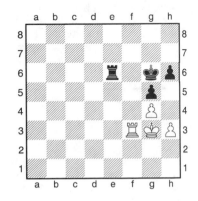

Facing this situation, the players might agree to a draw.

DRAW BY INSUFFICIENT MATING MATERIAL

A game can also be drawn if there is *insufficient mating material*—that is to say, if neither player has the pieces available for even a theoretical chance of checkmating the opponent's king. When this situation occurs, the game is automatically declared drawn.

STRICTLY DEFINED

Insufficient mating material is a situation where neither side has enough pieces on the board to checkmate the opposing king. In this case the game is drawn since it is impossible for a checkmate to occur.

The following are minimal combinations of pieces that can mate a lone king:

- Queen and king versus king
- Rook and king versus king
- Two bishops and king versus king
- 1 bishop, 1 knight, and king versus king
- 2 rooks and king versus king
- 1 queen, 1 rook, and king versus king

For example, if each player has only a king, the game is drawn because no player can win or lose with only a king.

DRAW BY PERPETUAL CHECK

A game can result in a draw by perpetual check, an unstoppable series of checks.

In the following figure, white is behind in material. To save the game, white forces a draw by perpetual check.

The black king cannot escape white's checks. (1. Qh6-g6+ Kg8-h8   2. Qg6-h6+ Kh8-g8 3. Qh6-g6+) This is a perpetual check.

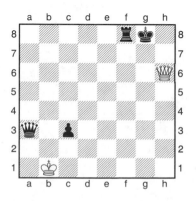

DRAW BY REPETITION OF POSITION

A game can be drawn by repeating the position: called draw by repetition of position or also known as the three-move repetition rule. A player can claim a draw when the same exact position is reached three times.

DRAW BY STALEMATE

A game can also be drawn because of a stalemate. As we mentioned in the last hour, a stalemate arises when on his or her next turn a player has no legal move to make. (See the following figure.)

PROCEED WITH CAUTION

A king is stalemated when he is not in check, and the only moves he could make would put him in check. In addition, there is also no other legal move. If this happens, the game is declared a draw.

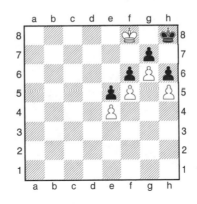

It's black's turn to move, but black has no legal move.

DRAW BY 50-MOVE RULE

If both players make 50 consecutive moves without capturing any material or moving a pawn, a player whose turn it is to move could claim a draw.

HOW A GAME IS LOST

Just as a game can be won in a number of ways, a game can be lost in a number of ways:

- A player resigns.
- A player is checkmated.
- A player runs out of time before completing the required number of moves.

These have all been discussed in the preceding sections. However, it is important to note that you can learn from your mistakes by analyzing the game to identify your problems. Sometimes you may be able to discuss your loss with the opponent who defeated you.

PROCEED WITH CAUTION

If you see that you are depleted of material or that no matter what you do you will ultimately be check-mated, it is considered rude not to offer to resign or force your opponent to play to the bitter end.

HOUR'S UP!

1. The chess value of a rook is
   a. 5
   b. 4
   c. 6
   d. 3

2. A knight is designated by which initial?
   a. K
   b. C
   c. N
   d. B

3. True or False: A player can lose without being checkmated.

4. A player signals his or her intention to resign by
   a. Inviting your opponent to dinner
   b. Tipping the king
   c. Tipping the queen
   d. Crying

5. True or False: The most popular chess notation method is called the "algebraic."

6. You have two pawns, two knights, one bishop and a king. What is the total value of your pieces?
   a. 10
   b. 12
   c. 9
   d. 11

7. An even position is likely to lead to what kind of result?

   a. A loss by either white or black

   b. A win by either white or black

   c. A stalemate

   d. A draw

8. What is the initial (symbol) for the king?

   a. R

   b. K

   c. N

   d. B

9. True or False: A chessboard is based on a grid system.

10. How many ranks are there?

    a. 6

    b. 64

    c. 8

    d. 12

PART II

Now That I Know the Basics, What Is the Next Step?

HOUR 5

Playing Your First Game

CHAPTER SUMMARY

LESSON PLAN:
There are three basic phases of the chess game.

In this hour you learn ...

- How to choose who gets white and who gets black.
- What the three phases of the game are.
- How to control the center of the board.
- How to strengthen your positions.
- How to defend your pieces.

Congratulations! Now that you are familiar with the rules and the pieces and how they move, you are ready to start the game!

HOW DO YOU START A GAME?

To start a game, you first must find an opponent. It could be a friend, a sibling, Mom or Dad, a neighbor, a classmate, and so on. Once you accomplish that, you need to decide who will play white and who will play black. You can decide that with a coin toss, or alternatively, you can take two pawns, one of each color, and put one in each hand. Hide your hands under the table or behind your back. Let your opponent choose a hand and whatever color pawn he picks, that is the color he will have.

The player who has white will make the first move. Now you are on your way. Have fun and good luck!

LEARNING THE THREE PHASES OF THE GAME

In a game of chess, there are usually three phases:

- Opening
- Middlegame
- Endgame

In the following three sections, the opening, middlegame, and endgame are illustrated with a three-minute game played over the Internet between FIDE Master Truong and Grandmaster Radjabov.

THE OPENING

The opening is the beginning stages of a chess game where the key ideas are:

- Controlling the center of the board, which means mastery of the center squares—d4, e4, d5, e5

- Developing your pieces—moving your pieces from their original squares to more effective squares

- Moving the king to safety by castling as soon as possible

The center of the board is considered the key battleground. Therefore, the player who controls the key battleground will have an advantage in the game.

FM Truong—GM Radjabov

3-minute Internet Blitz Game, 2001

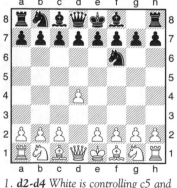

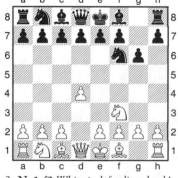

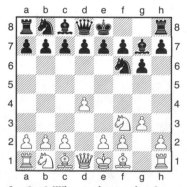

*1. **d2-d4** White is controlling c5 and e5. **Ng8-f6** Black is controlling e4 and d5.*

*2. **Ng1-f3** White is defending the d4 pawn and in the process applying more pressure on the e5 square. **g7-g6** Black is clearing the g7 square for the bishop on f8.*

*3. **g2-g3** White is clearing the g2 square for the bishop on f1. **Bf8-g7** Black is developing the bishop, clearing the path for the king to castle.*

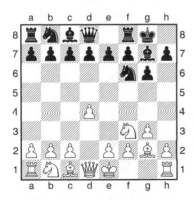

4. **Bf1-g2** *White is developing the bishop, clearing the path for the king to castle.* **0-0** *Black is moving the king to safety.*

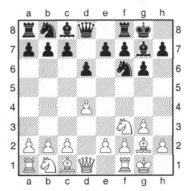

5. **0-0** *White moves the king to safety.* **d7-d6** *Black is controlling the e5 and c5 squares, clearing the c8-h3 diagonal for the bishop of c8.*

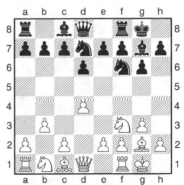

6. **b2-b3** *White is clearing the b2 square for the c1 bishop to move.* **Nb8-d7** *Black is strengthening the e5 and c5 squares.*

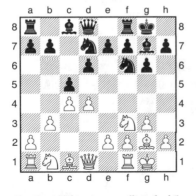

7. **c2-c4** *White is controlling the b5 and d5 squares.* **c7-c5** *Black is putting pressure on the d4 pawn and square.*

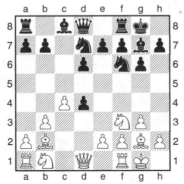

8. **Bc1-b2** *White is developing the bishop and providing reinforcement to the d4 pawn.* **c5xd4** *Black is eliminating a strong pawn from white that occupies the center.*

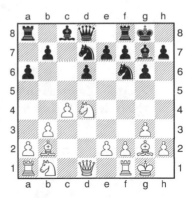

9. **Nf3xd4** *White is recapturing the pawn that's just been taken.* **a7-a6** *Black is preventing the knight on d4 from moving to the b5 square.*

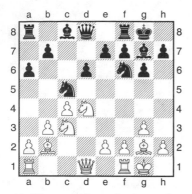

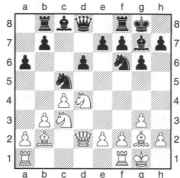

10. **Nb1-c3** *White is developing the knight, attacking the e4 and d5 squares.* **Nd7-c5** *Black is clearing the c8-h3 diagonal for the bishop on c8, putting pressure on the e4 square.*

11. **Qd1-d2** *White is developing the queen, clearing the d1 square for the rooks.* **Ra8-b8** *Black is protecting the b7 pawn, allowing the bishop on c8 to develop next move.*

All of white's pieces are developed and the rooks are connected (when the rooks protect each other without a piece in-between).

THE MIDDLEGAME

The middlegame is the phase that follows the opening and usually happens between moves 11 and 20. Admittedly, it's an ambiguous term. World Champion Alexander Alekhine once said, "Nobody has been able to define exactly when the middlegame begins or ends."

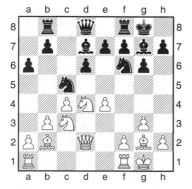

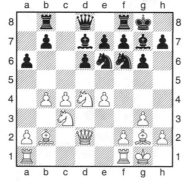

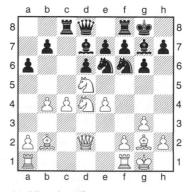

12. **e2-e4** *Now that white's pieces are developed, white wants to gain additional advantage by controlling more of the center.* **Bc8-d7** *Black is developing the last piece.*

13. **b3-b4** *White is pursuing the knight, black's most active piece that still remains in the rear.* **Nc5-e6** *Black quickly moves the knight away from danger.*

14. **Nc3-d5** *White is securing more extensive occupation of the center.* **Rb8-c8** *By placing the rook on the c file, black attacks the c4 pawn.*

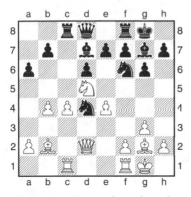

15. **Ra1-c1** *Putting the rook on the c file, white is defending the c4 pawn.* **Ne6xd4** *Black takes a strong piece from white.*

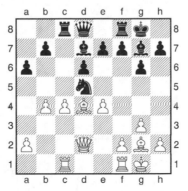

16. **Bb2xd4** *White recaptures the knight, maintaining its domination of the center.* **Nf6xd5** *Since black's position is very cramped, black is trying to exchange pieces to free up some spaces.*

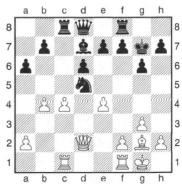

17. **Bd4xg7** *White eliminates an important piece that protects black's king.* **Kg8xg7** *Black recaptures the piece.*

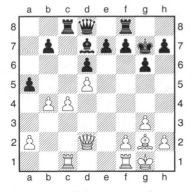

18. **e4xd5** *White recaptures the knight, maintaining its presence in the center.* **a7-a5** *Black is attacking the b4 pawn.*

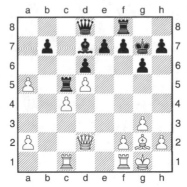

19. **b4xa5** *White captures the pawn.* **Rc8-c5** *Black gives the queen on d8 additional support to attack white's a5 pawn.*

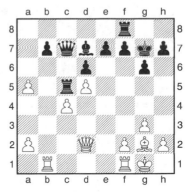

20. **Rc1-b1** *Putting the rook in the b file, white attacks the b7 pawn.* **Qd8-c7** *Black, defending the b7 pawn, is giving additional support for the rook on c5 so that it will be able to attack the c4 pawn.*

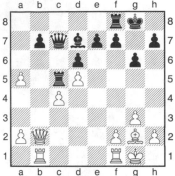

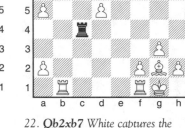

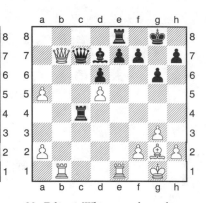

21. **Qd2-b2+** *White is checking black's king and attacking the b7 pawn.* **Kg7-g8** *Black is getting out of check.*

22. **Qb2xb7** *White captures the pawn.* **Rc5xc4** *Black captures the pawn.*

23. **Rf1-e1** *White puts the rook on the e file, attacking the e7 pawn.* **Rf8-e8** *Black is defending the e7 pawn.*

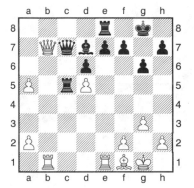

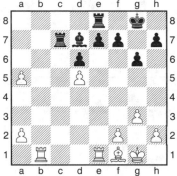

24. **Bg2-f1** *White attacks the rook at c4, giving support to the a5 pawn so that it can move to a6.* **Rc4-c5** *Black moves the rook out of danger, attacking the a5 and d5 pawn.*

25. **Qb7xc7** *White captures the queen.* **Rc5xc7** *Black captures the queen.*

The queens are off the board and most of the pieces are gone.

THE ENDGAME

The endgame is the last phase of the chess game where there are few pieces remaining. Because there are so few pieces, mating threats are less feared; therefore, the king can take a more active role. In addition, pawn promotions occur more frequently in the endgame.

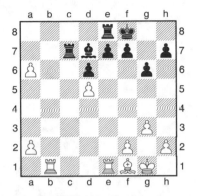

26. **a5-a6** White is advancing the passed pawn (a pawn without an opponent's pawn blocking it). **Kg8-f8** Black defends the e7 pawn, freeing the rook on e8 to make other moves.

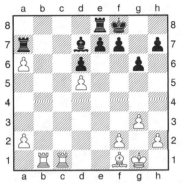

27. **Re1-c1** White moves the rook to the open c file, attacking the c7 rook. **Rc7-a7** Black moves the rook away from the attack, stopping the pawn on a6 from advancing.

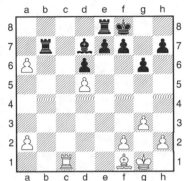

28. **Rb1-b7** White attacks the rook on a7 and bishop on d7. **Ra7xb7** Black captures white's rook.

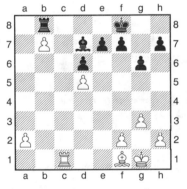

29. **a6xb7** White recaptures the rook. **Re8-b8** Black attacks the pawn on b7.

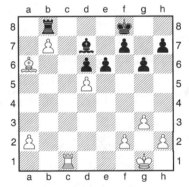

30. **Bf1-a6** White is protecting the b7 pawn. **e7-e6** Black is attacking the d5 pawn.

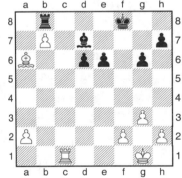

31. **d5xe6** White captures the pawn. **f7xe6** Black captures the pawn.

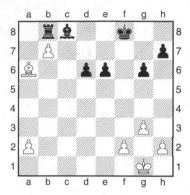

*32. **Rc1-c8+** White checks the king and attacks the rook on b8. **Bd7xc8** Black has no other choice but to capture the rook.*

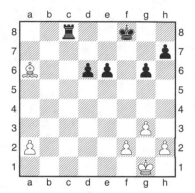

*33. **b7xc8(Q)+** White captures the bishop, queening the pawn. (The pawn is promoted because it has reached the final rank of black.) **Rb8xc8** Black has no choice but to capture the queen.*

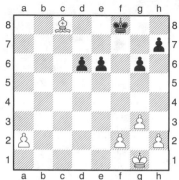

*34. **Ba6xc8** White captures black's rook. White is up a bishop. **Black resigns.** (Black's position is hopeless, being down a bishop.)*

Hour's Up!

1. True or False: Black always goes first.

2. True or False: One of the first things you want to do in a chess game is castle.

3. When we talk about developing your pieces we mean

   a. Getting your pieces out from their original positions at the start of the game

   b. Capturing your opponent's pieces

   c. Moving your pieces into strategic squares on the board

   d. Taking pictures of your pieces and sending the film to K-Mart for developing

4. In move 26, white is moving a passed pawn. This means

   a. The pawn is passing another white piece

   b. The pawn, in its initial move, can jump two squares—a special move

   c. The pawn is being passed by a black piece

   d. A pawn has no enemy pawn in front of it or next to it to stop it

5. Queening a pawn is an example of which of the following:

   a. Castling

   b. Mating

   c. Pawn promotion

   d. Stalemate

6. True or False: There are usually three phases to a chess game.

7. True or False: It is a bad idea to castle and keep your king safe.

8. True or False: In the first several moves by both white and black, the emphasis is on developing pieces and not on attacking or capturing their opponent's pieces.

9. True or False: In the model game presented in this hour, black resigned because white had a decisive material advantage.

10. A file is
    a. A vertical column of the chessboard
    b. The squares running across the chessboard
    c. The center of the chessboard
    d. A folder where you put your important documents

HOUR 6

A Guide to Basic Chess Games

By following these diagrams step-by-step, you will see how each player puts the minor pieces into play early in hope of gaining control over the center of board—the major battlefield on which the game is fought. What these diagrams show is strategy at work—why each move is significant and why if you make an error or don't pay attention, you can lose a material or positional advantage.

LEARNING HOW TO FOLLOW A CHESS GAME

With an explanation for each move, the following figures give you an idea of how a basic chess game is played.

CHAPTER SUMMARY

LESSON PLAN:

In this hour you learn how to play a basic chess game.

In this hour you learn …

- How to begin a game.
- How to deploy your pieces.
- How to control the center.
- How to attack and counter attack.
- How to defend your positions.
- How to gain positional advantage.
- How to gain material advantage.

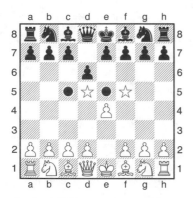

1. **e2-e4** *White occupies e4 and controls d5 and f5.* **d7-d6** *Black controls c5 and e5.*

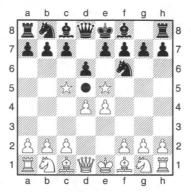

2. **d2-d4** *White occupies the d4 square and controls the c5 and e5 squares.* **Ng8-f6** *The knight attacks the e4 pawn while controlling d5.*

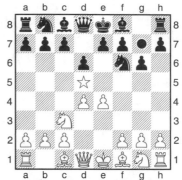

3. **Nb1-c3** *The white knight is protecting the e4 pawn while attacking the d5 square.* **g7-g6** *Black clears g7 for the bishop on f8.*

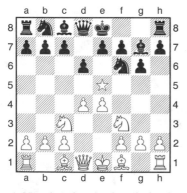

4. **Ng1-f3** *White develops the knight while putting more control on d4 and e5.* **Bf8-g7** *Black develops the bishop while clearing the space for the black king to castle.*

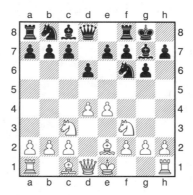

5. **Bf1-e2** *White develops the bishop while clearing space for the white king to castle.* **0-0** *Black brings the king to safety.*

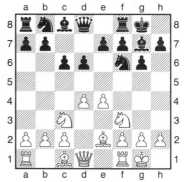

6. **0-0** *White brings the king to safety.* **c7-c6** *Black gives d5 more reinforcement.*

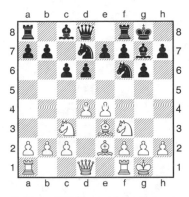

7. Bc1-e3 *White develops the last minor piece, giving additional protection for the d4 pawn.* **Nb8-d7** *Black develops the knight and gives additional support to e5.*

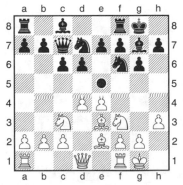

8. h2-h3 *Protecting the g4 square, white stops the knight on f6 from moving to g4 and attacking the white bishop on e3.* **Qd8-c7** *Black gives additional reinforcement to the central e5 square.*

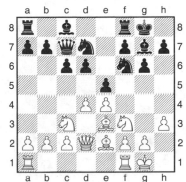

9. Qd1-d2 *White allows the two rooks to be connected and gives the bishop on e3 the backing to go to h6.* **e7-e5** *Now that black has enough support for the e5 square, black moves to occupy it.*

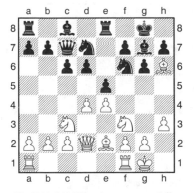

10. Be3-h6 *White's pieces are fully developed. Now, white starts to attack.* **Rf8-e8** *Black is adding more reinforcement for the e5 pawn.*

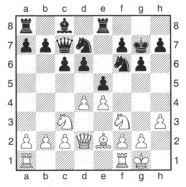

11. Bh6xg7 *White captures the bishop, an important piece that defends the black king.* **Kg8xg7** *Black recaptures the bishop.*

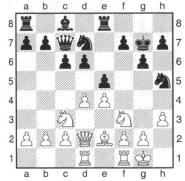

12. Ra1-d1 *White gives support to the queen on d2 to potentially attack black's pawn on d6 and to be on the d file in case it opens.* **Nf6-h5** *Black moves the knight to the h5 square to set up the attack on the white bishop on e2.*

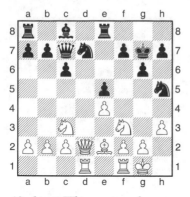

13. **d4xe5** *White captures the pawn and clears the d file for the queen and rook.* **d6xe5** *Black captures the pawn.*

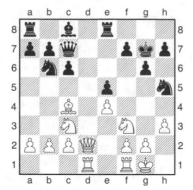

14. **Be2-c4** *White brings the bishop to a more active diagonal.* **Nd7-b6** *Black attacks the bishop on c4.*

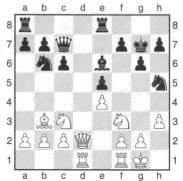

15. **Bc4-b3** *White retreats from the attack of the knight on b6.* **Bc8-e6** *Black tries to eliminate white's active bishop on the a2-g8 diagonal by offering a trade.*

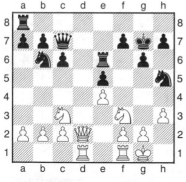

16. **Bb3xe6** *White captures the black bishop.* **Re8xe6** *Black captures the white bishop.*

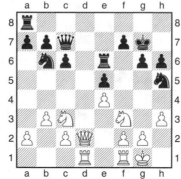

17. **b2-b3** *Protecting the c4 square, white stops the black knight on b6 from jumping to that square.* **h7-h6** *Protecting the g5 square, black stops the white knight from occupying that square.*

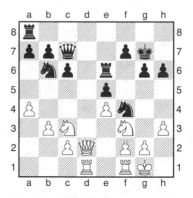

18. **a2-a4** *White's plan is to attack the knight on b6 on the next move.* **Nh5-f4** *Black brings the knight into play in front of the white king.*

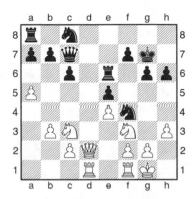

19. **a4-a5** *White is attacking the black knight.* **Nb6-c8** *Black moves the knight away from the attack.*

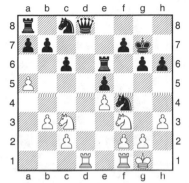

20. **Qd2-d8** *White is attacking the black queen on c7.* **Qc7xd8** *Black captures the white queen.*

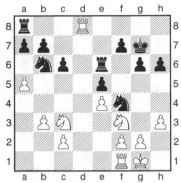

21. **Rd1xd8** *White captures the black queen.* **Nc8-b6** *Black is attempting to trade rooks.*

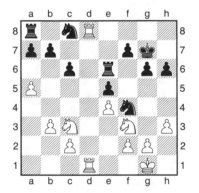

22. **Rf1-d1** *White is protecting the rook on d8. To take the knight on b6 would be a mistake because black could capture the white rook on d8 (if white plays 22. a5xb6, black will respond with Ra8xd8).* **Nb6-c8** *Now that the white rook is protected, the black knight must retreat from the attack of the white pawn on a5.*

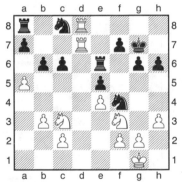

23. **Rd1-d7** *Penetrating black's territory, white is attacking the pawn on b7.* **b7-b6** *Black moves the pawn out of danger.*

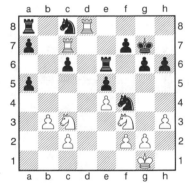

24. **Rd7-c7** *White is attacking the knight on c8 a second time using the pin.* **b6xa5** *Black captures the pawn since the knight on c8 cannot be defended. If the knight on c8 had moved, black's rook on a8 would have remained unprotected.*

GO TO ▶
For more info about pin, see Hour 14.

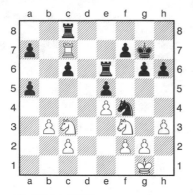

25. **Rd8xc8** White captures the knight. **Ra8xc8** Black captures the rook.

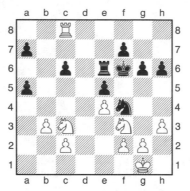

26. **Rc7xc8** White captures the rook. White won a piece. **Kg7-f6** Following the general endgame rule: Centralize your king!

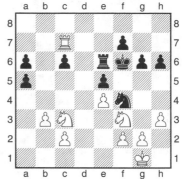

27. **Rc8-c7** White is attacking the pawn on a7. **a7-a6** Black moves the pawn away from the rook's attack.

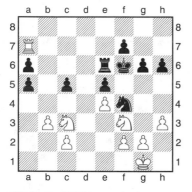

28. **Rc7-a7** White continues to chase the pawn on a6. **c6-c5** Black is clearing the sixth rank for the rook on e6 to protect the pawn on a6.

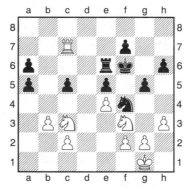

29. **Ra7-c7** Now that the a6 pawn is protected by the rook on e6, white is shifting gears to attack the black pawn on c5. **g6-g5** Black has no way of defending the c5 pawn. Black decides to give up that pawn by playing g6-g5, hoping to create some counter play on kingside.

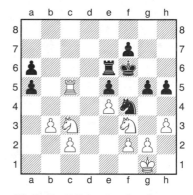

30. **Rc7xc5** Capturing the c5 pawn and attacking the a5 pawn, white continues to capture more material from black, increasing the advantage. **h6-h5** Black is attempting a desperate attack on the kingside.

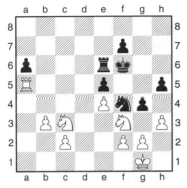

31. **Rc5xa5** *Capturing another pawn, white is accumulating more material advantage.* **g5-g4** *Attacking the knight on f3, black makes a desperate attempt to create some tension on the kingside.*

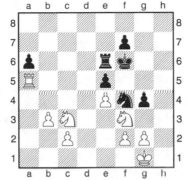

32. **h3xg4** *White captures the pawn.* **h5xg4** *Black captures the pawn.*

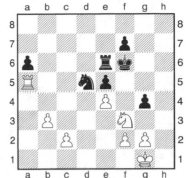

33. **Nc3-d5+** *Rather than moving the knight on f3 away from the attack of the black pawn on g4, white decides to attack by checking the black king.* **Nf4xd5** *Black captures the knight, stopping the check.*

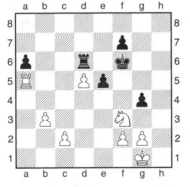

34. **e4xd5** *White captures the knight. Now the pawn is attacking the black rook on e6.* **Re6-d6** *Because the rook is more valuable than the knight, black is better off moving the rook away from the pawn's attack.*

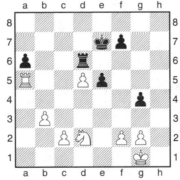

35. **Nf3-d2** *White is moving the knight away from the attack of the black pawn on g4. Now the knight on d2 is threatening to go to e4 next, checking the king while attacking the rook on d6 (this is known as forking).* **Kf6-e7** *Black is moving away from the potential check.*

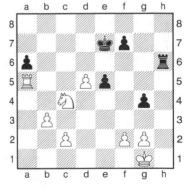

36. **Nd2-c4** *White is attacking the rook on d6 and the pawn on e5 at the same time (forking).* **Rd6-h6** *Black moves the rook away from attack; however, the pawn on e5 cannot be defended.*

GO TO ▶
For information on forking, see Hour 14.

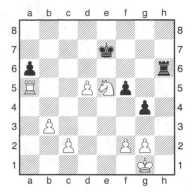

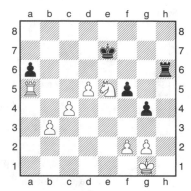

*37. **Nc4xe5** White captures the pawn, once again gaining more material advantage. **f7-f5** Black is now lost and is just gasping for air.*

*38. **c2-c4** White is marching his pawn to victory. **Black resigns** Being down one knight and two pawns, a decisive disadvantage, black decides it is time to surrender. Therefore, black resigns.*

REVIEWING THE GAME

Chess is played almost as if it were an actual battle in which strategic thinking is essential if you have any reasonable hope of winning. In our sample game, each player attacked, defended, and exploited each other's weaknesses. Each player tried to gain positional advantages and material advantages. As we have mentioned in earlier hours, at the end of the game your objective is either to capture the enemy's king or to gain such decisive material advantages that your opponent will choose to resign.

In moves 1 through 9, both players tried to control as much of the center of the board as possible while putting all their pieces out in play.

In moves 10 to 24, both players attacked and counterattacked while trying to gain positional and material advantage.

On move 25, white finally broke through black's defenses and gained material advantage after capturing the black knight on c8. From that point to the last move of the game, white solidified its material advantage by gaining more material advantages.

Finally, because too much material had been lost to mount a credible defense, black resigned.

HOUR'S UP!

1. In move 3, which player has the advantage?

   a. White

   b. Black

   c. Neither

2. In diagram 6, which player has the advantage?

   a. White

   b. Black

   c. Neither

3. In diagram 10, which player has connected the rooks?

   a. White

   b. Black

   c. Neither

   d. Both

4. Which is the best way to keep the king safe?

   a. Castling

   b. Controlling the center

   c. Developing the queen

   d. Putting the king in your pocket

5. Which of these pieces is the most important?

   a. Rook

   b. Knight

   c. Queen

6. True or False: In the basic game described in this hour, black decided to resign because of a material disadvantage.

7. On move 22, why didn't white capture the knight on b6 by playing a5xb6?

   a. White did not want to offend black

   b. White wanted to be nice

   c. Black could capture the white rook on d8

   d. Black could checkmate white immediately

8. In move 25, which player had the material advantage?

   a. White

   b. Black

   c. Neither

9. True or False: In moves 30–31, white gains substantial ground by capturing two pawns.

10. If white's pawn reached the last rank of black, white could promote the pawn for which piece?

    a. Queen

    b. Rook

    c. Bishop

    d. Any of the above

PART III

Okay, I Know How a Game Is Played, So How Do I Get Started?

Hour 7

The Right Way to Start a Game

During a chess opening, it's much more important to develop your pieces and ensure the safety of your king than it is to try to go after your opponent's pieces. Illustrating three variations of the opening phase in this hour, we see why.

CHAPTER SUMMARY

LESSON PLAN:

Getting off on the right foot is crucial for almost any enterprise you undertake in life, and it certainly holds true in chess as well.

In this hour you learn …

- How to plan the opening of a chess game.
- How to develop your pieces.
- How to protect your king.
- How to control the center of the board.
- Why attacking your opponent in the opening is likely to fail.

BASIC CHESS OPENINGS

The following are the basic objectives you need to keep in mind in the opening phase of any chess game:

- Control the center. The center is critical; it is the key battleground in the game of chess.

- Develop all your pieces as soon as possible. Remember, try not to move the same piece more than once unless it is necessary.

- Castle your king as early as possible. The king is your most important piece; therefore, make sure the king is safe.

- Do not try to attack until all your pieces are developed and your king is safe. Most attacks will not be successful unless you have all your troops and ammunition in place. That is why it is critical to bring out all your pieces as soon as possible.

ALTERNATIVE OPENING 1

The following is one of three openings that we look at in this hour.

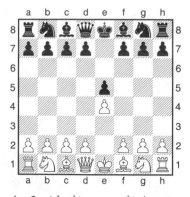 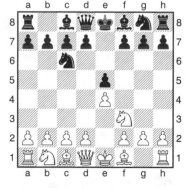 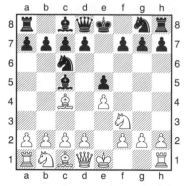

1. e2-e4 In this move, white's main purpose is to occupy the central e4 square while simultaneously exerting control over d5 and f5. In addition, by making this pawn move, the f1-a6 diagonal is open, which makes it possible for the white bishop on f1 to get out. e7-e5 Black does the same as white, occupying the e5 square while controlling d4 and f4. Similarly, black also opens the f8-a3 diagonal to allow a way out for the black bishop on f8.

2. Ng1-f3 By developing the knight, white is developing a minor piece and attacking both the e5 pawn and the central d4 square. In effect, white gains three advantages simultaneously. Nb8-c6 Because white starts the game, black is one move behind in the development of pieces. White is attacking the e5 pawn; therefore, black has to defend and protect that pawn. The knight's move in defense of the pawn protects the pawn on e5 while it controls d4.

3. Bf1-c4 White develops the bishop while controlling the center d5 square. Bf8-c5 Black also follows a similar strategy by developing the bishop and controlling the center d4 square.

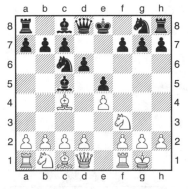

4. 0-0 *It is very important to make sure that you have the king in a safe position. Castling is the best move to do exactly that.* **d7-d6** *This move by black is important for two reasons: It adds more protection for the e5 pawn, and it clears the c8-h3 diagonal for the black bishop.*

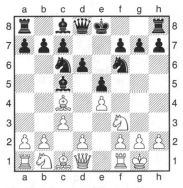

5. c2-c3 *White's move is based on one key idea: It gives additional support for d4. Because of its strategic value, this is a very important square, and if you are white you will want to put your d2 pawn on that square next.* **Ng8-f6** *Black is developing the knight and clearing space for the king to castle while attacking the pawn on e4.*

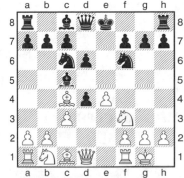

6. d2-d4 *White is following the strategy initiated in the previous move, putting the pawn on the d4 square while attacking black's bishop on c5; therefore, white does not need to waste time protecting the e4 pawn.* **e5xd4** *Black captures white's pawn, temporarily taking the pressure away from black's bishop on c5.*

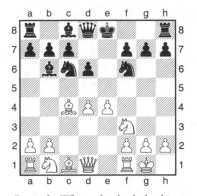

7. c3xd4 *White takes back the d4 pawn and once again is attacking black's bishop on c5.* **Bc5-b6** *Black moves the bishop to a safe square to prevent its capture.*

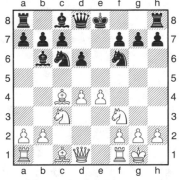

8. Nb1-c3 *White is developing the knight while protecting the e4 pawn.*

At this point of the game, the opening phase is almost complete. Black still needs to develop the bishop on c8 and the knight on g8 and to castle. White needs to connect the rooks soon by developing the queen and bishop.

What do we see so far? Both sides followed the basic objectives of chess openings:

- Developed their pieces as soon as possible.
- Moved their king to a safe place.
- Tried to control and occupy the center of the board.

ALTERNATIVE OPENING 2

Now, let's see a second example of chess openings.

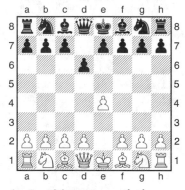

1. **e2-e4** *Moving in exactly the same way as in the previous example, white occupies e4 while controlling d5 and f5.* **d7-d6** *Black chooses a different strategy, preferring to occupy d6 while controlling c5 and e5.*

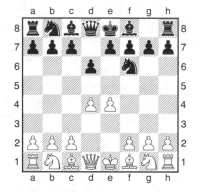

2. **d2-d4** *White now occupies d4 while controlling e5 and c5.* **Ng8-f6** *Black develops the knight while attacking the e4 pawn and controlling d5.*

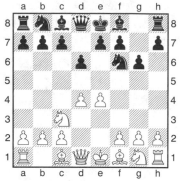

3. **Nb1-c3** *White develops the knight while protecting the pawn on e4.* **g7-g6** *Black clears the g7 square for the bishop on f8 to set the stage for the next move.*

4. **Bc1-e3** *This is a natural development move, forming part of white's opening strategy because it protects the d4 pawn.* **Bf8-g7** *Black is developing the bishop while clearing the way for the king to castle. When a bishop is developed to one of the long diagonals, the player is said to* fianchetto *the bishop.*

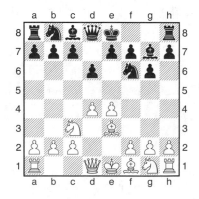

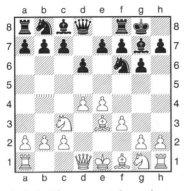

5. **f2-f3** *This move reinforces the pawn on e4.* **0-0** *Black moves the king to a safe place.*

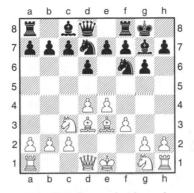

6. **Bf1-d3** *Following the plan, white is developing its other bishop while also supporting its e4 pawn.* **Nb8-d7** *Black is also developing its other knight while providing support to the e5 square.*

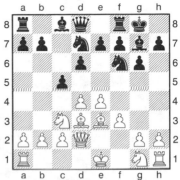

7. **Qd1-d2** *White protects the bishop on e3 while clearing the way for the king to be in a position for castling on the queenside.* **c7-c5** *Black occupies the c5 square while attacking the d4 pawn.*

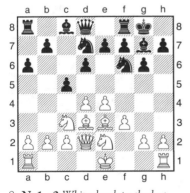

8. **Ng1-e2** *White develops the last piece. Now white has the option to castle on the kingside or queenside.* **a7-a6** *Black gives reinforcement to b5 to move the b7 pawn to b5.*

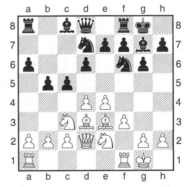

9. **0-0** *White castles on the kingside because it is a little safer than the alternative.* **b7-b5** *Black clears the b7 square for the bishop on c8 while giving support for the pawn on c5 to move to c4 next.*

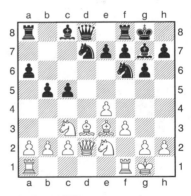

10. **d4xc5** *White captures the pawn, temporarily removing the threat of black playing c5-c4, which would trap white's bishop on d3.* **d6xc5** *Black reacts quickly, recapturing its pawn and renewing the threat of playing c5-c4 on its next move.*

*11. **Ne2-f4** White clears the way for the bishop on d3 so that it is able to retreat to e2, while also controlling d5 one more time. **Bc8-b7** Black develops the last minor piece, ending the opening phase of the game.*

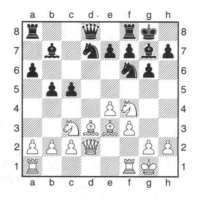

ALTERNATIVE OPENING 3

Here's a third possible way for both sides to open.

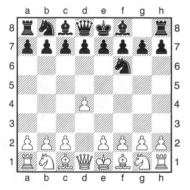

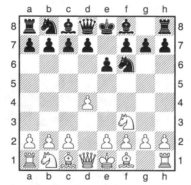

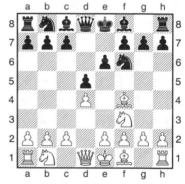

*1. **d2-d4** White occupies d4, controlling e5 and c5. **Ng8-f6** Black develops the knight, controlling d5 and e4.*

*2. **Ng1-f3** White develops the knight, defending the d4 pawn while controlling e5. **e7-e6** Black advances the pawn to clear the f8-a3 diagonal for the bishop on f8 while giving support to d5.*

*3. **Bc1-f4** White develops the bishop while increasing control of e5. **d7-d5** Black occupies d5 while increasing control of e4.*

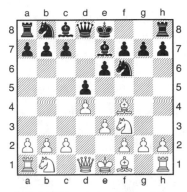

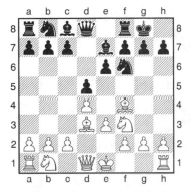

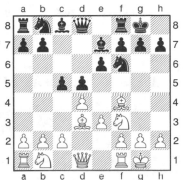

4. **e2-e3** *White clears the f1-a6 diagonal for the bishop on f1 while giving more support to the d4 pawn and the bishop on f4.* **Bf8-e7** *Black develops the bishop while clearing the path for the king to castle.*

5. **Bf1-d3** *White develops the bishop, controlling e4 while clearing the way for the king to castle.* **0-0** *Black follows through with the plan from its last move and castles, putting the king in a safer position.*

6. **0-0** *White does the same as black, putting the king in a safer position behind the h2, g2, and f2 pawns.* **c7-c5** *Black attacks the pawn on d4, trying to put more pressure in the center, which, as we have said before, represents the key battleground in a chess game.*

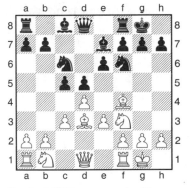

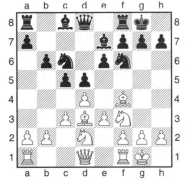

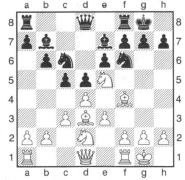

7. **c2-c3** *White protects the d4 pawn.* **Nb8-c6** *Black develops the knight while putting more pressure on the d4 pawn and e5.*

8. **Nb1-d2** *White develops the knight—white's last minor piece—while gaining more control over e4 and c4.* **b7-b6** *Black clears b7 for the bishop on c8.*

9. **Nf3-e5** *White centralizes the knight on the e5 center square while attacking the knight on c6.* **Bc8-b7** *Black develops the last minor piece while protecting the knight on c6.*

Now both sides are developed. This is where the opening phase of the game ends.

The examples above are just three random examples of thousands of possible opening variations.

REVIEWING THE IDEAS BEHIND THE CHESS OPENINGS

A chess game usually does not end in the opening. Therefore, the opening is not the time to try to checkmate your opponent. The opening phase of the game is the time to bring out all your troops, set them up, and make sure your king is in a safe place. Once all those things are accomplished, the middlegame begins and that is when attacks are made. And that's the subject of the next hour.

HOUR'S UP!

1. In the opening phase, clearing a diagonal will allow which piece to move?
   a. Rook
   b. Bishop
   c. Knight

2. True or False: It is important to develop all your pieces as soon as possible.

3. Which of the following is not the most advisable strategy to pursue in the opening of the game?
   a. Controlling the center
   b. Developing your pieces as quickly as possible
   c. Opening up diagonals for your bishops
   d. Keeping your king vulnerable by not castling

4. True or False: A game can end during the opening phase of a game.

5. True or False: Castling should occur as early as possible in the opening.

6. In general, the most important part of a chessboard is
   a. Queenside
   b. Kingside
   c. The center
   d. The color

7. In the three alternative openings in this hour, white began the game in exactly the same way in which two opening examples?

   a. Openings 1 and 3

   b. Openings 2 and 3

   c. Openings 1 and 2

8. True or False: The phase of the chess game following the opening is known as the middlegame.

9. True or False: In one move, a chess piece can accomplish three things: apply pressure to your opponent, gain more control over the center of the board, and defend one of your own pieces against capture.

10. True or False: It doesn't matter if you move the same piece more than once in the opening phase of a chess game.

Hour 8

Learning the Basics of Middlegames

CHAPTER SUMMARY

LESSON PLAN:

Now it's time to learn how to play the middlegame.

In this hour you learn …

- When the middlegame begins.
- How to develop an effective strategy.
- How to deploy your pieces to maximum effect.
- How to move decisively.

You can't be a successful chess player without a strategy. You aren't just moving pieces willy-nilly, responding to your opponent's move. Optimally, you should have a plan mapped out in your mind that you can execute, move-by-move, as the game progresses.

WHAT IS THE CHESS MIDDLEGAME?

Once all the minor pieces are developed, the rooks are connected, and the king is castled, the opening phase of the game ends and the middlegame phase begins.

In the following example taken from a classic game, you will be able to follow the strategies pursued by both players in the middlegame.

PLAYING THE MIDDLEGAME

J. R. Capablanca—D. Janowski

St.Petersburg, 1914

The figure below displays the board just as middlegame is about to begin.

1. e2-e4 e7-e5 2. Ng1-f3
Nb8-c6 3. Bf1-b5 a7-a6
4. Bb5xc6 d7xc6 5. Nb1-c3
Bf8-c5 6. d2-d3 Bc8-g4
7. Bc1-e3 Bc5xe3 8. f2xe3
Qd8-e7 9. 0-0 0-0-0
10. Qd1-e1 Ng8-h6

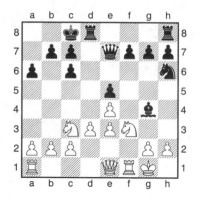

At this point in the game, black's last minor piece—the knight on g8—has been developed. This move signals the end of the opening phase of the game. Now, each side must formulate a plan and strategy to win the game. Let's take inventory:

Each player has

- One queen
- Two rooks
- Eight pawns

White has

- Two knights

Black has

- One bishop
- One knight

Therefore, both sides are even in material. White decided to castle on the kingside while black decided to castle on the queenside. So, what is the plan? How do you win in this situation?

Note that in the following middlegame, we begin with white's eleventh move (see the following figure), and then show black's eleventh move with white's twelfth move, and so on. Therefore, black's move shows an ellipsis (…) after the number, indicating that black's move is the continuation of the preceding move by white. This will better show the strategy of the middlegame.

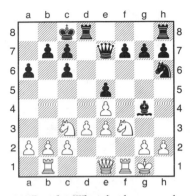

11. **Ra1-b1** *White decides to attack the black king on the queenside. To put the plan into effect, white moves the rook on the b file, giving support for the b2 pawn that will allow it to move up to b4 and later b5, destroying black's wall of defense.*

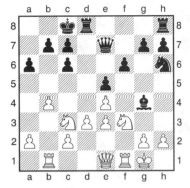

11... f7-f6 Black gives support to the e5 pawn, clearing the f7 square for black's knight on h6. **12. b2-b4** *White continues the plan to attack the black king on the queenside.*

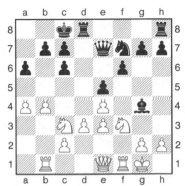

12... Nh6-f7 Black positioned the knight in such a way that he has two choices. Either he can play Nf7-d6 to help defend the queenside, or he can play Nf7-g5 to launch an attack on white's kingside. **13. a2-a4** *White continues to pursue his strategy, bringing more support for the eventual b4-b5, launching an attack on black's queenside. The next step in his plan is to play b4-b5, breaking up black's defenses.*

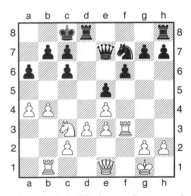

13... Bg4xf3 Black intends to get rid of the white knight on f3, allowing the knight on f7 to move to g5 and launch an attack on white's kingside. **14. Rf1xf3** *White recaptures the piece.*

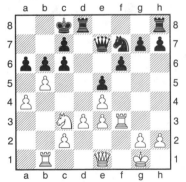

14... b7-b6 Black deploys the pawns so that they are in a position to hold off white's attack. **15. b4-b5** *Carrying out its strategy, white is attacking both a6 and c6 pawns.*

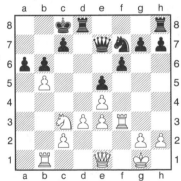

15... c6xb5 Black captures white's pawn, depleting the forces white has available to use for its attack. **16. a4xb5** *White recaptures the pawn, while continuing the attack and putting pressure on black's a6 pawn. White's objective is to break open either the a or b file, making it easier to attack the black king.*

16... a6-a5 Black is trying to protect the king. Therefore, black does not want to exchange the pawn on a6 with white's pawn on b5 because that would open up the a file. Instead, black tries to seal off the queenside by pushing the pawn on a6 to a5. 17. Nc3-d5 White wants to continue to break open black's queenside.

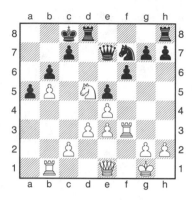

White's move is motivated by a number of considerations:

- It puts the queen on e7 under attack.
- The knight on d5 seals off the d file, which limits the power of the black rook on d8.
- The move puts pressure on the black pawns on b6 and c7.
- It clears the way for the white pawn on c2 to move to c4 and join the attack.

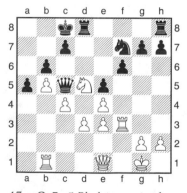

17... Qe7-c5 Black is escaping from the white knight attack. 18. c2-c4 Following its strategy, white is placing another pawn into the attack.

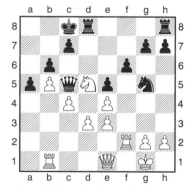

18... Nf7-g5 Black attacks the white rook on f3. 19. Rf3-f2 White moves the rook away from the attack of the knight. In addition, white is preparing to swing the rook on f2 to the queenside to renew the attack from another direction.

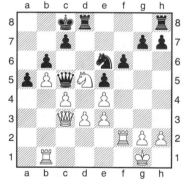

*19... Ng5-e6 Because black has not mounted much of an attack on the white kingside, black decides to bring the knight on g5 toward the queenside to aid with the defense.
20. Qe1-c3 White brings the queen into action, reinforcing d4 and making it possible for the pawn on d3 to occupy that square in the future.*

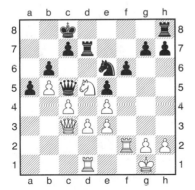

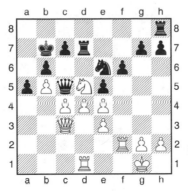

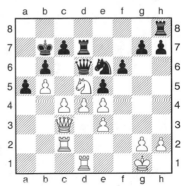

*20... **Rd8-d7** This move provides additional protection for the black pawn on c7 and clears the d8 square for the other black rook on h8.*

*21. **Rb1-d1** White's move adds more reinforcement for the white pawn on d3 to go to d4.*

*21... **Kc8-b7** Because black did not take the initiative earlier to counterattack, black is now in a dilemma. All that black can do is watch helplessly as white continues the attack on the queenside and in the center.*

*22. **d3-d4** White continues to pursue his plan, taking over the center, opening up files for the queen and rooks, and attacking the black queen on c5.*

*22... **Qc5-d6** Black withdraws the queen, moving away from the attack.*

*23. **Rf2-c2** White continues to focus on the queenside attack. By moving the rook to c2, white is preparing to play c4-c5, continuing the assault on the black queenside.*

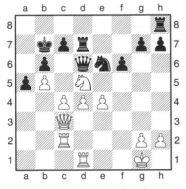

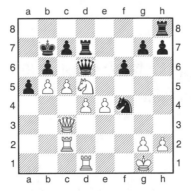

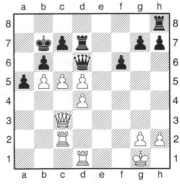

*23... **e5xd4** Capturing the white pawn, black reduces some of white's material, hoping to diminish the force of white's attack.   24. **e3xd4** White recaptures the pawn, while continuing to prepare for the next move of c4-c5, devastating black's forces in the process.*

*24... **Ne6-f4** Black continues trying to trade off as much material as possible. By exchanging pieces, it makes white's attack less dangerous. Black is making this move in the hope that white will take the knight with the white knight on d5.   25. **c4-c5** White, however, does not even bother dealing with the knight's attack. Instead, white marches its pawn to c5 in order to attack the black queen on d6.*

*25... **Nf4xd5** Black captures the key white knight while attacking the white queen on c3.   26. **e4xd5** White recaptures the knight while maintaining the attack on the black queen with the pawn on c5.*

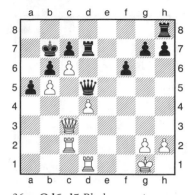

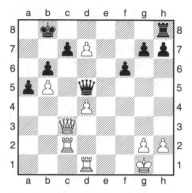

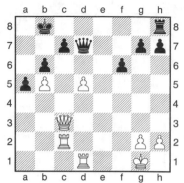

26... **Qd6xd5** *Black moves its queen to avoid direct attack by capturing the white pawn on d5.* 27. **c5-c6+** *Using a maneuver called the fork, white finally obtains a decisive breakthrough. By playing c5-c6 and checking the black king, white is also in a position to attack the black rook on d7. This gives white a decisive material advantage and thus the game.*

27... **Kb7-b8** *Black has no choice but to move its king out of check.* 28. **c6xd7** *Capturing the black rook, white now has a winning material advantage.*

28... **Qd5xd7** *Black captures the pawn. In spite of this minor victory, black is still lost.* 29. **d4-d5** *White advances the d pawn. Black's position is hopeless. Black simply resigns a few moves later.*

GO TO ▶
To learn more about the fork, see Hour 14.

GETTING A GRIP ON THE CHESS MIDDLEGAME

Once all the minor pieces are developed, the rooks are connected, and the king is castled, the middlegame phase of the game begins. At this point, you need to develop a strategy. In the game that we have just presented, the players had castled to opposite sides. White focused on the black king on the queenside. With that objective in mind, white started to move the pieces to the appropriate positions to formulate a devastating attack.

Black, on the other hand, lacked white's decisiveness. That's because black wasn't operating with any particular plan. Black shifted the pieces back and forth between the kingside and the queenside without ever presenting any real threats to his opponent's pieces. Due to black's indecisiveness, white was able to follow his plan without much resistance.

So what did we learn? Once a plan is formulated, follow through with it. Otherwise, your opponent will gain the upper hand. Of course, at a more advanced level, your opponent will try either to cross your plan or be more decisive about following through with a counterattack.

In addition, we saw that white, unlike his opponent, made certain to utilize all the pieces during the attack. By contrast, black never mobilized his pieces to optimum effect. For example, black never moved his rook on h8 until it was too late.

CREATING A WINNING STRATEGY FOR THE MIDDLEGAME

We use this game to show you the strategy from each side. When you go over the game, you will see that white tries to formulate an attack on the kingside as fast as possible, and black tries to counterattack on the queenside.

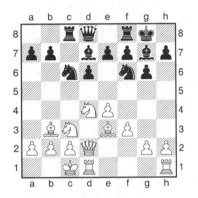

1. e2-e4 c7-c5   2. Ng1-f3
d7-d6   3. d2-d4 c5xd4
4. Nf3xd4 Ng8-f6
5. Nb1-c3 g7-g6   6. Bc1-e3
Bf8-g7   7. f2-f3 0-0
8. Qd1-d2 Nb8-c6
9. Bf1-c4 Bc8-d7
10. 0-0-0 Ra8-c8
11. Bc4-b3

At this point in the game, both sides are completely developed. Now is the time to form specific plans and strategies. When the two sides castle on the opposite side, the common plan of both players is to launch an immediate attack against the other's king.

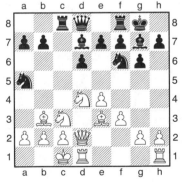

11... **Nc6-a5** Black fires the first shot, starting the launch of a queenside attack against the white king.

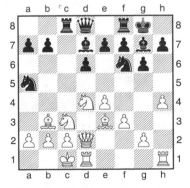

12. **h2-h4** Now it is white's turn to start a kingside attack. The purpose of this move is to play h4-h5 next to try opening the h file for a deadly attack.

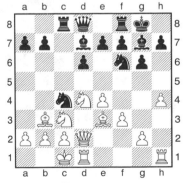

12... **Na5-c4** Black continues to pursue an attack on the white queenside. The black knight is directly attacking the white queen on d2.

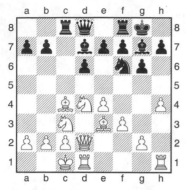

13. **Bb3xc4** *White gets rid of the active black knight, temporarily delaying black's kingside attack.*

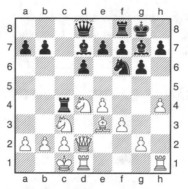

13... **Rc8xc4** *Black recaptures the bishop. The next plan is to put the queen behind the rook on c4 in an attempt to break through the c file and attack the white king.*

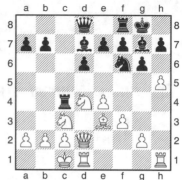

14. **h4-h5** *White does not allow black to continue the attack. Instead, white is beginning to launch an attack on the kingside, trying to open up the h file. White is even willing to sacrifice the h pawn to accomplish the goal of clearing the h file.*

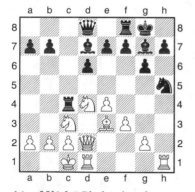

14... **Nf6xh5** *Black is forced to capture the white pawn. Otherwise, white will play h5xg6 on the next move, opening up the h file.*

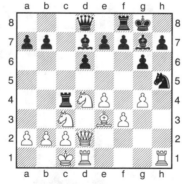

15. **g2-g4** *Since the black knight captured the white pawn on h5, the knight is temporarily closing up the h file. This move chases the knight away, clearing the h file for further attack.*

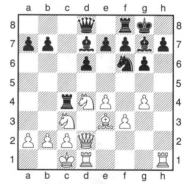

15... **Nh5-f6** *Black has no choice but to withdraw the knight. Once again, black has no opportunity to continue the attack against white on the queenside.*

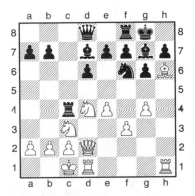

16. Be3-h6 *White is once again mounting a direct attack, stopping black from making progress on the queenside. This is a perfect example of executing a well-thought-out plan, seizing the opportunity to attack and never relinquishing the initiative.*

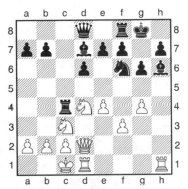

16... Bg7xh6 *Black captures the white bishop. Unfortunately for black, this move helps white to bring the queen into play, as you will see in the next move.*

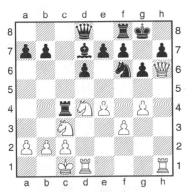

17. Qd2xh6 *White recaptures the bishop. All of a sudden, white has the queen and rook deployed directly on the most dangerous h file, putting severe pressure on the black king.*

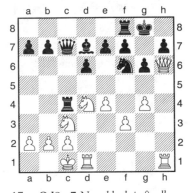

17... Qd8-c7 *Now black is finally making an attempt to revive some pressure on the queenside. Unfortunately, it is too late. White succeeds first with the dynamic attack on the kingside.*

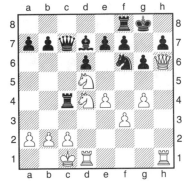

18. Nc3-d5 *White wants to capture the h7 pawn with the queen on h6 to checkmate. However, black has the knight on f6 protecting the position. Therefore, white will attempt to get rid of that knight.*

White's move to get rid of the knight is called *deflection*. This move poses many threats to black:

- Attacking the queen on c7
- Attacking the pawn on e7
- Attacking the knight on f6

STRICTLY DEFINED

Deflection is removing the guard—the piece that is guarding another piece or guarding against a checkmate.

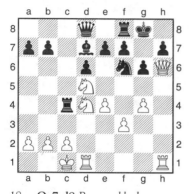

*18... **Qc7-d8** Because black cannot defend all three targets, he decides to protect the most valuable piece, the queen, by withdrawing it to d8 and defending the e7 pawn at the same time. The problem is the knight on f6, which protects the h7 pawn, is still under attack. If black would have played Nf6xd5, white could have checkmated black with Qh6xh7#.*

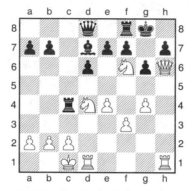

*19. **Nd5xf6+** White eliminates the black knight, the key black piece that protects the h7 pawn, thus accomplishing white's ultimate plan.*

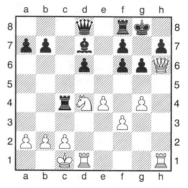

*19... **e7xf6** Black recaptures the knight, but it doesn't matter. Black is lost no matter what move he makes because the h7 pawn will fall next.*

*20. **Qh6xh7#** Mission accomplished! White finally captures the h7 pawn, checkmating black!*

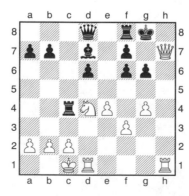

REVIEWING THE IDEAS BEHIND CHESS MIDDLEGAME

After all the pieces are developed, the middlegame phase of the game begins. In the preceding game, we described the strategy employed by both sides. White wanted to launch an attack against black on the kingside. At the same time, black wanted to launch an attack against white on the queenside.

White's plan was to open up the h file while black wanted to open up the c file. White sacrificed the h pawn to gain the momentum and initiative to attack. Black, on the other hand, was too busy defending the kingside, while failing to continue to attack on the queenside until it was too late.

In chess, every move counts, so don't waste time. Concentrate on developing your plan and relentlessly follow up with it. It is hard to win if you don't do anything and just pray that your opponent will make mistakes.

So what have we learned? Once the opening phase is over, you need to create a middlegame plan. Once a plan is formulated, follow it up as efficiently as possible even as you're trying to stop your opponent from attacking you.

HOUR'S UP!

1. True or False: Minor pieces must be developed before the middlegame can begin.
2. True or False: The middlegame phase follows the opening phase.
3. True or False: Usually, it is good to connect your rooks in the opening.
4. What is the first thing that you must do in commencing the middlegame?
   a. Launch an immediate attack.
   b. Advance your pawns.
   c. Develop a strategy.
   d. Pray that your opponent will blunder.
5. In the first game between Capablanca and Janowski, what piece was white threatening to capture with the check on move 27?
   a. Rook
   b. Queen
   c. Pawn
   d. Knight
6. True or False: White's strategy was to launch an attack directed at black's queenside.
7. True or False: Toward the end of the second game, the black queen was defending the h7 pawn against checkmate.

8. One major part of white's strategy in the second model game was to open which file?

    a. c

    b. f

    c. h

    d. a

9. One major part of black's strategy in the second model game was to open which file?

    a. c

    b. f

    c. h

    d. e

10. In the second game, which piece did white sacrifice in order to gain the momentum?

    a. Rook

    b. Bishop

    c. Knight

    d. Pawn

Hour 9

Learning the Basics of Endgames

You might have a material advantage and you might have outmaneuvered your opponent, but that's not enough—you need to checkmate your opponent's king. That's the objective of the endgame.

UNDERSTANDING OTHER CHESS SYMBOLS

Before we get started, the notation in this hour uses more symbols than you've had to up to now. The following is a list of symbols you are likely to see in the coming hours.

-	=	Move
x	=	Capturing a piece
+	=	Check
#	=	Checkmate
!	=	Good Move
!!	=	Brilliant / Incredible Move
?	=	Bad Move
??	=	Horrible Blunder
!?	=	Interesting Move
?!	=	Dubious Move
0-0	=	Castling on the Kingside
0-0-0	=	Castling on the Queenside
ep	=	*En Passant*
=	=	Even Position
+=	=	White has a Small Advantage

CHAPTER SUMMARY

LESSON PLAN:

Now that you have some idea how to open a game and how to apply a strategic plan to the middle-game, you are ready to learn the basics of the endgame.

In this hour you learn ...

- How to wrap up a chess game successfully.
- How to maneuver your opponent's king into a corner.
- Why trapping an opponent's king is the key to playing an effective endgame.
- How to win with various major and minor pieces.

=+	=	Black has a Small Advantage
+-	=	White has a Big/Winning Advantage
-+	=	Black has a Big/Winning Advantage
∞	=	Both sides have chances

Basic Chess Endgames

After you've played a hard-fought game trying to gain a decisive advantage, you want to be able to wrap the game up successfully. However, even though you may have a decisive advantage, the game is not over until it is over. Therefore, knowing how to execute the endgame strategy is critical. In this hour, you find detailed instructions on how to gain a win in basic endgame positions.

Example 1

In this first example of an endgame, white has a decisive advantage. Let's see how the game should be wrapped up by examining the following figures.

White has a king and two pawns remaining. Black has just a king.

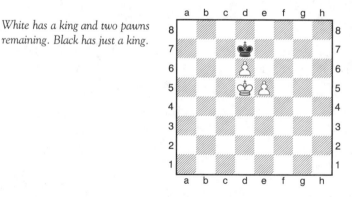

White has two *connected pawns*. White's objective is to promote one pawn to a queen.

STRICTLY DEFINED

Pawns are considered connected if two or more of them are on files beside each other. They pose more of a threat because they can provide reinforcement to each other.

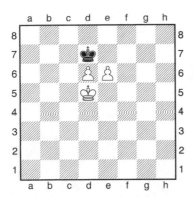

*1. **e5-e6+** Because the black king is blockading the white pawn on d6, white needs to move the e pawn to force the black king to move away. The pawn is protected by the white king on d5.*

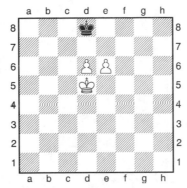

*1... **Kd7-d8** Black's king is in check, so black must withdraw the king.*

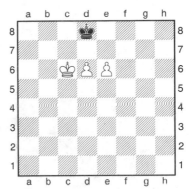

*2. **Kd5-c6** White's king moves forward, blocking the possibility of the black king from moving forward. Now the black king can only move sideways.*

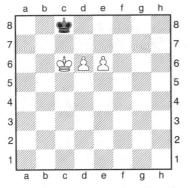

*2... **Kd8-c8** Moving to the other side (Kd8-e8) would not be any better for black's situation.*

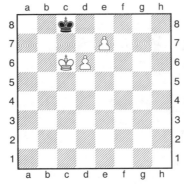

*3. **e6-e7** Once again white takes away space from the black king and is preparing to queen. Now the black king cannot even move back to the d8 square.*

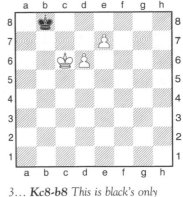

*3... **Kc8-b8** This is black's only move.*

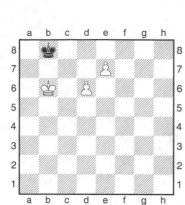

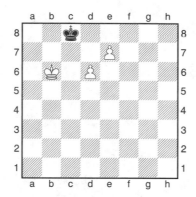

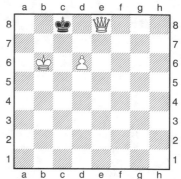

4. Kc6-b6 This is the most precise move by white because it stops black from moving the king up.

4... Kb8-c8 Black has to continue to move his king sideways.

5. e7-e8(Q)# White advances the pawn to the eighth rank, becomes a queen, and checkmates the black king.

EXAMPLE 2

In this second endgame example, white is up by a rook, which is a decisive material advantage. The question now is how to finish off black. See the following figures.

1. Rc7-c6 White is confining the black king to the corner. White does not want the king to get beyond the b file or the eighth rank. By moving the rook to c6, black is limited to only one legal move.

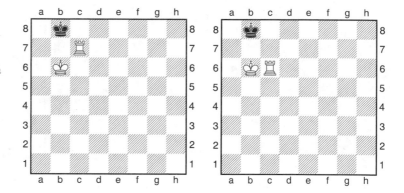

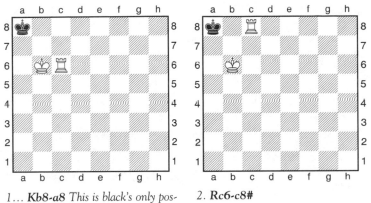

1... **Kb8-a8** *This is black's only possible move.*

2. **Rc6-c8#**

EXAMPLE 3

In this third endgame example, white is up a queen. This is a completely winning advantage, but black does not resign. How does white checkmate black? See the following figures.

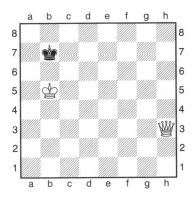

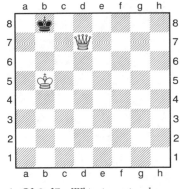

1. **Qh3-d7+** *White is cutting down the black king's escape routes.* **Kb7-b8** *Black has no choice but to withdraw the king.*

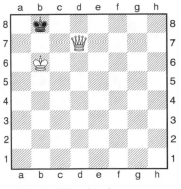

2. **Kb5-b6** *The white king is coming to help the queen checkmate black.*

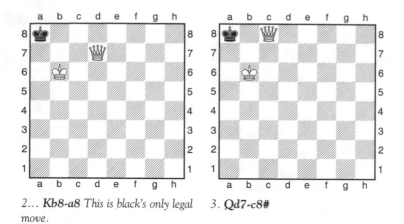

2... Kb8-a8 This is black's only legal move.

3. Qd7-c8#

EXAMPLE 4

As in the previous examples, the way to checkmate the opponent's king in the endgame is to force the king into a corner. (See the following figures.)

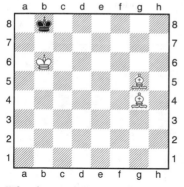

White has two bishops, and black has none. This is enough of a material advantage to score a victory.

1. Bg5-f4+ White puts the black king in check.

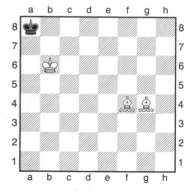

1... Kb8-a8 Black has no other choice but to move into the corner.

2. Bg4-f3# Now that the other bishop on f4 is blocking the black king from getting out, white easily mates black.

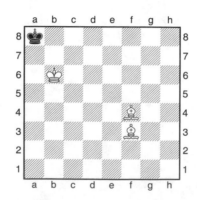

EXAMPLE 5

In this example, white has one bishop and one knight more than black. This is also enough to win. But how specifically does white win? See the following figures to find out.

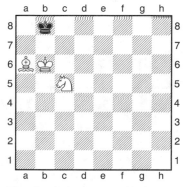

The white bishop on a6 is blocking the black king from getting out of the corner. Now is the time for the white knight to join in and work together with the bishop to mate the king.

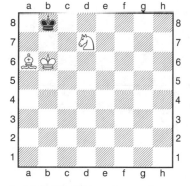

*1. **Nc5-d7+** White is forcing the black king into the corner.*

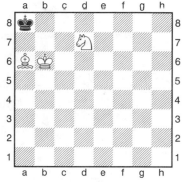

*1... **Kb8-a8** This is black's only legal move.*

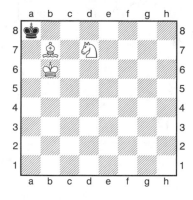

*2. **Ba6-b7#** Here the attack is coming from two directions. The white knight is stopping the king from moving to b8, and the white king on b6 is stopping the king from moving to a7. That means that the black king has nowhere to go.*

EXAMPLE 6

In the following example, white has only one pawn more than black; however, if the game is correctly played, white should win. But how? See the following figures.

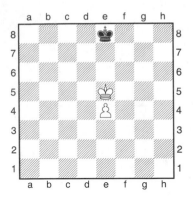

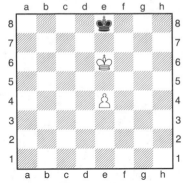

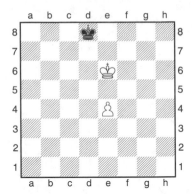

1. **Ke5-e6** *White stops the black king from being able to move forward. White also forces black to move the king to one side or the other.*

1... **Ke8-d8** *Black has no choice but to move the king sideways. (If black had played Ke8-f8, white would have answered with Ke6-d7.)*

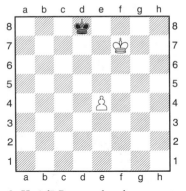

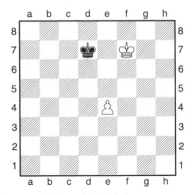

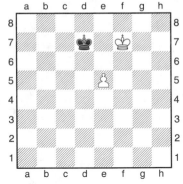

2. **Ke6-f7** *Because the white pawn is on the e file and white needs e8 for the pawn to queen, white plays the king to f7 to control e8.*

2... **Kd8-d7** *The black king cannot stop the advance of the white e pawn.*

3. **e4-e5** *White pursues his strategy by marching the pawn forward.*

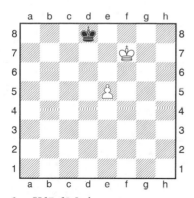

3... **Kd7-d8** *It does not matter where the black king moves, the white pawn will just march down the e file and become a queen.*

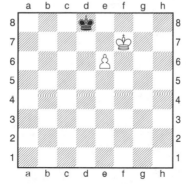

4. **e5-e6** *White continues to advance the pawn toward the eighth rank.*

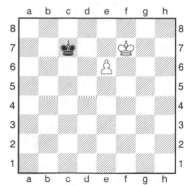

4... **Kd8-c7** *Black is completely helpless because white controls the e8 square.*

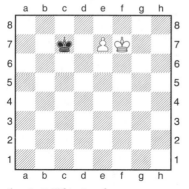

5. **e6-e7** *White is only one move away from queening the pawn.*

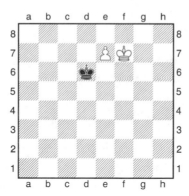

5... **Kc7-d6** *It does not really matter what black plays. White will queen the pawn next move.*

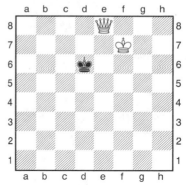

6. **e7-e8(Q)** *White reaches the goal of queening the pawn. Now black is down by a full queen in material. This is considered a completely winning position for white.*

The game could continue the following way:

6... **Kd6-d5**

7. **Qe8-e3 Kd5-d6**

8. **Qe3-e4 Kd6-c5**

9. **Qe4-d3 Kc5-c6**

10. **Qd3-d4 Kc6-c7**

11. **Qd4-d5 Kc7-b6**

12. **Qd5-c4 Kb6-b7**

13. **Qc4-c5 Kb7-b8**

14. **Qc5-e7** (With the past moves, white has forced the black king to the edge of the board, and with the Qc5-e7 move, white makes sure black's king stays there.) **Kb8-c8**

15. **Kf7-e6** (Now it is time to bring in the king to help.) **Kc8-b8**

16. **Ke6-d6 Kb8-c8**

17. **Kd6-c6 Kc8-b8**

18. **Qe7-b7#**

There are numerous other ways to checkmate proceeding from the previously diagramed position; however, this is the most systematic one.

Reviewing the Ideas Behind Chess Endgames

From some of the examples that we have presented, you can see that the way to mate your opponent in an endgame is by forcing the opposing king into a corner or at least to the edge of the board. Once the King is trapped in the corner, it is much easier to checkmate. But when the king is in the corner, it is also easier to be careless and accidentally stalemate your opponent. You want to checkmate and not stalemate your opponent. Keep that in mind when you are faced with that situation.

Hour's Up!

1. True or False: It is easier to checkmate the king when it is in the center.
2. True or False: A lone queen can checkmate a lone king without the help of the king.
3. True or False: Two bishops can checkmate a lone king only in the corner.

4. Which of these can checkmate a lone king?
   a. Bishop
   b. Knight
   c. 2 Knights
   d. 1 Bishop and 1 Knight

5. True or False: It is easier to checkmate with the queen than with a bishop and a knight.

6. While trying to checkmate a lone king, you should try to avoid which of the following?
   a. *En passant*
   b. Playing precisely
   c. Checking the king
   d. Stalemate

7. When trying to avoid checkmate, the king should be where?
   a. Corner
   b. Center
   c. Side

8. True or False: A king and pawn can always win against a lone king.

9. True or False: A king and pawn cannot win against a lone king without promoting the pawn to a queen or rook.

10. True or False: Pawns are considered more powerful if they are connected.

PART IV

I Am Confident Now.
How Do I Get Better?

HOUR 10
Chess Openings I

There are thousands of opening variations. It is impossible even for professional chess players to be experts in all of them. In this hour, we look at openings beginning with e2-e4.

KING PAWN OPENINGS (E2-E4)

Once you get the general idea of how the different openings start, you can develop a more extensive opening repertoire that better suits your playing style. There are many specialized books written on each opening.

For example, let's say you start the game as white with e2-e4. It's difficult in the early stages of learning chess to look at various games where white opens with other moves, so let's look at some basic opening replies to e2-e4, shall we?

RUY LOPEZ

This king pawn opening is named after the player Ruy Lopez, and is also known as the Spanish Opening.

CHAPTER SUMMARY

LESSON PLAN:
You should build an opening repertoire that is comfortable for you, one tailored for playing white and the other for playing black.

In this hour you learn …

- What opening choices you have as white and as black.
- Why control of the center is sometimes worth a sacrifice.
- What various openings—the French Defense, the Sicilian Defense, and the Ruy Lopez—look like.

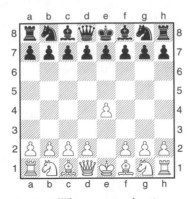

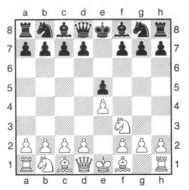

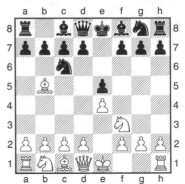

1. e2-e4 White occupies the e4 center square, controlling the d5 center square, and at the same time clearing the f1-a6 diagonal for the bishop on f1.

1... e7-e5 Black occupies the e5 center square, controlling the d4 center square, and at the same time clearing the f8-a3 diagonal for the bishop on f8. 2. Ng1-f3 White develops the knight and at the same time is attacking the center pawn on e5. (If white had played f2-f4 instead, that would have been the king's gambit, which was very popular in the nineteenth century.)

2... Nb8-c6 Black develops the knight and at the same time defends the e5 pawn. 3. Bf1-b5 White develops the bishop and attacks the knight on c6, a move that makes the pawn on e5 vulnerable.

SCOTCH OPENING

This opening was used and given its name by a chess team from Edinburgh Chess Club in a correspondence match against the London Chess Club.

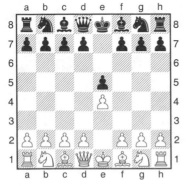

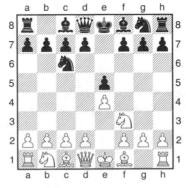

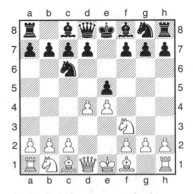

1. e2-e4 e7-e5 The Scotch Opening begins the same as the Ruy Lopez.

2. Ng1-f3 Nb8-c6

3. d2-d4 White occupies the d4 center square, attacking the e5 pawn while clearing the c1-h6 diagonal for the bishop on c1. (The Italian game would have been started if white had played Bf1-c4 instead of d2-d4.)

PETROFF DEFENSE

Also known as the Russian Defense, this opening is named after Alexander Petroff (1794–1867), the best Russian player of his time.

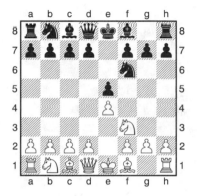

1. e2-e4 e7-e5   2. Ng1-f3 Ng8-f6 Symmetrical development.

PHILIDOR DEFENSE

This opening is named after Francois-Andre Danican Philidor (1726–1795), the best chess player of his time.

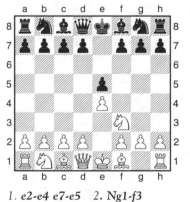

1. e2-e4 e7-e5   2. Ng1-f3

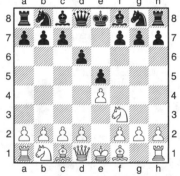

2... d7-d6 Black defends the pawn on e5 and at the same time opens the h3-c8 diagonal for the bishop. The drawback is that it also blocks the a3-f8 diagonal for the bishop on f8.

French Defense

French Defense was the name given after a Paris team defeated London using this opening in a correspondence match in 1834.

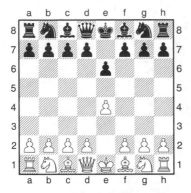
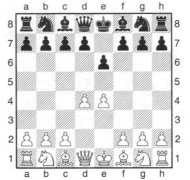
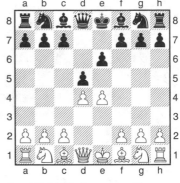

1. e2-e4 e7-e6 Black defends d5 with a plan to play d7-d5, and at the same time clears the a3-f8 diagonal for the bishop.

2. d2-d4 White occupies d4 while controlling e5 and at the same time clears the c1-h6 diagonal for the bishop.

2… d7-d5 Black occupies d5, attacking the e4 pawn.

Sicilian Defense

The Sicilian Defense opening was named by the player Jacob Henry Sarratt (1772–1819). He named it after the homeland—Sicily—of Pietro Carrera who first published it in 1617.

1. e2-e4 c7-c5 Black controls d4 with the c pawn. The idea behind this move is that if white decides to play d4 at a later time, black will play c5xd4, eliminating one of white's center pawns. This still leaves black with two center pawns, which would better enable black to control the center squares.

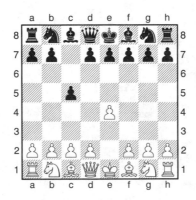

The center is the key battleground. Whichever side controls the center usually controls the game.

CARO-KANN DEFENSE

This defense gets its name after British player Horatio Caro (1862–1920) and Viennese player Marcus Kann (1820–1886).

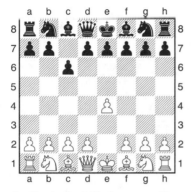

1. e2-e4 c7-c6 Black protects d5, giving reinforcement for the pawn on d7 to play d5 next.

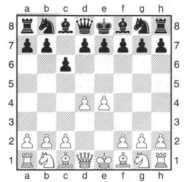

2. d2-d4 White occupies d4 while controlling e5.

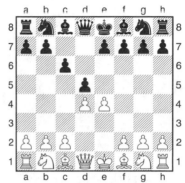

2... d7-d5 Black occupies the d5 square, attacking the e4 pawn, while opening up the h3-c8 diagonal for the bishop. The idea here is that if white captures the pawn with e4xd5, black will capture back with c6xd5, maintaining two center pawns while white only has one left.

PIRC DEFENSE

This defense is named after Yugoslav Grandmaster Vasja Pirc (1907–1980).

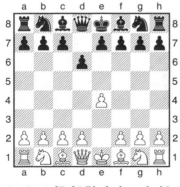

1. e2-e4 d7-d6 Black clears the h3-c8 diagonal for the bishop while controlling e5.

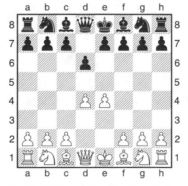

2. d2-d4 Controlling the e5 and c5 squares.

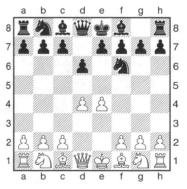

2... Ng8-f6 Black develops the knight while attacking the e4 pawn.

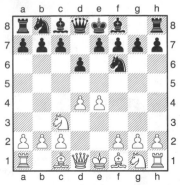

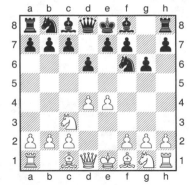

3. **Nb1-c3** *White develops the knight while defending the e4 pawn.*

3... **g7-g6** *Black clears g7 for the bishop. This is called bishop fianchetto.*

ALEKHINE DEFENSE

This defense is named after world champion Alexander Alekhine (1892–1946).

1. *e2-e4* **Ng8-f6** *Black develops the knight and at the same time attacks the e4 pawn.*

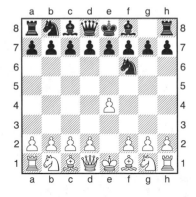

SCANDINAVIAN OPENING

The Scandinavian Opening, also known as the Center Counter Opening, was named after the Scandinavians in the nineteenth century, because it was very heavily analyzed by a group of Scandinavian players.

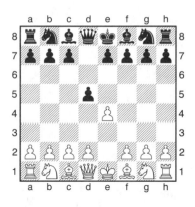

1. e2-e4 d7-d5 Black occupies d5 and clears the h3-c8 diagonal while attacking the e4 pawn.

MODERN DEFENSE

The Modern Defense was at one time known as the Robatsch Defense and the Abbazia Defense.

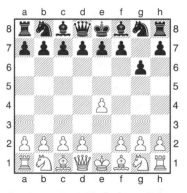

1. e2-e4 g7-g6 Black clears g7 for the bishop.

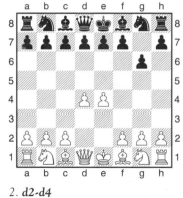

2. d2-d4

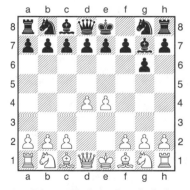

2... Bf8-g7 Black develops the bishop while putting pressure on the d4 pawn.

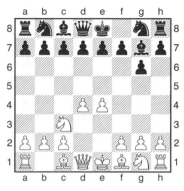

3. Nb1-c3 White develops the knight and protects the e4 pawn.

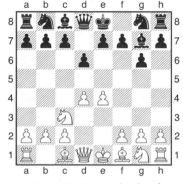

3... d7-d6 Black controls e5 and stops the white pawn from playing e4-e5, while clearing the h3-c8 diagonal for the bishop.

HOUR'S UP!

1. True or False: 1. **e2-e4 e7-e5** 2. **Ng1-f3 Ng8-f6** is called the Philidor Defense.

2. Openings are considered as which of the following?

   a. Beginning of the game

   b. Middle of the game

   c. Ending of the game

   d. Fork

3. True or False: The Sicilian Defense starts with 1. **e2-e4 c7-c5**.

4. True or False: 1. **e2-e4 g7-g6** is called the Banana Split Defense.

5. An opening starting with 1. **e2-e4** is which of the following?

   a. Unusual

   a. Queen Pawn Opening

   a. King Pawn Opening

   a. Gambit

6. The game that starts with 1. **e2-e4 g7-g6** is called

   a. Caro-Kann

   b. Modern Defense

   c. Sicilian Defense

   d. Military Defense

7. The purpose of playing 1. **e2-e4** is which of the following?

   a. It has no meaning

   b. To allow the king to get out for a stroll

   c. To allow the knight on g1 to develop

   d. To occupy the center and open up the f1-a6 diagonal for the bishop.

8. True or False: Games that start with 1. **e2-e4 d7-d5** are called the Scandinavian.

9. 1. **e2-e4 e7-e6** is called

   a. The French Defense

   b. The Moscow on the Hudson Defense

   c. The Bulgarian Attack

   d. The Modern Defense

10. True or False: 1. **e2-e4 Ng8-f6** is called the Alekhine Defense.

HOUR 11

Chess Openings II

CHAPTER SUMMARY

LESSON PLAN:

The objective in this hour, as in the last one, is to familiarize you with various opening choices that you find appropriate to your taste when you are playing white and when you are playing black.

In this hour you learn ...

- What opening choices you have as white and as black.
- Why controlling the center is sometimes worth a sacrifice.
- What various openings—the Queen's Gambit or the Nimzo-Indian Defense—look like.
- How an opening can influence the course of the game.

Now we consider some other special openings besides e2-e4. As we said in the last hour, there are so many opening variations that even professional chess players can't remember them all, let alone take time to analyze them!

QUEEN PAWN OPENINGS (D2-D4)

Now that you've gotten a sense of how to develop your pieces in the first phase of the game by using various openings, particularly e2-e4, let's look at some basic openings that apply to d2-d4.

QUEEN'S GAMBIT ACCEPTED

White opens the game with the queen pawn and on move 2, white is sacrificing the c4 pawn. By black accepting the sacrifice and take the pawn, the opening becomes the Queen's Gambit Accepted.

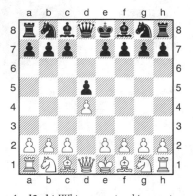 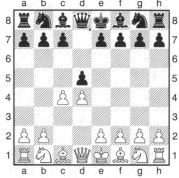

1. **d2-d4** *White occupies d4, opening the c1-h6 diagonal for the bishop on c1 while controlling e5.* **d7-d5** *Black occupies d5, opening the h3-c8 diagonal for the bishop while controlling e4.*

2. **c2-c4** *White attacks the d5 pawn. The idea is to eliminate one of black's center pawns with white's c pawn while maintaining both white center pawns. Because of the importance of the center, white is willing to sacrifice the c4 pawn. If black plays d5xc4, white could freely play e2-e4 because black would no longer control e4.*

Black's move in the following figure actually demonstrates "Queen's Gambit Accepted."

2... **d5xc4** *Black is willing to give up control of the center e4 square in exchange for the free pawn. This is part of white's strategy: to give up a pawn for full control of the center.*

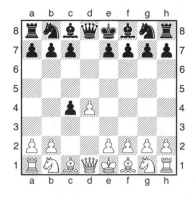

QUEEN'S GAMBIT DECLINED

When black declines to accept the gambit by not taking the pawn on c4, the opening becomes Queen's Gambit Declined.

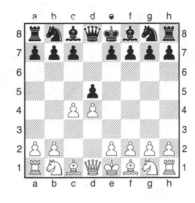

1. d2-d4 d7-d5   2. c2-c4

Black's move in the following figure demonstrates "Queen's Gambit Declined."

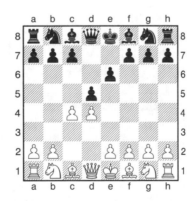

2... e7-e6 White is willing to give up the c4 pawn for black to relinquish the center e4 square. In this opening, black declines the free pawn offer, choosing to stay in control of e4.

SLAV DEFENSE

The Slav Defense is a form of the Queen's Gambit Declined. The main difference in the Slav Defense: Black plays c7-c6 on the second move.

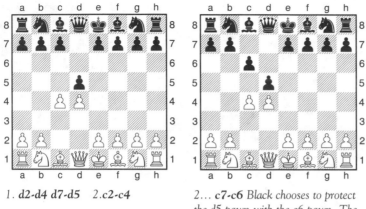

1. **d2-d4 d7-d5** 2. **c2-c4**

2... **c7-c6** *Black chooses to protect the d5 pawn with the c6 pawn. The idea behind this move is that if white captures the d5 pawn by playing c4xd5, black will capture back with c6xd5. In this scenario, both sides retain two center pawns.*

QUEEN'S INDIAN DEFENSE

In the Queen's Indian Defense, white chooses to play Ng1-f3 on the third move and black responds with b7-b6 to fianchetto the bishop on the queenside.

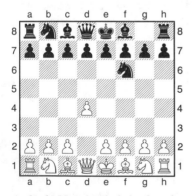

1. **d2-d4 Ng8-f6** *Black develops the knight while controlling e4, thus stopping white from playing e2-e4.*

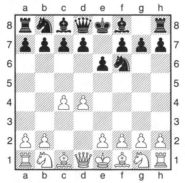

2. **c2-c4 e7-e6** *Black controls d5 and at the same time clears the a3-f8 diagonal for the black bishop.*

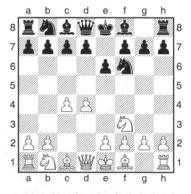

3. **Ng1-f3** *White develops the knight, controlling e5.*

Black's response below to white's opening moves constitutes the Queen's Indian Defense.

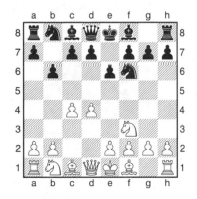

3... b7-b6 Black clears b7 for the bishop, bringing reinforcement for the center.

BOGO-INDIAN DEFENSE

The Bogo-Indian Defense is an alternative to the Queen's Indian Defense and is named after Grandmaster Efim Bogoljubow (1889–1952). The key difference is black does not fianchetto the queenside bishop. Instead, black develops the other bishop while putting the white king in check with Bf8-b4+.

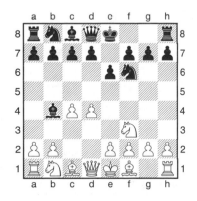

1. d2-d4 Ng8-f6   2. c2-c4 e7-e6   3. Ng1-f3 Bf8-b4+ Black develops the bishop while checking the white king, trying to disrupt white's normal development.

NIMZO-INDIAN DEFENSE

This is named after Grandmaster Aaron Nimzowitsch, one of the best players in the world in his day.

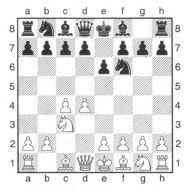 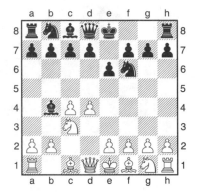

*1. **d2-d4** Ng8-f6 2. **c2-c4** e7-e6 3. **Nb1-c3** White develops the knight with the idea of playing e2-e4 next.*

*3... **Bf8-b4** Black is pinning the white knight, stopping white from playing e2-e4. If white should play e2-e4, black could take the pawn with Nf6xe4.*

GO TO ▷
For more on pinning, see Hour 14.

DUTCH DEFENSE

The Dutch Defense is so called because Elias Stein, its developer, lived in the Netherlands.

*1. **d2-d4 f7-f5** This is an unortho-dox way of controlling e4. The idea here is for black to be a little more prepared for a future kingside attack by black.*

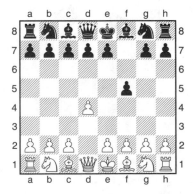

OTHER IMPORTANT OPENINGS

The following two openings are not queen pawn openings.

ENGLISH OPENING

The English Opening is so named because the English player Howard Staunton used it six times against Saint Amant in a match.

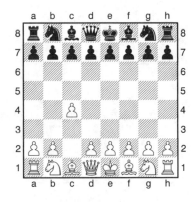

1. c2-c4 Rather than controlling the center with the d or e pawn, in this opening, white chooses to do it with the c pawn.

LARSEN OPENING

This opening is named after the famous Danish grandmaster Bent Larsen (1935–).

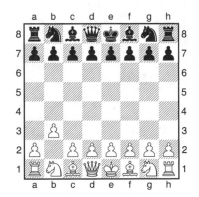

1. b2-b3 In this opening, white gives up the center occupancy in exchange for an early fianchetto of the queenside bishop. This opening was named after Danish grandmaster Bent Larsen, formerly one of the best players in the world.

USING THE OPENINGS

The following game, played by two grandmasters in early 2002, demonstrates how a game is continued after the opening.

GM Tkachiev—GM Sadvakasov

> 1. d2-d4 d7-d5
> 2. c2-c4 d5xc4

Queen's Gambit Accepted.

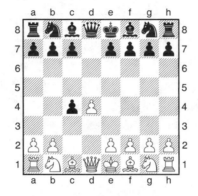

> 3. e2-e3 Ng8-f6
> 4. Bf1xc4 e7-e6
> 5. Ng1-f3 c7-c5
> 6. 0-0 a7-a6

Black is planning to play 7… b7-b5 to attack the white bishop on c4, as well as to clear the b7 square to develop the black bishop on c8.

> 7. Bc4-b3 b7-b5
> 8. a2-a4

White wants to break up the strong black pawn chain of a6, b5, and c5.

> 8… b5-b4
> 9. Nb1-d2 Bc8-b7
> 10. e3-e4!

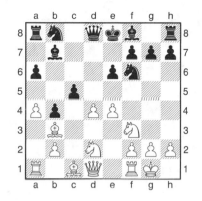

White is willing to sacrifice the pawn on d4 to gain some initiatives and exploit the fact that black has not castled.

10... c5xd4

11. e4-e5 Nf6-d7

12. Nd2-c4

This move gives reinforcement to the white pawn on e5 and allows the white knight on f3 to capture the black pawn on d4. In addition, this move provides a potential future threat of Nc4-d6+.

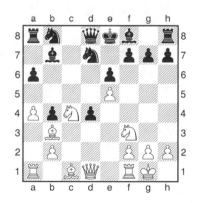

12... Bf8-e7

13. Nf3xd4 Nd7-c5

Black cannot castle here because most of his pieces are located on the queenside of the board. Therefore, it is not safe for the king to be on the kingside. If black plays 13... 0-0, white will play 14. Qd1-g4. With the white queen in front of the black king and the assistance of the two white bishops on c1 and b3 (potentially moving to c2) pointing in the direction of the black king, black would be in a very dangerous position.

14. Qd1-g4

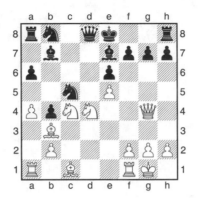

14... g7-g6

15. **Bc1-h6!**

This stops black from castling. Black is now forced to leave his king in the middle, something everyone should avoid.

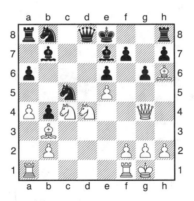

15... **Nc5xb3**

16. **Nd4xb3 Nb8-d7**

17. **Ra1-d1**

The white rook is placed on an open file, pinning the black knight on d7. With white in this position, you can see that white is in total control. The white king is safe and his pieces are where they are supposed to be—attacking black. In the meantime, the black king cannot castle, and his pieces are no threat to white.

When you play white, you should try to control the tempo of the game, maintaining and enhancing the advantage of having the first move. When you play black, do your best to neutralize white's advantage as soon as possible.

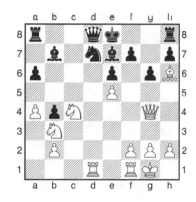

17... **Ra8-c8**

18. **Rf1-e1 Bb7-c6**

19. **Nc4-d6+**

Black is forced to take the knight with the bishop on e7. This weakens the e file for black, allowing white to mount a deadlier attack on the black king.

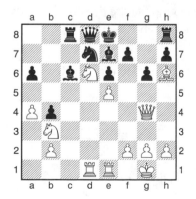

19... **Be7xd6**

20. **e5xd6**

White is threatening to do the following: 21. Re1xe6+ f7xe6   22. Qg4xe6+ Qd8-e7
23. Qe6-e7#

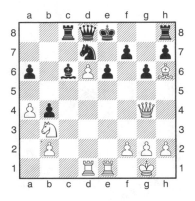

20... **e6-e5**

Black has to defend against the mate threat. If black plays 20... Qd8-f6, white will reply with
21. Nb3-d4 and threaten to take the e6 pawn with the knight on next move, thus busting
open the e file. If black plays 20... Nd7-f8, white will play 21. Nb3-c5 with the same idea of
capturing the e6 pawn on the knight's next move. This will open up the e file to launch a
mating attack.

21. **Nb3-c5!**

Because the black knight on d7 has to defend the e5 pawn, white is willing to sacrifice his
knight to attack the black knight.

If black takes the knight, 21... Nd7xc5, white will play 22. Re1xe5+ Qd8-e7   23. Qg4xc8#,
or if 22. Nc5-e6   23. Re5xe6+ Qd8-e7   24. Re6xe7 with an overwhelming advantage, and
white will soon mate black.

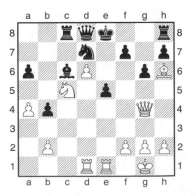

21... Qd8-a5

22. Qg4xd7+!!

Now white is sacrificing his own queen, eliminating the key defensive knight on d7 to checkmate black. Black has only one legal move: taking the queen with his bishop.

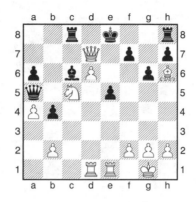

22... Bc6xd7

23. Re1xe5+

White finally breaks through the e file, and black is now in big trouble.

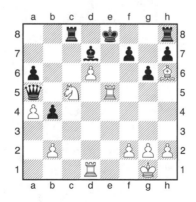

23... Bd7-e6

If black were to move 23... Ke8-d8, white would checkmate black with 24. Bh6-g5+ f7-f6 25. Bg5xf6#

24. d6-d7+!

White checks the king and forks the c8 rook. Black cannot capture the pawn with his bishop on e6 because of the pin by the white rook on e5.

GO TO ▶

For more on the fork and pin, see Hour 14.

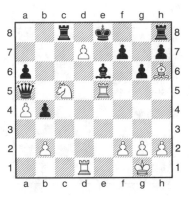

24... **Black resigns.**

There is no defense to this situation. Black has only two legal moves. If black plays 24... Ke8-e7, white will win with 25. Bh6-g5+ f7-f6   26. Re5xe6+ Ke7-f7   27. Re6xf6+ Kf7-g7 28. Nc5xe6+ Kg7-g8   29. d7xc8+(Q) Qa5-d8   30. Qc8xd8#.

If black plays 24... Ke8-d8, white will win with 25. Nc5xe6+ f7xe6   26. d7xc8(Q)+ Kd8xc8 27. Re5xa5, putting white up a rook and a bishop, a completely decisive advantage.

Hour's Up!

1. True or False: The Dutch Defense starts with 1. **d2-d4 f7-f5**.

2. True or False: After 1. **d2-d4**, white opens up the f1-a6 diagonal for his bishop on f1.

3. True or False: In the Bogo-Indian Defense, black gives a check on his third move.

4. With which does the Larsen Opening start?

    a. 1. d4

    b. 1. e4

    c. 1. b3

    d. 1. c4

5. With what does the English Opening start?

    a. 1. d4

    b. 1. e4

    c. 1. b3

    d. 1. c4

6. True or False: With 1. **d2-d4**, white occupies the center.

7. True or False: In our model game, both sides castled.

8. In our model game, black chose the following opening:

    a. Nimzo-Indian Defense

    b. Queen's Gambit Accepted

    c. Queen's Gambit Declined

    d. Bogo-Indian Defense

9. In our model game on move 22, white sacrificed his

    a. Queen

    b. Rook

    c. Bishop

    d. Knight

10. True or False: In our model game, black resigned because he could not avoid checkmate or loss of significant material.

HOUR 12

Developing a Sharp Eye for Middlegames

This hour provides you with numerous checkmate examples using any one of several different pieces, even those you might have obtained by pawn promotion. In addition to the smothered mate (not to be confused with a murder mystery), you learn how to make a two- or three-move combination that leads to checkmate.

HELPFUL AND FUN PUZZLES FOR CHESS MIDDLEGAMES

These are some mate-in-one puzzles that will improve your chess skills.

CHAPTER SUMMARY

LESSON PLAN:

In this hour, we deepen your understanding of the middlegame.

In this hour you learn …

- How to distinguish among different checkmate patterns.
- How a smothered mate works.
- How a back rank mate works.
- How to checkmate by pawn promotion.

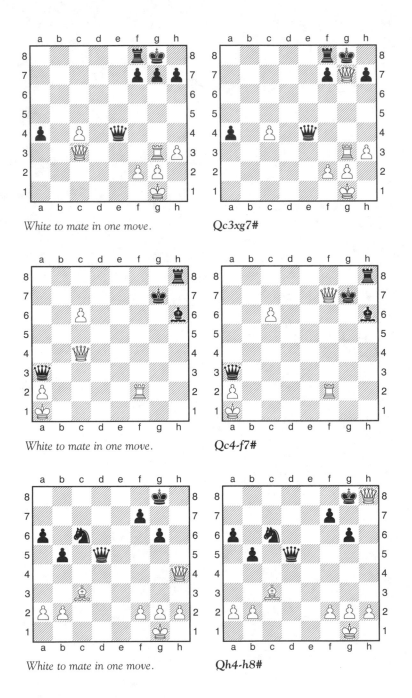

White to mate in one move.

Qc3xg7#

White to mate in one move.

Qc4-f7#

White to mate in one move.

Qh4-h8#

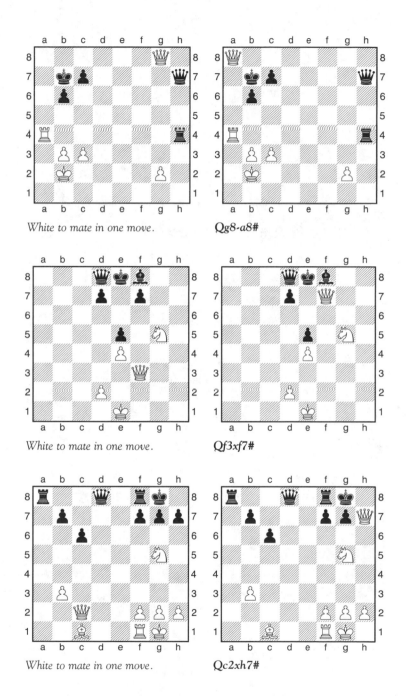

White to mate in one move.

Qg8-a8#

White to mate in one move.

Qf3xf7#

White to mate in one move.

Qc2xh7#

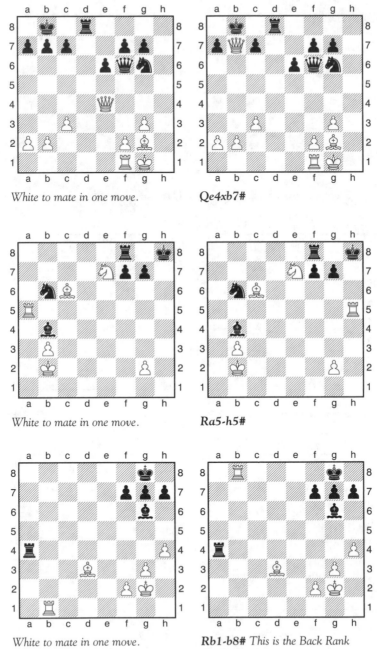

White to mate in one move.

Qe4xb7#

White to mate in one move.

Ra5-h5#

White to mate in one move.

Rb1-b8# *This is the Back Rank checkmate.*

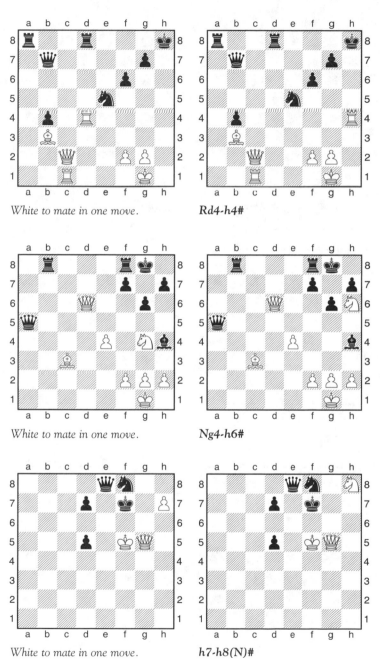

White to mate in one move.   **Rd4-h4#**

White to mate in one move.   **Ng4-h6#**

White to mate in one move.   **h7-h8(N)#**

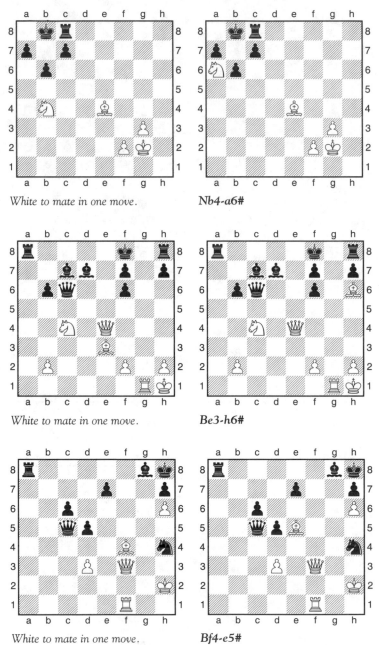

White to mate in one move.

Nb4-a6#

White to mate in one move.

Be3-h6#

White to mate in one move.

Bf4-e5#

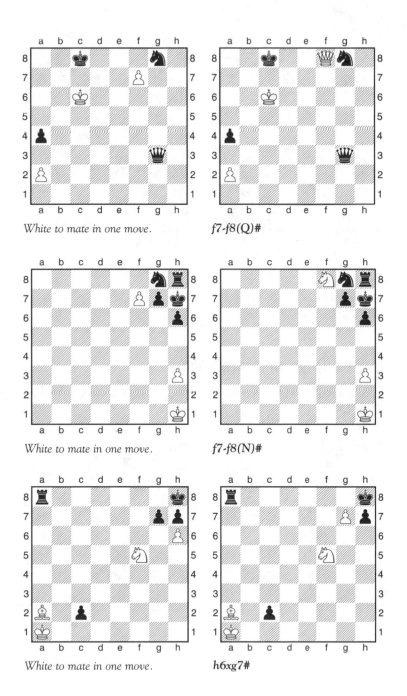

White to mate in one move.

f7-f8(Q)#

White to mate in one move.

f7-f8(N)#

White to mate in one move.

h6xg7#

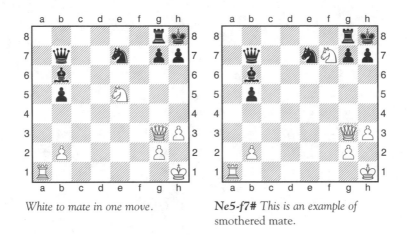

White to mate in one move.

Ne5-f7# *This is an example of* smothered mate.

STRICTLY DEFINED

A smothered mate is a checkmate in which the king was unable to escape because his own pieces are blocking him.

Learning Different Types of Mate Tricks

In this section, you will learn to recognize various mating patterns. In the following example, white mates in two moves.

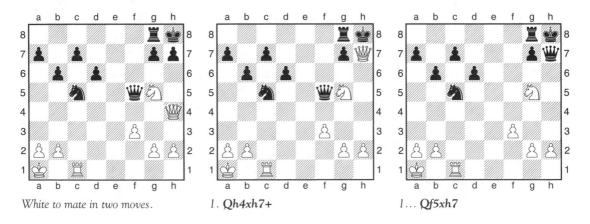

White to mate in two moves.

1. Qh4xh7+

1... Qf5xh7

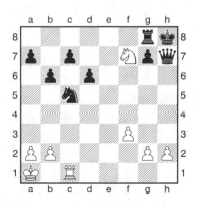

2. Ng5-f7# *Another example of smothered mate.*

In this next example, white mates in three moves.

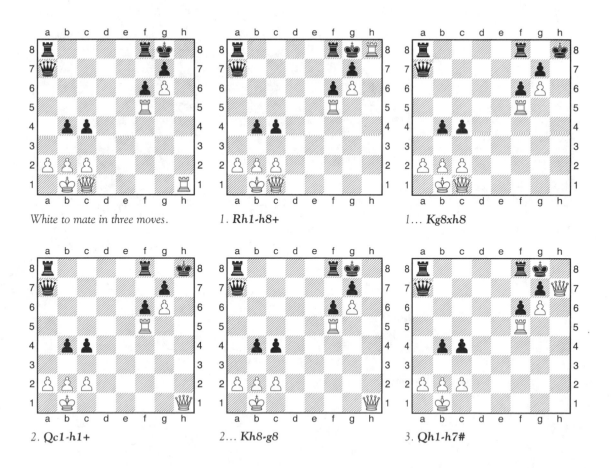

White to mate in three moves.

1. Rh1-h8+

1... Kg8xh8

2. Qc1-h1+

2... Kh8-g8

3. Qh1-h7#

And in the next example, white again mates in three moves.

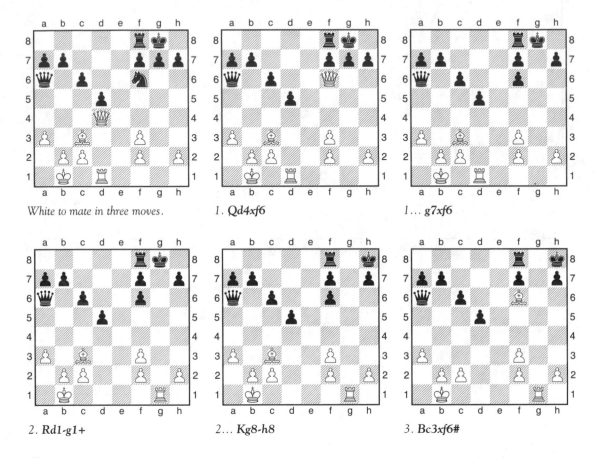

White to mate in three moves.   *1. Qd4xf6*   *1... g7xf6*

2. Rd1-g1+   *2... Kg8-h8*   *3. Bc3xf6#*

HOUR'S UP!

1. True or False: A back rank mate occurs on the fourth rank.

2. True or False: At least two pieces are needed to create a checkmate against the king.

3. True or False: A smothered mate can occur on move one.

4. True or False: You can never checkmate by promoting a pawn.

5. When you checkmate your opponent, you:

   a. Lose

   b. Draw

   c. Win

   d. Take a midgame break for tea

6. Which of the following cannot be used to check your opponent?

    a. Bishop

    b. Knight

    c. Queen

    d. King

7. Checkmate can occur in the:

    a. Opening

    b. Middlegame

    c. Endgame

    d. All of the above

8. True or False: Back rank checkmate occurs on the first or eighth rank.

9. True of False: Sometimes you may have to sacrifice material to create a checkmate.

10. True or False: There is always only one way to checkmate a king.

HOUR 13

Developing an Understanding for Chess Endgames

This hour builds on the endgame lessons that you have learned in the previous hours.

LEARNING THE BASICS OF CHECKMATING

In the endgame phase of chess, there are a few basic rules you must remember.

- A king and a queen can mate a lone king.
- A king and a rook can mate a lone king.
- A king and a bishop cannot mate a lone king.
- A king and a knight cannot mate a lone king.
- A king and two bishops can mate a lone king.
- A king and two knights cannot mate a lone king unless the other side helps by playing very badly.
- A king, a bishop, and a knight can mate a lone king.
- A king and a pawn may be enough to mate a lone king only if the pawn can advance to become a queen or rook.

It is very important to know these rules because they come in handy when the game reaches the endgame phase. Knowing these rules gives you a leg up when you play and increases the chances that you will achieve a victory.

CHAPTER SUMMARY

LESSON PLAN:

It's one thing to understand the basics of the endgame, but it's another to acquire the skills and experience to bring a game to a successful conclusion.

In this hour you learn …

- What combinations of pieces can mate an opponent's king.
- What combinations of pieces cannot mate an opponent's king.
- How to win from difficult positions.
- How to secure a material advantage in the endgame.
- Why queening is so important in the endgame.

SOLVING COOL ENDGAME PUZZLES

To give you an idea how these rules work in practice, take a look at some of the helpful and cool endgame puzzles that follow.

EXAMPLE 1

In this exercise, both sides have three pawns. It is white's turn to move.

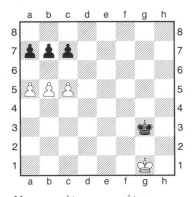

How can white get one of its pawns to break through to queen and achieve a winning position?

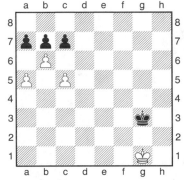

1. **b5-b6** This is a great move and the only move that can give white a win. The white pawn on b6 is attacking both the black a7 and c7 pawns.

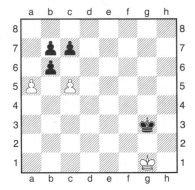

1... **a7xb6** Black has to capture the white pawn on b6 with either the c7 or a7 pawn. If black captures with the c7 pawn, white would play a5-a6.

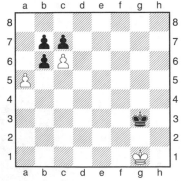

2. **c5-c6** Once again, a great move and the only move that can deliver a win for white. White is attacking the black pawn on b7.

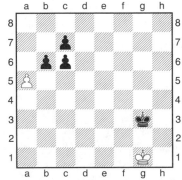

2... **b7xc6** Black has no choice but to capture the white pawn on c6. If black were to capture the white pawn on a5, white would play c6xb7, which makes it possible for white to queen its b7 pawn on the next move, thus obtaining a decisive material advantage.

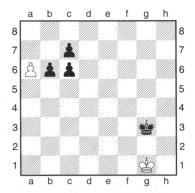

3. **a5-a6** Now that the black pawn is no longer on b7, white freely advances its a5 pawn. Black cannot stop white from promoting his pawn in the next few moves. Once white promotes the pawn to a queen, white will have a winning advantage.

EXAMPLE 2

The winning idea in this exercise is for white to advance the pawn to the eighth rank and obtain a queen. Unfortunately, the white rook is in the way, blocking the pawn from advancing.

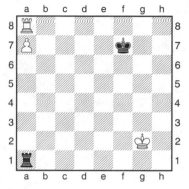

If the rook moves out of the way, the pawn on a7 is left unprotected, and black can capture it. So, how can white win?

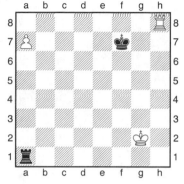

1. **Ra8-h8** White is clearing the a8 square for the white pawn on a7 to advance.

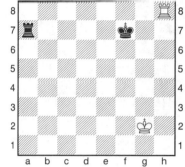

1... **Ra1xa7** Black has no choice but to capture the white pawn on a7. If black does not take the pawn, the pawn will advance to a8 in the next move.

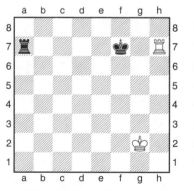

2. **Rh8-h7+** Now white is capable of mounting an attack known as a skewer. By checking the black king, white forces the king to move away, thus leaving the black rook on a7 unprotected.

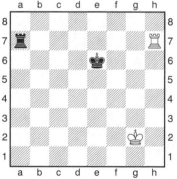

2... **Kf7-e6** Black has no choice but to move the king away from the seventh rank.

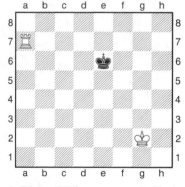

3. **Rh7xa7** White captures the black rook, obtaining a decisive material advantage.

GO TO ▶
To learn more about the skewer, see Hour 14.

EXAMPLE 3

In this exercise, white is down a pawn. However, white has an advanced pawn on h7, just one square away from promotion to another queen. But will the pawn be able to advance?

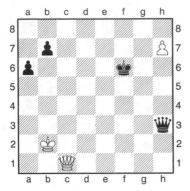

The problem seems to be that the black queen is attacking the h7 pawn while keeping the pawn from advancing to h8. Can white utilize the h7 pawn and win in this position?

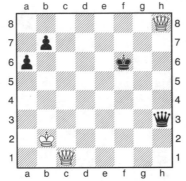

1. **h7-h8(Q)+** *White queens the pawn while checking the black king and attacking the black queen.*

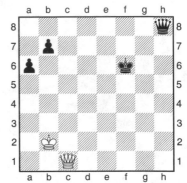

1... **Qh3xh8** *Black has no choice but to capture the white queen on h8. Otherwise, black would lose the queen on h3.*

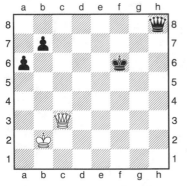

2. **Qc1–c3+** *White now has a skewer on hand with this check.*

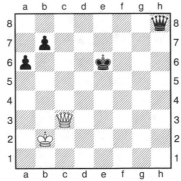

2... **Kf6-e6** *Black has to move the king out of the a1-h8 diagonal, leaving the queen unprotected.*

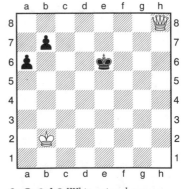

3. **Qc3xh8** *White wins the queen and obtains a decisive material advantage.*

EXAMPLE 4

In this exercise, white's objective is to advance the b pawn. How can white protect its pawn?

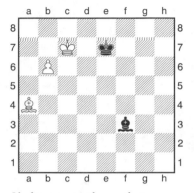

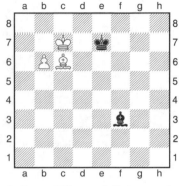

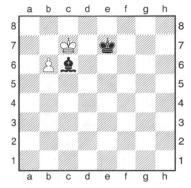

If white tries to advance the pawn now, black can capture the pawn with its bishop, leaving white only one bishop—and one bishop is not enough to win the game. Therefore, white cannot allow black to capture its pawn when the pawn advances.

1. **Ba4-c6** This is a brilliant move by white. While attacking the black bishop, white is also blocking the black bishop from controlling b7.

1... **Bf3xc6** Black has very few choices remaining. If black does not capture the white bishop, white is free to advance the b pawn.

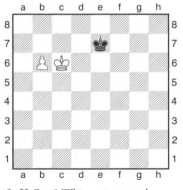

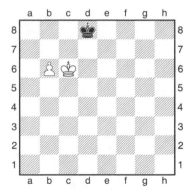

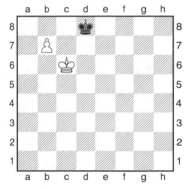

2. **Kc7xc6** White recaptures the bishop.

2... **Ke7-d8** Black is hoping to move the king to c8 to stop the b pawn from advancing.

3. **b6-b7** By advancing the pawn to b7, white automatically stops the black king from moving to c8.

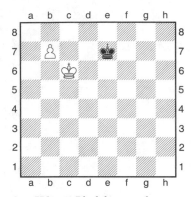

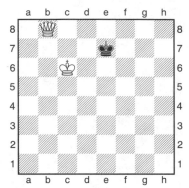

3... **Kd8-e7** Black has no other choice but to move the king elsewhere, being completely helpless to stop the white pawn from promoting to queen.

4. **b7-b8 (Q)** White queens his pawn, obtaining a winning endgame.

EXAMPLE 5

In this exercise, the only way that white can win is by queening the pawn on d6. If white advances the pawn to d7 now, the black knight can capture it. That would leave white only a knight, which is not enough to win the game.

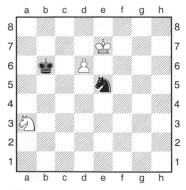

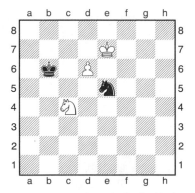

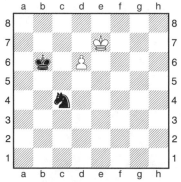

White needs to move the black knight away from the occupation of the d7 square so the white pawn can advance without being captured.

1. **Na3-c4+** White checks the black king while attacking the black knight.

1... **Ne5xc4** Black has no choice but to accept the sacrifice and capture the white knight. Otherwise, the black knight would be captured.

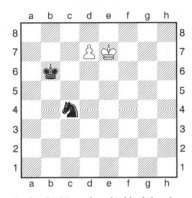

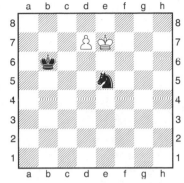

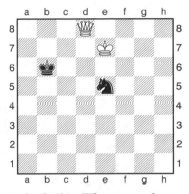

2. **d6-d7** *Now that the black knight relinquishes the control of d7, the white pawn can advance.*

*2... **Nc4-e5** The black knight returns to the previous square, hoping to capture the white pawn.*

3. **d7-d8(Q)+** *White queens the pawn and wins the game by having decisive material advantage.*

HOUR'S UP!

1. True or False: A king and a rook cannot mate a lone king.

2. True or False: A king and two knights cannot mate a lone king unless the opponent plays very badly.

3. A king and a pawn may be enough to mate a lone king only if

   a. The pawn is on a rank.

   b. The pawn can be promoted to a bishop.

   c. The pawn can be promoted to a rook.

   d. The pawn can be promoted to a knight.

4. True or False: A king and a knight can mate a lone king.

5. True or False: A king, a bishop, and a knight can mate a lone king.

6. True or False: The game is a drawn if both sides only have a lone king.

7. True or False: One bishop (besides the two kings) is not enough to win a game.

8. True or False: You can never win a pawn endgame with an equal number of pawns for each side.

9. True or False: A king and two bishops cannot mate a lone king.

10. A skewer is a tactic involving

    a. An attack on one piece.

    b. A defense of one piece.

    c. An attack on two pieces.

    d. A defense of two pieces.

HOUR 14

Learning Essential Chess Tactics

There are several well-established tactical moves that, if you apply correctly, can gain you a decisive material advantage and produce more consistent wins. Through a set of models, we show you how these tactical moves work, and you'll examine some puzzles that will hone your tactical skills.

WHAT IS A PIN?

A *pin* is a *tactic* by which attacking one piece, you indirectly attack a piece behind it. That makes the second piece vulnerable to capture if your opponent moves the first piece under attack (the pinned piece) out of the way. A pin is only valuable if the piece being indirectly attacked (the piece behind) is the king or a more valuable piece than the piece being pinned.

CHAPTER SUMMARY

LESSON PLAN:

Now that we've covered the basics of the opening, middlegame, and endgame, it's time to consider actical elements (chess combinations).

In this hour you learn …

- How to pin.
- How to fork.
- How to skewer.
- How to mount a discovery attack.
- How to create *zugzwang*.

STRICTLY DEFINED

A pin is a direct attack on one piece and an indirect attack on the piece behind it. A pin is only valuable if the piece being indirectly attacked is the king or a more valuable piece than the pinned piece.

A tactic is defined as a move that takes advantage of short-term opportunities in the game by improving your position or undermining your opponent's position.

PIN EXAMPLE 1

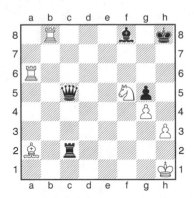

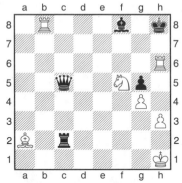

The white rook on b8 is pinning the black bishop on f8. White will utilize that pin to mate black.

1. **Ra6-h6#** The bishop on f8 is not allowed to capture the rook on h6 because that would leave the black king in check. Therefore black has no escape.

PIN EXAMPLE 2

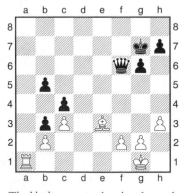

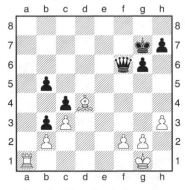

The black queen is placed in front of the king. How can white pin the black queen?

1. **Be3-d4** The white bishop is pinning the black queen, which cannot escape. Black will lose the queen, giving white the decisive material advantage.

PIN EXAMPLE 3

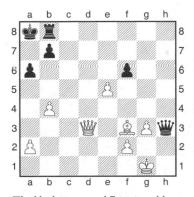

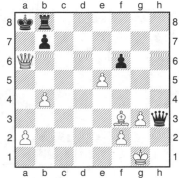

The black pawn on b7 is pinned by the white bishop on f3. How can white checkmate black in one move?

1. **Qd3xa6#** *The black pawn on b7 cannot capture the white queen on a6 because it is pinned by the white bishop on f3.*

PIN EXAMPLE 4

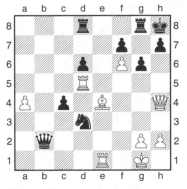

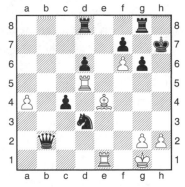

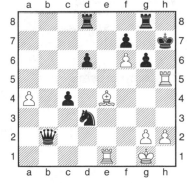

White will attempt to force the black king into a pin by the bishop on e4. What is the right move?

1. **Qh4xh7+** *With this beautiful combination, white is giving up his queen to achieve his goal.* **Kh8xh7** *Black has only one legal move: to capture the queen.*

2. **Rd5-h5#** *White is using the bishop on e4 to pin the black pawn on g6. Now, white can checkmate black with Rd5-h5 because the black pawn on g6 cannot capture the white rook.*

Pin Example 5

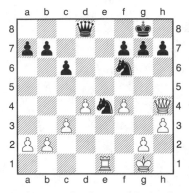
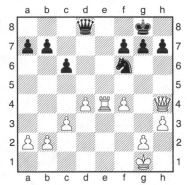

In this example, the pin of the knight on f6 will result in white winning the knight on e4. How does white do this?

1. **Re1xe4** White captures the black knight with the rook. Even though the black knight on f6 can capture the white rook, black cannot do it because the black knight is pinned by the queen on h4. If 1... Nf6xe4   2. Qh4xd8#.

What Is a Fork?

A *fork* is a two-pronged attack against two or more of the opponent's pieces on the same move. If you are the one being attacked, you generally can defend one piece but seldom both.

STRICTLY DEFINED

A fork is a two-pronged attack against two or more of the opponent's pieces on the same move.

FORK EXAMPLE 1

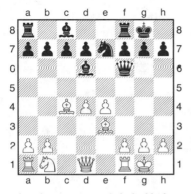

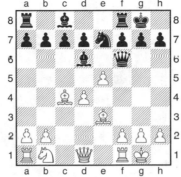

The white pawn can fork the black bishop and the black queen. What is the move?

1. **e4-e5** By attacking both the bishop and the queen, white gains a material advantage.

FORK EXAMPLE 2

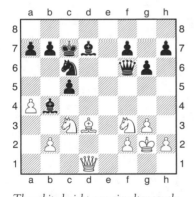

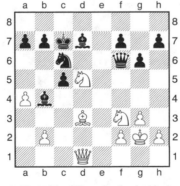

The white knight can simultaneously check the black king while attacking the black queen, giving white a decisive material advantage. Can you find the move?

1. **Nc3-d5+** White checks the black king on c7 and attacks the black queen on f6. The black king needs to get out of check. Then, white captures the black queen and thus gains a winning material advantage.

Fork Example 3

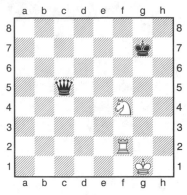

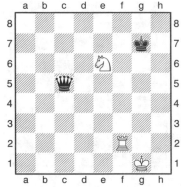

In this example, white again forks with the knight. Where should the knight go to fork the black king and queen?

1. **Nf4-e6+** White is forking the king on g7 and the queen on c5, giving white a decisive material advantage.

Fork Example 4

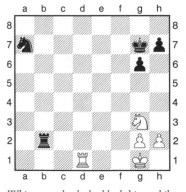

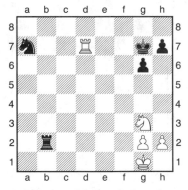

White can check the black king while attacking the black knight at the same time. Can you find the way to do it?

1. **Rd1-d7+** White is checking the king and winning the knight on a7.

WHAT IS A SKEWER?

The *skewer* is a tactic that consists of an attack on an opponent's valuable piece, forcing it to move and leave behind another piece that is vulnerable to capture. It's been described as the reverse pin.

STRICTLY DEFINED

The skewer is a tactic consisting of an attack on an opponent's valuable piece, forcing it to move and leave behind another piece that is vulnerable to capture.

SKEWER EXAMPLE 1

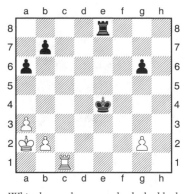

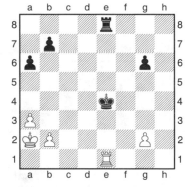

White has a chance to check the black king. When the black king has to move, the black rook is exposed and can be captured. Let's find it.

*1. **Rc1-e1+** The white rook checks the black king on e4. The king has no choice but to move away from the e file. When that happens, the black rook on e8 is exposed.*

SKEWER EXAMPLE 2

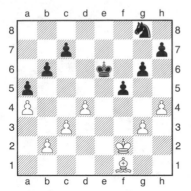

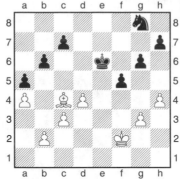

White has a check coming up. Because the black king has to move out of the way, the black knight is placed under attack. Where is this check?

1. **Bf1-c4+** When black has to move the king out of the a2-g8 diagonal, white has the opportunity to capture the black knight on g8, giving white a decisive material advantage.

SKEWER EXAMPLE 3

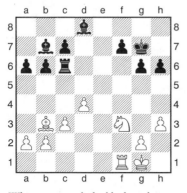

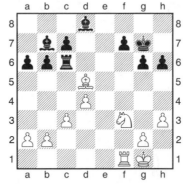

White can attack the black rook on c6 in the next move with the b3 bishop. When the rook has to move out of the h1-a8 diagonal, the black bishop on b7 is left hanging and can be captured. Where should the white bishop go?

1. **Bb3-d5** White attacks the black rook on c6. Black must move his rook out of danger, but that makes it possible for the black bishop in b7 to be captured.

SKEWER EXAMPLE 4

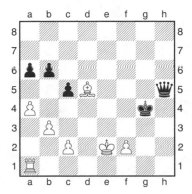

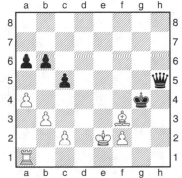

In this example, the white bishop is currently under attack. White has a move that can get the bishop out of danger and also result in checking black. When black is forced to move the king, the black queen can be captured, giving white a winning position. What move can accomplish all this?

1. **Bd5-f3+** With this move, white is able to save the bishop from the queen attack mounted by black. At the same time, white is now checking black. When the black king on g4 moves, the queen on h5 will be under direct attack by the white bishop on f3. White can then capture the queen, putting black in a losing position.

WHAT IS A DISCOVERY ATTACK?

A *discovery attack* occurs when one piece moves and uncovers an attack by a piece behind it. It is extremely powerful because both pieces can create an attack at the same time. Most commonly, a discovery attack involves a check or a capture, which can often lead to either a gain of material or sometimes even to checkmate.

STRICTLY DEFINED

A discovery attack occurs when one piece moves and uncovers an attack by a piece behind it, usually involving a check or a capture. It is extremely powerful because both pieces can create an attack at the same time.

DISCOVERY ATTACK EXAMPLE 1

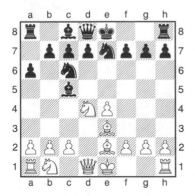

White can make a move that simultaneously attacks the black queen on d8 and the black bishop on c5. When black is forced to defend against the attack on the queen, the black bishop can be captured, giving white a decisive material advantage. Can you find this move?

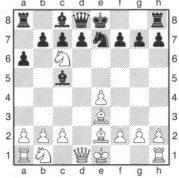

1. **Nd4xc6** With this move, the white knight is attacking the queen on d8. In the meantime, the white bishop on e3 is attacking the black bishop on c5.

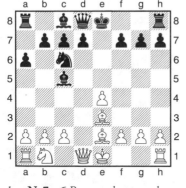

1... **Ne7xc6** Because the queen has more value, black needs to defend it by recapturing the knight on c6, giving up the bishop on c5 because black cannot defend both the queen and the bishop simultaneously.

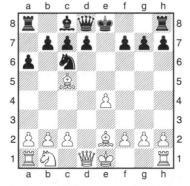

2. **Be3xc5** White captures the black bishop, giving white a substantial material advantage.

DISCOVERY ATTACK EXAMPLE 2

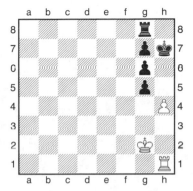 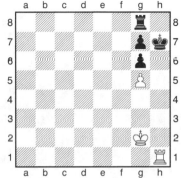

White has the opportunity in the next move to capture a pawn. At the same time, from the discovery, the white rook can checkmate the black king. Can you find this discovery?

1. **h4xg5#** White captures the black pawn on g5 while clearing the h file for the white rook on h1 to checkmate the black king on h7.

DISCOVERY ATTACK EXAMPLE 3

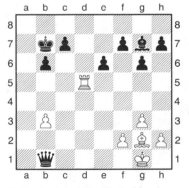 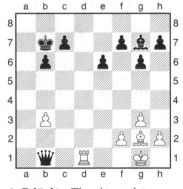

White has just been checked by the black queen. How can white give a countercheck and win black's queen with the help of a discovery?

1. **Rd5-d1+** The white rook is attacking the black queen on b1. The white bishop on g2 is checking the black king on b7. Black must defend the king, but that means that it will lose the queen, giving white a winning advantage.

DISCOVERY ATTACK EXAMPLE 4

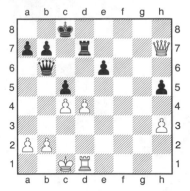

This example is a little harder to see. White is looking for a way to win a full rook with the help of a discovery against the black king and queen. Can you find this tricky combination?

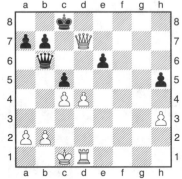

1. **Qh7xd7+** White captures the black rook on d7, preparing for the discovery on the next move.

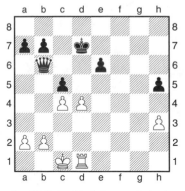

1... **Kc8xd7** Black has no choice but to capture back the white queen.

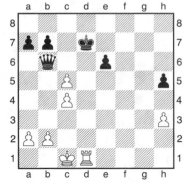

2. **d4xc5+** The white rook on d1 is checking the black king on d7 while the white pawn on c5 is attacking the black queen on b6. While black is defending the king from check, white will capture the black queen, thus obtaining a winning position.

JUST A MINUTE

The ability to find moves that will defend your pieces is one of the signs of a master player. Remember, you can't stop an attack if you can't see it.

What Is a Zugzwang

Zugzwang is a German word for a position in which whoever has the obligation to move will have no choice but to move into a worse position. In chess you can't just say, "I pass" as you can in some other games. So you have to move even if that puts you in a difficult or dangerous situation.

STRICTLY DEFINED

Zugzwang is a German word for a position in which whoever has the obligation to move will have no choice but to worsen his or her position.

Zugzwang Example 1

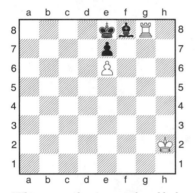

White can make a move where black has no choice but to make a losing move. Can you find this zugzwang?

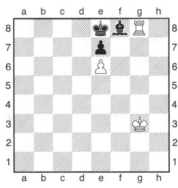

1. **Kh2-g3** Even though the move in this example does not present a direct threat to black, it gives an important purpose, putting black in zugzwang.

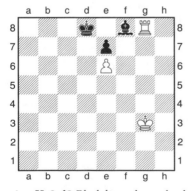

1... **Ke8-d8** Black has only one legal move, but this move leaves the bishop on f8 unprotected.

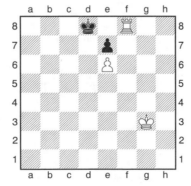

2. **Rg8xf8+** By winning the bishop and obtaining a decisive position, white has one more rook than black.

ZUGZWANG EXAMPLE 2

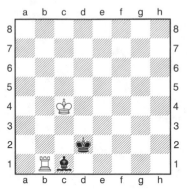

White can make a move that forces the black king to abandon the bishop on c1, giving white a decisive advantage. How is that possible?

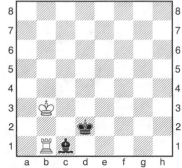

1. **Kc4-b3** This move puts black in zugzwang. The black bishop has nowhere to move.

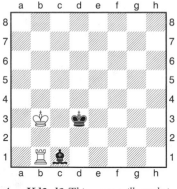

1... **Kd2-d3** This move will result in the loss of the bishop for black, but black does not have a better alternative.

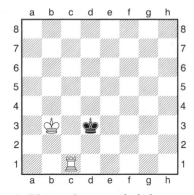

2. **Rb1xc1** Capturing the bishop, white gains a winning material advantage.

ZUGZWANG EXAMPLE 3

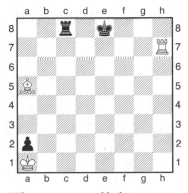

White wants to put black in a zug-zwang where the black king and the black rook have to be separated, making it easier for white to capture. How can it be done?

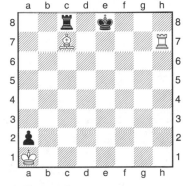

1. **Ba5-c7** By causing a zugzwang, white is forcing black to move the rook away from the king.

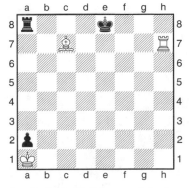

1... **Rc8-a8** Black has no choice but to move the rook away from the king. After 1... Ke8-f8, white's answer would be the same as next move Rh7-h8+ winning the rook.

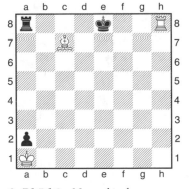

2. **Rh7-h8+** Now white has a skewer to win the black rook on a8.

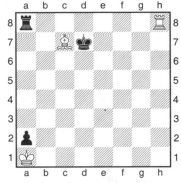

2... **Ke8-d7** Black has no choice but to move the king up.

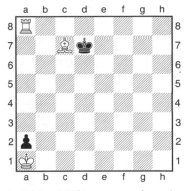

3. **Rh8xa8** White captures the rook, obtaining a winning position.

HOUR'S UP!

1. True or False: Tactics are important in making short-term gains in a game.

2. Which one of the following tactics consists of an indirect attack on an opponent's piece?

   a. Pin

   b. Fork

   c. Discovery

   d. Zugzwang

3. In which one of the following tactics is an attack blocked by your own piece?

   a. Pin

   b. Discovery

   c. Fork

   d. Skewer

4. Which one of the following tactics consists of an attack against two pieces at the same time?

   a. Checkmate

   b. Fork

   c. Skewer

   d. Zugzwang

5. Which one of the following tactics is intended to force a bad move by your opponent?

   a. Skewer

   b. Fork

   c. Zugzwang

   d. Discovery

6. True or False: It is important for a player to learn tactics because he or she might fail to see a chance to exploit an opponent's mistakes.

7. True or False: A discovery check can also be checkmate.

8. True or False: A fork occurs when you move one piece out of the way, thus putting an opponent's vulnerable piece under capture.

9. True or False: A pin is only valuable if the piece being indirectly attacked is more valuable than the piece being pinned.

10. Zugzwang is a valuable tactic because

    a. It is certain to lead to a mate.

    b. It will lead to the capture of a valuable piece.

    c. It gives the player using this tactic more control over the game.

    d. It will force the opponent to worsen his or her position.

HOUR 15

Essential Chess Tactics Workshop

This hour consists of 34 exercises designed to improve your skills at using the pin, the fork, the skewer, the discovery attack, and the zugzwang. Answers to these exercises are found in Appendix E, but first try finding the solutions yourself.

CHAPTER SUMMARY

LESSON PLAN:
You have learned the basic tactics of the pin, the fork, the skewer, the discovery attack, and the zugzwang. It's now time to work on these basic tactics and get a feel for when each should be applied and what advantages each offers in a game.

In this hour you learn ...

- How to put the pin into practice.
- How to put the fork into practice.
- How to put the skewer into practice.
- How to put the discovery attack into practice.
- How to put the zugzwang attack into practice.

PRACTICING PIN EXERCISES

The following exercises will help you to recognize various pin patterns.

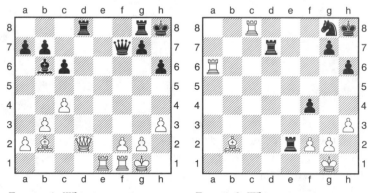

Exercise 1: White to mate in one move. Exercise 2: White to mate in one move.

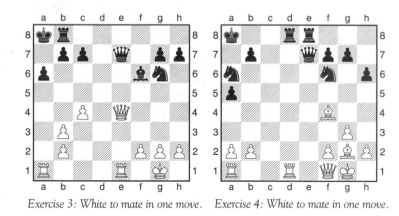

Exercise 3: White to mate in one move. Exercise 4: White to mate in one move.

PRACTICING FORK EXERCISES

The following exercises will help you to recognize various fork patterns.

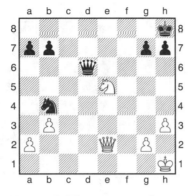

Exercise 5: White to move and win
the black queen.

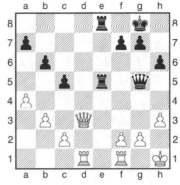

Exercise 6: White to move and fork
the rook and queen.

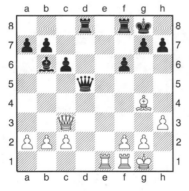

Exercise 7: White to move and win
the black queen.

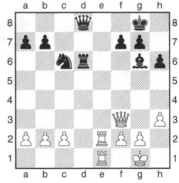

Exercise 8: White to move and win
the black queen.

PRACTICING SKEWER EXERCISES

The following exercises will help you to recognize various skewer patterns.

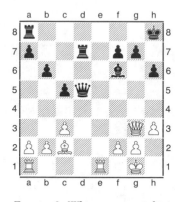

Exercise 9: White to move and win the black rook.

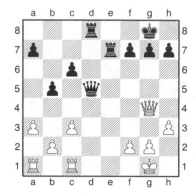

Exercise 10: White to move and win the black rook.

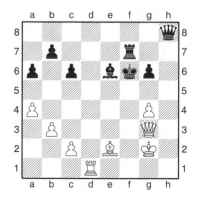

Exercise 11: White to move and win the black queen.

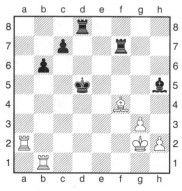

Exercise 12: White to move and win the black rook.

PRACTICING DISCOVERY ATTACK EXERCISES

The following exercises will help you to recognize various discovery attack patterns.

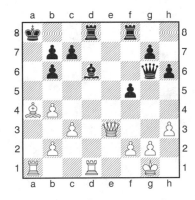

Exercise 13: White to move and win the black queen.

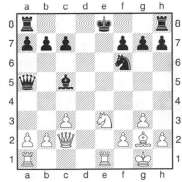

Exercise 14: White to move and win the black queen.

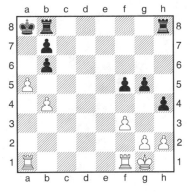

Exercise 15: White to mate in one move.

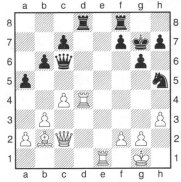

Exercise 16: White to move and win the black queen.

PRACTICING ZUGZWANG EXERCISES

The following exercises will help you to learn how to set up zugzwang positions.

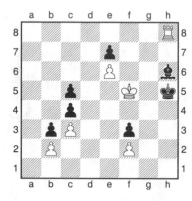

Exercise 17: White to mate in two moves.

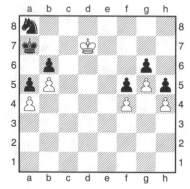

Exercise 18: White to move and win the black knight.

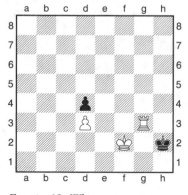

Exercise 19: White to mate in two moves.

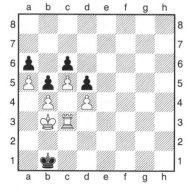

Exercise 20: White to mate in two moves.

HOW TO APPLY THE PIN, FORK, SKEWER, DISCOVERY ATTACK, AND ZUGZWANG IN A GAME

Now that you have begun to recognize patterns for these tactics, you can see how they are applied in the following exercises.

1. e2-e4 e7-e6	4. Nc3xe4 Ng8-f6	7. Bf1-d3 Bf8-d6
2. d2-d4 d7-d5	5. Ne4xf6+ Qd8xf6	8. 0-0 0-0
3. Nb1-c3 d5xe4	6. Ng1-f3 h7-h6	9. Qd1-e2 b7-b6?

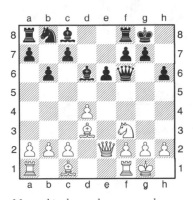

Now white has a chance to make a fork, attacking the black rook and threatening checkmate at the same time. Can you find it?

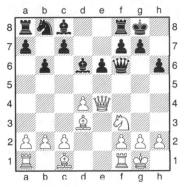

10. **Qe2-e4** *White attacks the black rook on a8 and threatens checkmate on h7. Black has no choice but to defend the mate threat on h7 and give up the rook on a8.*

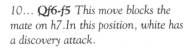

10... **Qf6-f5** *This move blocks the mate on h7. In this position, white has a discovery attack.*

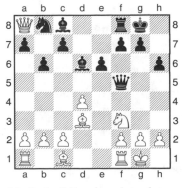

11. **Qe4xa8** *By taking the rook on a8, the white bishop on d3 is attacking the black queen on f5 while the white queen on a8 is attacking the black knight on b8.*

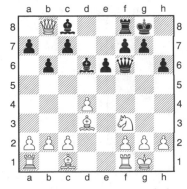

11... **Qf5-f6** 12. **Qa8xb8** *Black can create a discovery attack in this position.*

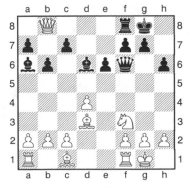

12... **Bc8-a6** *By making this move, the black rook on f8 is attacking the white queen on b8.*

13. Qb8xa7 Ba6xd3	17. Bc1-e3 Qe5xb2	20. Rb1xb5 Qa2-e6
14. c2xd3 e6-e5	18. Qa7xc7 b6-b5	21. Rf1-e1 Rf8-e8
15. d4xe5 Bd6xe5	19. Ra1-b1 Qb2xa2	22. h2-h3 g7-g6
16. Nf3xe5 Qf6xe5		

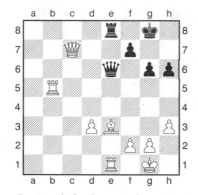

Can you find a skewer in this position?

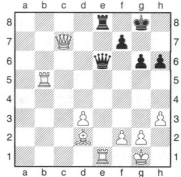

23. **Be3-d2** By putting the bishop on d2, white is attacking the black queen on e6. If the black queen moves out of the attack, the black rook on e8 will be under attack.

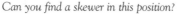

23... Qe6xe1+	26. Rb5-b8 Re8xb8	28. Qb8-f8 f7-f5
24. Bd2xe1 Re8xe1+	27. Qc7xb8+ Kg8-h7	29. h3-h4 h6-h5
25. Kg1-h2 Re1-e8		

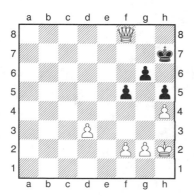

White can create a zugzwang right here, forcing black to make a move that will result in the loss of at least a pawn. Can you find the next white move?

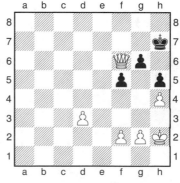

30... **Qf8-f6** Black is now in zugzwang. If black plays 30. Kh7-h6, then 31. Qf6-h8#. If black plays 30... Kh7-g8, black loses the pawn on g6.

30... **f5-f4**

31. **Qf6xf4 Kh7-g7**

32. **Qf4-g5 Kg7-h7**

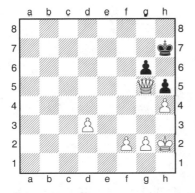

Once again, white can create a zugzwang that forces black to lose at least a pawn or else risk getting mated.

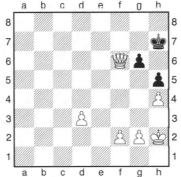

33. **Qg5-f6** After this move, black is stuck. Black has no good move.

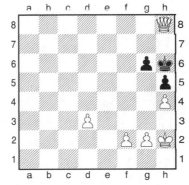

33...**Kh7-h6** 34. **Qf6-h8#** If black plays 33... Kh7-g8, white can capture the pawn on g6. Either way, black is lost.

HOUR'S UP!

1. True or False: Black made a big mistake on move nine.

2. White used the following tactic on move 10 to win material.

   a. Fork

   b. Pin

   c. Discovery attack

   d. Zugzwang

3. With move 11, white created a

   a. Fork

   b. Pin

   c. Discovery attack

   d. Zugzwang

4. Black's mistake on move 22 allowed white to use which of the following tactical elements in order to win material?

    a. Fork

    b. Pin

    c. Discovery attack

    d. Skewer

5. What did white create with move 30?

    a. Fork

    b. Pin

    c. Discovery attack

    d. Zugzwang

6. True or False: With the fork on move 10, white won a queen.

7. True or False: White made a fork by threatening checkmate and the black rook simultaneously.

8. True or False: After move 27, white was up a rook and a pawn.

9. True or False: Black won the game.

10. At the end of the game, white checkmated with his

    a. Queen

    b. Rook

    c. Bishop

    d. Knight

HOUR 16

Five Essential Rules for Winning and Enjoying Chess

It's not enough merely to know the rules of chess. What's important is to be able to keep a cool head in the heat of a game so that you can apply the rules when it counts. That takes practice and experience.

RULE 1: DEMONSTRATING PROPER DISCIPLINE IN CHESS OPENING DEVELOPMENT

In the following example, you find that white does not follow the opening development rules on many occasions.

CHAPTER SUMMARY

LESSON PLAN:
There are five essential rules that should be followed in every game of chess you play.

In this hour you learn …

- How to exercise discipline in openings.
- How foolish blunders can wrest defeat out of the jaws of victory.
- Why analyzing your opponent's moves is so important.
- Why learning from mistakes can lead to victory in the future.
- Why impulsive moves can cost you the game.

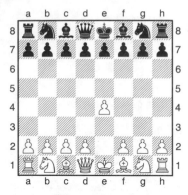

1. e2-e4 White occupies the e4 center square and controls the d5 center square, a normal opening for white.

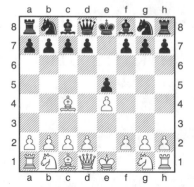

1... e7-e5 Black occupies e5 and controls d4, a normal development for black. *2. Bf1-c4* White develops the bishop and puts more control on the d5 square. No problem so far.

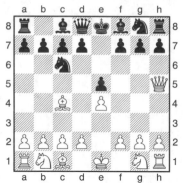

2... Nb8-c6 Black continues with normal development, moving out the knight from b8. *3. Qd1-h5* Here is the first thing white should NOT do!

Don't bring out the queen prematurely; it is more important to have normal piece development. A better move would have been 3. Ng1-f3. White is aiming for a checkmate with Qh5xf7. However, if you play against decent players, the chances of this mate happening are nil. Therefore, it would be much better to develop the pieces normally.

3... g7-g6 Black is blocking the threat of the checkmate and clearing g7 for the bishop on f8. In the meantime, black is attacking the white queen on h5, forcing white to move the queen again. *4. Qh5-f3* Another bad move!

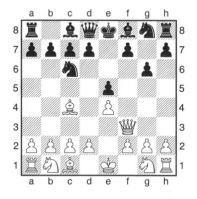

The following explains black's g7-g6 move:

- It would not have helped if black had played 3... Ng8-f6 because white could have played 4. Qh5xf7#

- If black had played 3... Ng8-h6, development would have been a problem because the knight does not belong to that side. The natural development of the knight is f6, which would enable it to put pressure on the center.

- If black had played 3… Qd8-e7, the black queen on e7 would have blocked the a3-f8 diagonal for the black bishop on f8.
- If black had played 3… Qd8-f6, the black queen on f6 would have blocked the black knight on g8 from developing to f6, a natural square for the knight.

White, on the other hand, is moving the queen too many times rather than developing other pieces. White has no choice now but to move the queen again because of the direct attack of the pawn on g6. This is the consequence of bringing the queen out prematurely. Also, by moving the queen to f3, white is blocking that square from the white knight on g1, preventing it from developing to the natural square. Moreover, the queen can once again be a target of future attack with Nc6-d4. A better move would have been retreating with 4. Qh5-d1.

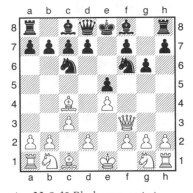

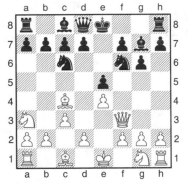

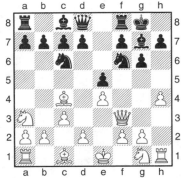

4… **Ng8-f6** *Black once again is defending against the threat of Qf3xf7# while developing another minor piece, not wasting any valuable time.* 5. **c2-c3** *Another questionable move by white. The pawn on c3 is stopping the white knight on b1 from developing to that natural square. White still has many pieces left to develop.*

5… **Bf8-g7** *This is normal development of the black bishop while preparing for castling next.* 6. **Nb1-a3** *This move is questionable because the knight is taken out of the action— placing it away from the center. Because the white pawn is on c3 and the knight couldn't develop to c3, white should have prepared to develop the knight to d2 by playing 6. d2-d3.*

6… **0-0** *Black is following all the rules, castling to make the king safe.* 7. **h2-h4** *Instead of developing other pieces, white is violating the rules of opening and trying to attack prematurely.*

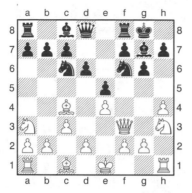

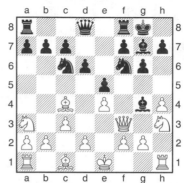

7... d7-d6 *Black is clearing the h3-c8 diagonal for the bishop on c8 to develop.* **8. Ng1–h3** *Another mistake. Because the queen is on f3, white could not develop his knight on that square; however, e2 would still be better than h3.*

8... Bc8-g4 *Black develops the last minor piece and even attacks white's queen.*

Let's take a look at the game after eight moves: White has not castled. The white bishop on c1 is stuck. Both white knights developed in a less-than-ideal location. Black in the meantime is fully developed, and black pieces are where they are supposed to be. Black is in good shape. This is an example how not to play as white, in contrast to a perfect development for black.

RULE 2A: ADJUST YOUR PLANS ACCORDING TO YOUR OPPONENT'S MOVES

Ask yourself after each one of your opponent's moves: What is the purpose of that move?

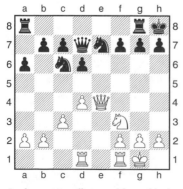

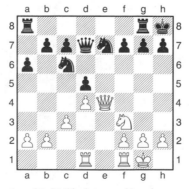

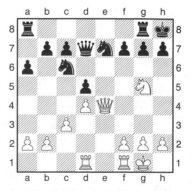

In the position illustrated here, black is up by a knight and is dominating the game. With a little focus and attention, black should win easily.

1... d6-d5 *Black is attacking the white queen on e4.*

2. Nf3-g5 *White is in a losing position so he is trying to set up a desperate trap, hoping black will be careless.*

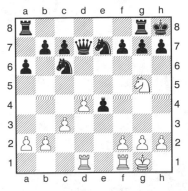

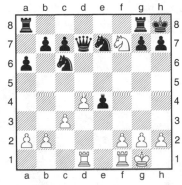

2... **d5xe4** *Black was not looking at white's last move too carefully. Black saw that white posed a checkmate threat with 3. Qe4xh7; however, black failed to pay attention to the threat posed by 3. Ng5xf7# as well. If black had paid careful attention to white's last move, black would have seen both threats. The proper response by black would have been 2... Ne7-g6, stopping both mate threats. Black, however, assumes that 2... d5xe4 eliminates the 3. Qe4xh7#.*

3. **Ng5xf7#**

So, what have we learned here? Always ask yourself: What is the purpose of each of your opponent's moves? Don't assume that your opponent blundered or just made a harmless move. Always look at the whole board!

RULE 2B: NEVER UNDERESTIMATE YOUR OPPONENTS AND THEIR MOVES

At the time of this game, white was a world famous grandmaster while black was a young up-and-coming international master, definitely not equal to the grandmaster yet.

GM Yacov Murey—IM Zsuzsa Polgar

France, 1988

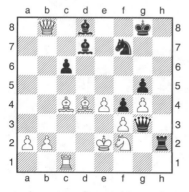

At the position illustrated here, white is completely dominating. Because black is an underdog, white underestimates his opponent and misunderstands her next move, assuming that it is only meant to delay the inevitable resignation on her part.

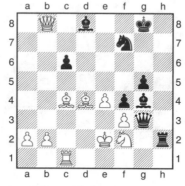

1... **Bd7xg4** Black is setting up a desperate trap.

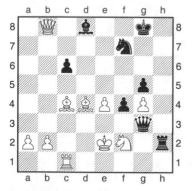

2. **f3xg4** White assumes that it is a blunder and takes the black bishop immediately, feeling very confident. A better move would have been 2. Rc1-c3, then white would still have numerous winning threats.

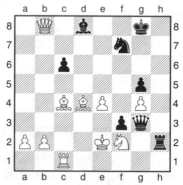

2... **f4-f3+** After this discovery, white loses his queen on b8, leaving black with decisive material advantage. Taken by surprise, white is shocked, wondering how he could have overlooked such an elementary trap. He immediately resigns.

RULE 2C: NEVER OVERESTIMATE YOUR OPPONENTS AND THEIR MOVES

At the time of this game, both players were well-known world class grandmasters. White achieved a superior position and could have checkmated in two moves because black made a horrible blunder. To everyone's amazement, white did not see the two-move checkmate.

GM Szabo—GM Reshevsky
Zurich, 1953

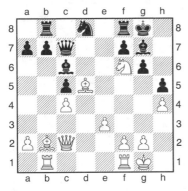

White has just moved the knight to f6 to check black.

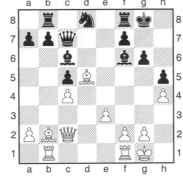

*1… **Bg7xf6??** Here's the horrible blunder that allowed white to checkmate black in two moves! Black still could have avoided the immediate trouble by moving out of the check by 1… Kg8-h8.*

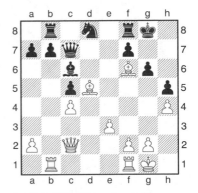

*2. **Bb2xf6??** White played this move instead of checkmating. After a series of bad moves on the part of both players, the two players agreed to a draw.*

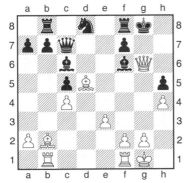

*Instead of playing 2. **Bb2xf6**, all white had to do was play 2. Qc2xg6+ and he would have had a checkmate in the next move.*

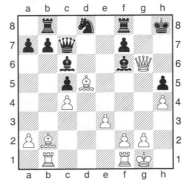

2… Kg8-h8 Black has to get out of check. If black plays 2… Bf6-g7, white would play 3. Qg6xg7# Black cannot capture the white queen with the pawn of f7 because it is pinned.

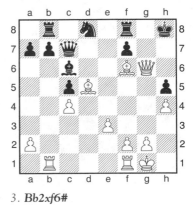

*3. **Bb2xf6#***

After the game when he was asked about the shocking oversight of an elementary mate in two moves, white responded: "Well, you don't just look for mates in two against Reshevsky."

So, what have we learned? Never overestimate your opponent, even if he or she is one of the best in the world. The best thing to do is play the board and not the opponent.

Rule 3: Be Accurate and Double-Check All Your Moves or Tactics

When you map out tactics, make sure you double-, triple-, or even quadruple-check all possibilities. Don't get so excited that you make a move as soon as you find a good line. More often than not, faulty calculations occur, and it can cost you your game.

In the following example, white fought hard for several hours and achieved a winning position. With only a few moves left before victory, white got careless and did not double-check the last move.

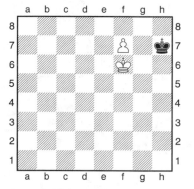

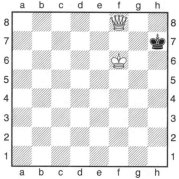

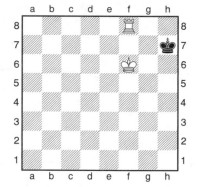

Instead of having a mate in two, white stalemated black and gave away a win.

1. *f7-f8(Q)??* White is happy that his pawn has made it to the eighth rank for promotion. But rather than double-checking which piece to promote to, white chooses to make it a queen without thinking. This is a horrible blunder because black cannot move and is stalemated! The game is declared a draw.

Had white double-checked his last move and played 1. *f7-f8(R)*, choosing to become a rook rather than a queen, he would have won.

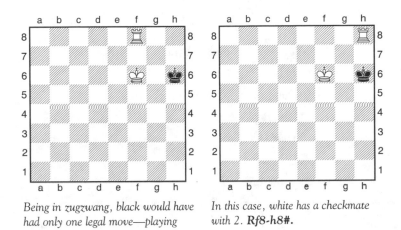

Being in zugzwang, black would have had only one legal move—playing 1... Kh7-h6.

In this case, white has a checkmate with 2. Rf8-h8#.

So, what have we learned? Don't take any move for granted no matter how good it may look. Make sure you double-check before making the move.

RULE 4: LEARN FROM YOUR OWN MISTAKES

When you play a tournament chess game, you are required to keep score. When you play chess on the Internet, the game score is kept automatically. In either case, when the game is finished, go through the game to figure out where you made your mistakes. Some mistakes may not be so obvious to a novice. Therefore, when you analyze your game, it might be helpful to get some advice or help from an expert chess player.

You can also use a chess software program to help you analyze your game. Most computer software can recommend the best moves to you and point out where your mistakes were made.

The more time you spend going over your games, the more you will learn, and chances are, you will not repeat the same mistakes in the future.

GO TO ▶
To find out more about chess software programs, see Appendix B.

RULE 5: HAVE FUN! ENJOY! WIN WITH GRACE AND CLASS! LOSE WITH DIGNITY!

Chess is a great game and is meant to be fun. Enjoy the competition, the challenge, and the artistic side of chess. Sometimes you win, sometimes you lose, but always conduct yourself with grace and class. This is the most important rule!

Hour's Up!

1. True or False: You should never analyze your opponent's moves.

2. When you find a good combination, you should

    a. Close your eyes and play it, hoping for the best.

    b. Pray that it will work.

    c. Double-check your calculations.

    d. Take many deep breaths.

3. True or False: Chess is life or death.

4. True or False: Studying your own game is a good way to improve.

5. When your opponent makes a move you think is a blunder, you should

    a. Assume it is a blunder, laugh hysterically, and make a responding move right away.

    b. Try to figure out the idea behind that move to see if it is really a blunder or if it is a trap.

    c. Ignore it and assume it is a trap.

    d. Think about what is for dinner.

6. When you play against a much stronger opponent, you should

    a. Never overestimate your opponent's move and play normally.

    b. Assume all your opponent's moves are perfect.

    c. Get nervous and make a blunder.

    d. Pray that you don't hyperventilate.

7. After you win a game, you should

    a. Scream out loud.

    b. Insult your opponent.

    c. Walk away.

    d. Shake hands and behave sportsmanlike.

8. When you lose a game, you should

    a. Go cry in the bathroom.

    b. Go have a big dinner.

    c. Go over the game and see where you went wrong.

    d. Throw the chess pieces against the wall.

9. True or False: You should always assume that a weaker opponent will blunder against you and lose.

10. True or False: You should never make a move on impulse.

HOUR 17

Mastering Basic Chess Etiquette

In addition to being professional, courteous, and sportsmanlike, chess is also supposed to be fun—win, lose, or draw. Unfortunately, some people take it too seriously and behave badly.

WHEN DO I RESIGN?

When you are way down in material (such as by a queen, a rook, or even a knight or bishop) without any prospect of compensation (for example, queening is impossible and you have no positional advantage), it is okay to resign. It is also okay to resign when you are about to get mated and there is no defense.

On the other hand, there is no rule requiring you to resign in a completely lost position. You can play on until you get mated; it is a personal decision. However, if you feel that the position is hopeless, it is probably best to resign and save time and further humiliation. That is considered good sportsmanship.

In the following figure, for instance, it is appropriate for black to resign because black is down by a rook and a bishop.

CHAPTER SUMMARY

LESSON PLAN:

Chess is supposed to be a game in which two minds collide at the chessboard, in a professional, courteous, and sportsmanlike manner.

In this hour you learn ...

- When resignation is appropriate.
- How to resign.
- When to draw.
- What happens if you accidentally touch the pieces.
- What you do when pieces require adjusting.
- How to avoid distracting or annoying behavior in a game.
- How to behave in a simul.

It would be perfectly appropriate for black to resign.

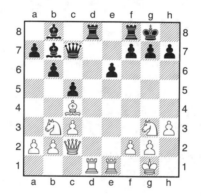

Some players, however, do not believe in resigning against anyone. They believe in the concept of "It's not over till it's over". Even though it is their right to persist, we disagree. In the following figure, should black resign because he is behind in material?

In our opinion, black should not resign in this case because black has some compensation with the perfectly placed bishop pair, pointing at the white king.

Objectively, if the position in the preceding figure were played between two grandmasters, white would have a winning position, and there would be almost no chance for a surprise. However, if this position were played by two chess novices, white wouldn't necessarily have the advantage. In this case, anything could go wrong as illustrated in the following sequence of figures.

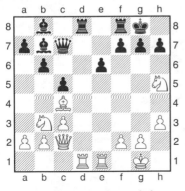

Let's say white is careless and plays 1. **Ng3-h5**.

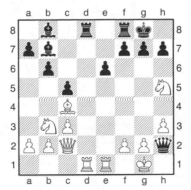

Black can mate white with 1... **Qc7-h2+**.

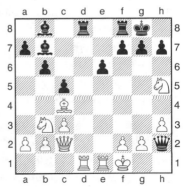

The white king has no choice but to play 2. **Kg1-f1**.

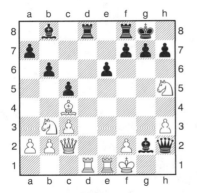

2... **Bb7xg2+** Black captures a pawn, forcing the white king to the e file.

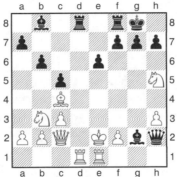

Again, white only has one legal move, 3. **Kf1-e2**.

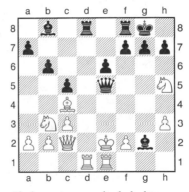

Black continues to check the king with 3... **Qh2-e5+**.

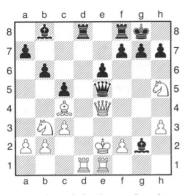

Again, the only legal move for white is 4. **Qc2-e4**.

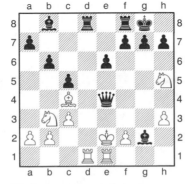

Black mates white with 4... **Qe5xe4#**. Look how fast the tide can turn with just one bad move.

When it comes to resigning, each player should use his or her judgment. If you play against a novice and you have a lost position, you can hope that your opponent will make a mistake, allowing you to save the game or even win it as shown in the preceding example. However, if you play against a very experienced player, a chess master or chess professional, the chances of that happening are just about none. In the meantime, hours could be wasted continuing to play when the outcome is all but inevitable.

There is nothing more annoying for a player than to have a tournament game all but completely won, yet have to sit for another few hours while the opponent continues to play. If you do the same in a friendly game at a local club or park, chances are your opponent will refuse to play with you again.

The bottom line is simple: Resigning is a personal decision. Don't do it because that is what your opponent wants. Only resign when you objectively feel that your position is hopeless and that you have absolutely no chance to save it. Don't drag out a lost game just because you are a sore loser or you want to annoy your opponent.

HOW DO I RESIGN?

Knowing how to resign is just as important as knowing when to resign. The traditional way of resigning is to tip your king over on its side. This is the universally known method of resigning. The next step would be to extend your hand to congratulate your opponent. This shows true sportsmanship. Even better would be to take the extra step and praise your opponent by telling your opponent that he or she played well. I believe in showing a touch of class, no matter how badly you lose.

Some players do not tip their king. Instead, they stop the clock, extend their hand, and say, "I resign." This is acceptable as well.

What you don't want to do is behave badly by knocking the pieces over, saying something obnoxious, cussing, or just walking away and making your opponent wait around. Unfortunately, some players cannot handle losses and behave in this manner. Let's just hope that there are not too many of these players around.

Since I began playing chess at the age of five, I have only experienced two extreme cases of poor sportsmanship. One incident occurred in the early 1980s when I was one of the top juniors playing against a well-known international master, one of the best players in the United States. I won the game. Rather than resigning and congratulating me for a well deserved win, my opponent grabbed a bunch of pieces, threw them 20–30 feet across the room, knocked the remaining pieces off the table, and stormed out of the room. He subsequently withdrew from the tournament. I was quite stunned.

The other occasion occurred a few years later in the mid-1980s during a big international tournament with some of the best players from all over the world. In one of the games, I played against one of the best-known legends in chess. I won a spectacular game. Rather than resigning with class, my opponent knocked all the pieces over, got up, refused to shake hands, and left. Some players behave better than others after a loss, but in general, most chess players behave decently.

THE POST-GAME ANALYSIS

It is very common for tournament players to spend a considerable amount of time going over the game in the analysis room after it is finished. This is called a "post-mortem" or "post-game analysis" session. It is important to be respectful during these sessions.

Sometimes, you can learn a lot more during these sessions because you find out what was going on in your opponent's mind during the game. You can pick your opponent's brain by asking for an explanation as to what kind of ideas and strategies were guiding his or her play. It will help you understand why you lost. One additional benefit of these sessions is that friendships often develop this way.

WHEN DO I OFFER A DRAW?

Usually, a draw is offered when a player feels that the position is equal and neither side can really checkmate the other. However, this is to be determined 99 percent of the time solely by the players, and not by a third party, such as a spectator, friend, or arbiter.

In the figure, for instance, neither side can make any progress with the king or bishop.

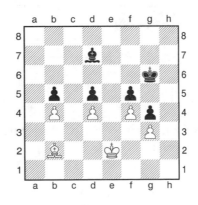

In a position like this, a draw offer is definitely appropriate.

In this next example, shown in the following figure, it is also appropriate to offer a draw because there is no realistic chance that either side can win.

As long as black and white move only their kings, there would be no way for the other side to break through.

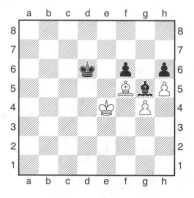

However, in the example shown in the following figure, it would be inappropriate for black to offer a draw because black is way behind in material and is about to get mated when white plays Qf7-g8# in the next move.

Qf7-g8#. *This is not an appropriate time for black to offer a draw.*

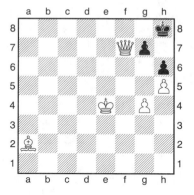

How Do I Offer a Draw?

During a tournament game, the draw offer can be made right after you have just made a move but before you start your opponent's clock. It is inappropriate to offer a draw while it is your opponent's move.

If you offer a draw while it is still your move, your opponent has the right to ask to see your move first. Then once you make a move, your opponent has the option to accept or decline.

It is generally known as bad etiquette to repeatedly offer a draw to your opponent. Try not to offer a draw again until there are significant changes in the game position.

WHAT IS THE "TOUCH-MOVE" RULE?

Touch-move means if you touch a chess piece, you must move it. The touch-move rule is used in every tournament. There is an exception, however, when the piece that a player touches has no legal move. Only in that case can the player move another piece.

In the example shown in the following figure, let's say white touched the king. Under normal circumstances, white would have to move the king. However, because the white king cannot move to g1 because black has a bishop on b6 guarding that square, white may move any other piece. Just try not to make a habit of it.

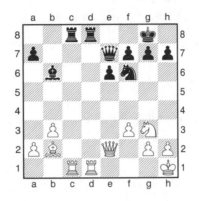

The white king cannot move to g1 because black has a bishop on b6 guarding that square.

When a player lets go of the piece he has just moved, that move is final. Even though the player may have forgotten to press his clock, no changes can be made.

WHAT IS A HAND HOVER?

Hand hover occurs when a player keeps his hand over a piece for a long period of time but without touching or moving it. This kind of gesture is a very big distraction and it's annoying besides. It's best not to reach for the piece until you are sure about where to move it.

J'ADOUBE

"J'adoube" is a French word meaning "I adjust." Sometimes in the course of a game, one or more of your pieces or pawns may not be centered in a square, meaning they are touching another square. This can be distracting for a player. In order for a player to adjust the pieces or pawns properly, he or she must first announce "J'adoube" or "I adjust" prior to touching the pieces.

J'adoube is French for "I adjust." It is uttered in advance of straightening a piece that may not be centered properly, thus posing a distraction.

When a player makes the announcement "J'adoube" before touching any piece or pawn, the touch-move rule is temporarily waived. Just don't say the words after you touch a piece. If that happens, the touch-move rule is in full effect.

General Rules of Chess Etiquette

The following are generally accepted rules of etiquette that are observed by most chess players:

- It is considered rude and inappropriate for a player to eat or have a meal at the playing table.
- Basic refreshments such as water, coffee, tea, or soda are okay provided one does not make a mess.
- When you chew gum, chew quietly. Don't annoy your opponent by chewing loudly or blowing bubbles.
- Smoking at the playing table is not allowed.
- Refrain from singing while playing. You may be Pavarotti but do not perform while playing chess.
- There should be no communication with your opponent until after the game, except to resign, offer a draw, or announce J'adoube.
- Don't make a draw offer to your opponent after every move once it is refused or rejected.

Although the following are not rules, it is recommended to do the following:

- Try to show up to your game in a timely manner. While you are not forfeited unless you are an hour late or more (with regular time limit), it is considered rude to be tardy.
- Don't adjust the chess pieces with each move. It is quite annoying for your opponent.
- It may sound too basic to even mention, but don't cough or sneeze at your opponent.
- Shake hands before the game. It is customary.
- Have you ever seen the sign: "No shirt, no shoes, no service"? The same rule holds true in chess. Proper attire should be worn while playing.
- Don't whistle while you are playing. It is annoying and distracting to your opponent.
- No trash talking before, during, or after the game. Be courteous.

- If you intend to listen to a Walkman during a game, don't play it too loud and definitely use headphones.
- Don't do anything to annoy your opponent or other players who may be sitting next to you.

GENERAL ETIQUETTE WHEN PLAYING IN A SIMUL

In a *simul*, a strong and experienced chess player plays many other players at their respective chess boards simultaneously—as few as 4 players or as many as a few hundred players.

STRICTLY DEFINED

A simul is short for simultaneous exhibition in which a strong chess player may take on just a few opponents or as many as a few hundred challengers at the same time.

Below are some common etiquette rules to remember when participating in a simul:

- The person who is giving the simul (or moving among the other players), known as the "simul giver," always gets the white pieces in every game. The exception is when a simul giver consents to give the opponent the white pieces.
- The person who is participating in the simul, known as "the participant," should never make a move while the simul giver is occupied at another board. It is hard for the simul giver to remember who moved where on every board.
- When the simul giver is playing at the board of the participant, the latter must make a move immediately.
- If the participant can't find a good move, he or she must say "pass." It is common to have a maximum of three passes per game. "Pass" means the participant is asking the simul giver to move on to another board to give him or her a little more time to find a reply.

HOUR'S UP!

1. True or False: It's inappropriate to offer a draw when it's your opponent's move.
2. True or False: If you offer a draw before you move, your opponent has the right to ask you to make the move.
3. True or False: It's acceptable to continue to make draw offers throughout the game even if they are rejected.

4. If you touch one of your pieces, you must
    a. Move that piece.
    b. Move another piece.
    c. Resign immediately.
    d. Offer a draw.

5. The words "I adjust" are said when
    a. Your piece is accidentally touched.
    b. An opponent's piece is accidentally touched.
    c. A mistaken move is made.
    d. A piece is not properly centered on a square and you want to fix it.

6. A hand hover is considered bad etiquette because
    a. A player can hide the move.
    b. The gesture is distracting.
    c. Waiting too long to move is illegal.

7. One of the behaviors listed below is considered unacceptable during a tournament game. Which one is it?
    a. Concentrating on your game
    b. Making good moves
    c. Drinking water
    d. Smoking

8. True or False: A player forfeits the game if he or she shows up half an hour late in a regular time control tournament.

9. True or False: If a player forgets to press his or her clock, the move just made is not considered final.

10. In a simul, "the participant" usually has how many passes per game?
    a. Two
    b. Three
    c. Four
    d. One

PART V

I Feel Good. I Want to Play in Tournaments or Competitively.

Hour 18

Playing Different Types of Tournaments

Chapter Summary

LESSON PLAN:

Now that you have learned how to play chess, you may want to get some tournament experience under your belt.

In this hour you learn ...

- Where you can find tournaments in your neighborhood or online.
- How to join the United States Chess Federation (USCF).
- How you can earn USCF official ratings.
- How to play round-robin and Swiss-system tournaments.
- What sudden death is.
- How to read a chess wall chart.

Opportunities to play in tournaments are available practically every day of the week. Tournament play can either occur over-the-board (OTB), through mail correspondence, or on the Internet. There is nothing to be nervous about. Tournament directors (TD) are there to help you and guide you through the process.

Local, National, and International Tournaments

Most local area chess clubs frequently run tournaments. Usually, these club tournaments attract the club members and players from the local area. Trophies are awarded to the winners. The entry fees for these tournaments are very reasonable. Most clubs require you to be a club member and a member of the United States Chess Federation (USCF). Some may not, but only USCF sanctioned events can be officially rated.

Entering Your First Tournament

When you enter your first tournament, you are considered unrated, that is, someone who has no official rating. Once you complete your first official USCF-sanctioned rated tournament, you will receive a USCF rating based on your performance in the tournament. The more you win, the higher your rating will be and vice versa. For more information regarding the USCF ratings, visit the official rating website of the USCF: http://www.uschess.org/ratings. You can also check out this section: http://uschess.org/ratings/info for rating information.

INTRODUCTION TO USCF-RATED TOURNAMENTS

Many USCF members find that participation in USCF-rated chess tournaments is one of their favorite benefits. Sanctioned tournaments are sponsored by the USCF or one of its many affiliated organizations. Players compete against other federation members under the direction of certified tournament directors. There are tournaments everywhere; there's probably one in your area.

ROUND-ROBIN TOURNAMENTS

In a *round-robin tournament*, you play one game with every other player in the tournament. One common type of round robin in the United States is a quad, in which four players of approximately equal ability are grouped into a section. These three-round tournaments are usually played in a single day, and no one is eliminated. The person with the highest score at the end of the tournament is the winner. Round-robin tournaments are much more common in other parts of the world (especially Europe) than in the United States. In Europe and other places, round-robin tournaments normally include 10–14 players.

STRICTLY DEFINED

A round-robin tournament is a chess tournament in which each player plays a game with every other participant.

DOUBLE ROUND ROBIN

Double round robin is the same as round robin except you play each of the other players twice: one game as white and one as black.

SWISS-SYSTEM TOURNAMENTS

The *Swiss-system tournament* is the most common tournament format in the United States and can accommodate a large number of players. In a Swiss-system tournament, no one is eliminated. Normally, as you continue to win games, you face progressively stronger opposition, with the result that those participants who are not so successful end up playing against each other.

STRICTLY DEFINED

A Swiss-system tournament is one in which large numbers of players participate, no player is eliminated, and as the games progress, stronger players are paired with stronger players and weaker players with other weaker players.

Toward the end of the event, you will probably find yourself matched against players who are playing more or less on your level. Many tournaments have special prizes for new players and novices.

In Swiss-system events, players are paired with each other according to the following general principles:

- A player is not paired with any other player more than once.
- Players with the same score are paired whenever possible.
- Colors are assigned to players by the director as fairly as possible. Alternating the colors is the ideal.

For the first round, the players are ranked according to their last-published USCF rating. The top player in the upper half of the field is then paired against the top player in the lower half of the field, and so on. The top-ranked player's color in the first round is normally allocated by lot, and then colors alternate down the halves.

In the second round, the director uses the same principles to pair each of the three score groups (those who won, those who drew, and those who lost). These pairing procedures continue through the rest of the tournament. In some large tournaments, various "accelerated pairings" are used in early rounds.

The wall chart is important in a Swiss tournament. The wall chart, which lists the players and their results, enables everyone to see exactly what is happening in the event. After a wall chart is posted, players normally help the directors by proofreading the entries that interest them.

The following sample wall chart shows John Doe as the top-rated player in the event (because he is ranked No. 1). Doe's USCF identification number is 12345678; his last published rating was 2467. (Rating is a number measuring your playing strength. Average club players are usually rated between 1300–1600 while professionals are usually between 2500–2700.)

Player's Full Name	Rating	Round 1	Round 2	Round 3	Round 4
JOHN DOE	2467	W 35	B 21	B 3	W 12
ID No. 12345678		1.0	2.0	2.0	2.5

In round 1, John Doe had white against player 35 and won (for a total of 1 point). In round 2, he had black against player 21 and won (for a cumulative total of 2). In round 3, he had black against player 3 and lost (still a cumulative total of 2). In round 4, he had white against player 12 and drew (for a cumulative total of 2.5).

MATCH PLAY

Match play occurs when two players are playing a series of games against one another in a match. This is not a very popular format except on the world class level. Match play is usually used for the World Chess Championship where the challenger plays a match against the World Champion for the title. Usually, match play has an even number of games (4, 6, 8, 10, and so on). For example, in 1996, the then challenger Zsuzsa Polgar (Hungary) defeated the reigning World Champion Xie Jun (China) by the score of 8.5–4.5 to capture the Women's World Champion title.

CHESS CLOCKS

Another standard part of a sanctioned tournament is the chess clock. Usually, players must bring their own. These special timers are really two separate clocks and dials in a single case. When a player makes a move, he presses a button that stops his clock and starts his opponent's clock.

In tournament play, any player who has not completed the prescribed number of moves in the allotted time loses, unless his opponent has insufficient mating material. Some typical time controls are 40 (or 50) moves in two hours, or 40 (or 45) moves in an hour and a half.

Sudden-death (SD) time controls have become popular. Sudden-death games must be completed within the prescribed time, no matter how many moves it takes. If a player runs out of time, his opponent wins only if the opponent has sufficient remaining material to make checkmate possible.

STRICTLY DEFINED

Sudden-death time refers to games that must be completed within a certain time period regardless of how many moves it takes.

RECORDING GAMES

In a tournament game in which time controls are used, it is necessary for the players to keep a record of the game to know how many moves have been made. Because a player must make a certain number of moves in the allotted time, if the player does not fulfill the requirement of moves, the player forfeits and loses the game. For example, 40/90 SD (sudden death)/60 means that each player has to make 40 moves in 90 minutes. Once the 40th move is completed by both sides, each player will receive an additional 60 minutes added on to the clock, and the game has to be completed during that time. This record will also be a useful study tool.

FYI Score keeping is not required for events with time controls of Game/10 to Game/29. Game/10 means each player has 10 minutes to finish the entire game. Game/29 means each player has 29 minutes to do the same.

There are two notational systems that are commonly used in the United States—descriptive and algebraic. The "In Writing" flier describes these and other systems. Just write to the U.S. Chess Federation 3054 NYS Route 9W, New Windsor, NY 12553 and request a free copy.

GO TO ▷
To refresh your memory about notation for recording games, see Hour 4.

CHESS SETS AND BOARDS

A player should bring a chess set and board when participating in a tournament; the organizer does not supply chess equipment. Pieces should be made of plastic, wood, or a material similar in appearance.

The king's height should be 3.375–4.50 inches and the diameter of the king's base should be 40–50 percent of the height. The other pieces should be proportionate in height and form. The conventional *Staunton pattern* is the standard.

STRICTLY DEFINED

The Staunton pattern is named after Howard Staunton (1810–1874), a leading player in the 1840s. The set was registered by Nathaniel Cook in March 1849. It was inspired by the Parthenon frieze in the British museum. Staunton recommended the chess set in the *Illustrated London News* and that is how the Staunton pattern came about.

The pieces should be the color of naturally light and dark wood (for example, maple, boxwood, walnut, or ebony) or approximations of these colors. Black and white pieces are perfectly acceptable.

Chessboards must be opaque and fabricated from a smooth material that allows easy movement of the pieces. They can be made out of wood, paper, cardboard, leather, cloth, or marble. Chessboard colors should offer high contrast between light and dark sections, yet remain pleasing to the eye. Good color combinations include green or brown with ivory or buff, and walnut or teak with maple or birch. The colors and finish should allow extended examination without eyestrain. Squares that do not exactly match the colors of the pieces are popular because they allow ready distinction between empty and occupied squares. For example, the green and buff vinyl roll-up board is the most commonly used at tournaments. Boards for standard sets should have squares of approximately 2.0–2.5 inches.

CONDUCT OF PLAYERS

Tournament players are not allowed to look at personal or published chess material during a game. They are also not allowed to receive either solicited or unsolicited advice from a third party concerning a game in progress. Players are also forbidden to distract or annoy their opponents. Conversation, *skittles*, and other noisy activities should not take place in the playing room.

STRICTLY DEFINED

In the chess world, skittles means casual chess analysis, usually done following the game.

These rules and other relevant regulations can be found in the USCF Official Rules of Chess (catalog number C929CP), available from U.S. Chess. Call or write for details 3054 NYS Route 9W, New Windsor, NY 12553 1-845-561-CHES (2437).

If you are forced to withdraw from an event or miss a round of play, make sure that you tell the director in advance. Players who fail to do so are subject to a penalty.

RATINGS

USCF ratings are of special interest to many players. These numbers reflect a player's standing relative to other USCF players. There are two separate rating systems for over-the-board (OTB) chess—regular and "quick" ratings—and one rating system for correspondence chess. Quick ratings are used for events with time controls of Game/10 to Game/29, and regular ratings are calculated for tournaments with time controls of Game/30 or slower.

A person's OTB and correspondence ratings are printed on his or her *Chess Life* or *School Mates* mailing label. For more information on either rating system, contact the Federation's New Windsor office:

U.S. Chess Federation
3054 NYS Route 9W, New Windsor, NY 12553
Phone:(914) 526-8350
Fax: (914) 561-2437
www.uschess.org
E-mail: techdir@uschess.org

Novice OTB ratings are often 800 or less, and Master ratings start at 2200. Most tournament players are rated between these levels.

CORRESPONDENCE CHESS TOURNAMENTS

Correspondence chess is the major form of chess competition for some USCF members. A number of members play in both correspondence and OTB tournaments.

In a typical correspondence section, you play six games—three with white and three with black. Moves are exchanged on postcards, and play is governed by the official chess rules that are specially modified for correspondence chess. Some games may actually take up to two years to complete, although that is not often the case.

The USCF also offers e-mail correspondence chess tournaments to those who have CompuServe or Internet access. You must be a USCF member, have a computer with a modem, and subscribe to CompuServe or an Internet service provider. These games can be rated as correspondence games. A variety of correspondence tournaments are available.

OFFICIAL USCF TIME CONTROL REGULATIONS

The following are official regulations for USCF-rated tournaments.

REGULAR RATING SYSTEM

The duration of the first time control must be at least 30 minutes for each player. The first period may be sudden death. If a non-sudden-death control is used, the rate of play must be equal to or slower than an average of 60 moves per hour. The tournament director has the option to shorten the basic time control.

The rate of play for any non-sudden-death controls must be equal to or slower than an average of 60 moves per hour. It is recommended that secondary and subsequent controls allow one hour per player.

The important thing is a format and time control that appeals to you. Some players prefer slow time controls and others prefer faster play. Variety in time controls is important to help keep members with different preferences involved in regulation events.

QUICK AND REGULAR RATING SYSTEMS

The USCF has two separate rating systems. A player's regular rating is affected if the tournament's primary time control is at least 30 minutes. A player's quick rating is affected if a tournament has a single sudden-death time control between SD/10 to SD/29 (10 minutes through 29 minutes inclusive for each player). Check www.uschess.org under "Ratings" or ask the USCF to mail "The USCF Rating" flier for more information on how ratings are calculated.

SUDDEN-DEATH CONTROLS

Sudden-death time controls (SD) are common for primary, secondary, and tertiary time controls. Games using sudden-death time controls must be completed within the prescribed time, regardless of the number of moves. Sudden-death time controls offer advantages to players and organizers alike because they guarantee a round will finish by a predictable time. Tournaments with a time control of SD/30 are often called action chess.

QUICK CHESS

A quick chess event is intended for a player who wishes to play many games in one day and not have the results affect his or her regular rating. Sudden-death rules are used in quick chess events, but score keeping is not required.

BLITZ CHESS

Blitz chess (G/5) is not rated by the USCF. Sudden-death controls of less then 10 minutes are not permitted in USCF-rated play.

INTERNET RATINGS

The USCF does not normally rate individual play over the Internet. A few events such as the National Collegiate Chess League (NCCL) have been rated in the over-the-board system, but they have specific requirements such as having a certified TD at every site.

Official chess ratings of members of the United States Chess Federation can be found at http://uschess.org/ratings/info.

In addition, you can also look up listings by rank of the highest-rated players by the various categories listed below (http://uschess.org/ratings/top50).

- Overall (regardless of gender or age)
- Top 100 Correspondence Players (regardless of gender or age)
- Top 100 Quick Chess Players (regardless of gender or age)

Age-Restricted Lists:

- Age 65 and Over
- Under Age 21
- Age 18
- Age 17

- Age 16
- Age 15
- Age 14
- Age 13
- Age 12
- Age 11
- Age 10
- Age 9
- Age 8 and Under

Gender-Restricted Lists:

- Women (regardless of age)
- Girls Under 16
- Girls Under 13

Source: www.uschess.org

USCF CLASS TITLES

USCF's class norms system is similar to the system FIDE (the World Chess Federation) uses to determine grandmaster and international master titles. There is no time limit to earn a class title.

Each player's membership record contains his or her present title (if any) and has separate fields for the number of norm points he or she has earned toward the next two titles, as illustrated in the following table.

NAME	ID	EXP.	ST	REGULAR
DOE, JOHN	12345678	0893	WV	1575*c2

The norm code system consists of a letter representing the player's current title and a norm number. The norm number is the number of points earned toward the next norm title. John Doe (shown in the preceding table) has a norm code of c2, which means he currently holds the Certified Class C title (1400) and two points toward the Advanced Class C title (1500). The following table shows the USCF's levels, titles, and abbreviations.

Level	Title	Abbreviation
1000	Certified Class E	e
1100	Advanced Class E	E
1200	Certified Class D	d
1300	Advanced Class D	D
1400	Certified Class C	c
1500	Advanced Class C	C
1600	Certified Class B	b
1700	Advanced Class B	B
1800	Certified Class A	a
1900	Advanced Class A	A
2000	Certified Expert	x
2100	Advanced Expert	X
2200	Life Master	m
2300	Advanced Life Master	M
2400	Senior Life Master	s
2500	Star Master	S
2600	2-Star Master	t
2700	3-Star Master	T
2800	4-Star Master	u
2900	5-Star Master	U

Source: www.uschess.org

INTERNATIONAL CHESS COMPETITION

International chess competition is governed by the World Chess Federation (FIDE). FIDE has its own rating list, separate from the USCF.

FIDE posts their list of the World Top-Ranked Players as follows:

- Top 100 Players
  www.fide.com/cgi-bin/read.cgi?html=top100men
- Top 50 Women
  www.fide.com/cgi-bin/read.cgi?html=top50women
- Top 20 Boys (under 21)
  www.fide.com/cgi-bin/read.cgi?html=top20juniors

- Top 20 Girls (under 21)
  www.fide.com/cgi-bin/read.cgi?html=top20girls
- 32 Best Players
  www.fide.com/cgi-bin/download.pl

For a list of all the countries that are affiliated with FIDE and the four zones (Europe, Americas, Asia, and Africa) visit: www.fide.com/cgi-bin/federations.pl.

Hour's Up!

1. True or False: The first time you enter a tournament, you are considered unrated.
2. True or False: Correspondence chess can be played by either e-mail or regular mail.
3. In Swiss-system tournament play
   a. Players of equal performance end up being paired with each other.
   b. The weaker players are gradually eliminated.
   c. Each player gets to play against every other player.
4. A quad, in which four players participate, requires how many rounds?
   a. Two
   b. Three
   c. Four
5. True or False: A chess player in a tournament cannot receive literature or advice from a third party.
6. True or False: In a Swiss-system tournament, no player is paired with any opponent more than once.
7. True or False: In sudden-death play, both players must play a prescribed number of moves.
8. True or False: In a draw, each player is awarded half a point.
9. True or False: The results of blitz tournaments are not rated by the United States Chess Federation.
10. Match play occurs when
    a. Two players (usually top-ranked) play against each other in a tournament.
    b. Players are paired in a Swiss-system tournament.
    c. Players are paired in a round robin.

Hour 19

Playing Chess Against Others on the Internet

CHAPTER SUMMARY

LESSON PLAN:

There are advantages—and some disadvantages—to playing chess on the Internet.

In this hour you learn …

- Why Internet chess is convenient.
- Why Internet chess is cost effective.
- What problems can arise while playing Internet chess.
- How much Internet chess costs.
- What sites and servers are best for Internet chess.

Despite some drawbacks, the Internet offers a great opportunity for players, especially novices, to learn and play the game at their convenience (which is not true in over-the-board games). Usually, the costs are reasonable and some sites are even free of charge. A list of sites is included at the end of this hour with comments about each site's features, design, costs, and types of players who tend to use them.

WEIGHING THE PROS AND CONS OF INTERNET CHESS

Some of us are so busy with our daily lives that between our jobs, family, and other obligations, it is hard to play chess over-the-board. That is why Internet chess has thrived in the past seven to eight years. What can Internet chess offer that regular over-the-board chess can't?

THE PROS

Overall, the advantages of Internet chess outweigh the disadvantages.

FLEXIBILITY

You can play chess 24 hours a day, 7 days a week, 365 days a year online. Some players sneak in a game here and there during their lunch hour. Some love to get in a game or two before they head to school or work. Others enjoy playing late at night and into the wee hours of the morning after the kids or spouse have gone to bed. This kind of flexibility would be difficult to achieve when trying to arrange a game over an actual chessboard.

CONVENIENCE

For those of you who do not live in or near a metropolitan area like New York, Chicago, or Los Angeles, it may be hard to find a chess club or a chess tournament. Many chess enthusiasts face this dilemma. Even if you live in a big city, it is not always easy or convenient to go to a chess club or attend a chess tournament. Internet chess solves this problem. There is a game or a tournament available online at almost any time.

COST

Let's do some basic math. Add the cost of getting to a chess club or tournament—if you drive there's the expense of gas, tolls, parking, and the wear and tear on the car. And public transportation, when it exists, has its costs, too; moreover, buses and subways do not always run when you need to get somewhere. In addition, you have to pay an entry fee or club membership for over-the-board competition. It is quite expensive to play a lot of chess over-the-board. On an Internet chess server, however, the annual membership for 24 hours a day, 7 days a week, 365 days a year ranges from $0 to $60. That is nothing compared to what you pay to play over-the-board chess. That makes it a very appealing alternative.

TIME

When you play over-the-board chess, commuting time may take up a large chunk of your day—time you'd prefer to spend on other activities. In addition, many chess clubs are only open one or two days a week. Most chess tournaments take place on a weekend. If your job requires putting in time on the weekend, or if family responsibilities have priority, then kiss the chess activities goodbye. With Internet chess, on the other hand, you can play at any time and on any day. That is a very attractive alternative to spending so much time lugging yourself back and forth to a chess club or chess tournament.

QUANTITY OF GAMES

Another problem with over-the-board chess is the number of games you get to play. Most tournaments entail 3–6 rounds in a given weekend event. To spend two days sitting around just so you can play a few games can be quite frustrating. The same caveat applies to chess clubs. On the other hand, with Internet chess, some people can actually play 100–200 games a day! For a chess enthusiast, this is a dream come true.

QUALITY OF GAMES

Let's say you are a novice. Some novices do not like to play against people who are very experienced in the game. They feel intimidated and uneasy about playing against someone so much better than they are. By the same token, most chess experts and masters do not want to play weaker competition. With over-the-board chess tournaments, a player cannot choose the opponent. With Internet chess, however, you can seek games with certain types of players that have a certain skill level, and you can play them within a time limit that is suitable for you. This is a lot more appealing to many players.

SOCIAL ENVIRONMENT

When you play Internet chess, you can meet people from all over the U.S. and all over the world. You may play chess against a five-year-old boy or an eighty-year-old woman. Moreover, the Internet players you meet represent any number of different ethnic, religious, and socio-economic backgrounds with a wide range of experiences. We have played people from Europe, Asia, Africa, Central and South America, as well as residents of nearly every state in the union.

THE CONS

With all the advantages to the Internet, playing chess online does have some disadvantages.

CHEATING

Cheating is a very serious problem in Internet play. On every Internet chess server, there are players who cheat by using the assistance of computer software or a strong player to help them find the best moves. The problem is how to prove it. Catching cheaters is difficult—even for the best experts—because they are as prone to making errors as anyone else. Charging a player with cheating is a personal call and, as you know, when it comes to making an assessment about human behavior, perfection is an unattainable ideal.

Even if we are charitable and say that an expert is right about calling out a cheater 90 percent of the time (which is unlikely to be the case), that means he is going to be wrong the other 10 percent of the time. And if he makes a mistake and wrongly accuses an innocent player of cheating, he can ruin someone's reputation for life.

UNSPORTSMANLIKE CONDUCT

Another problem with Internet chess is unsportsmanlike conduct. Just as in baseball, basketball, or football, some players are very sore losers. They do not like to resign or be checkmated. Therefore, if they feel that they are losing, they disconnect from the Internet to avoid a loss. This will cause the game to be adjourned to resume later. Needless to say, this kind of behavior can be quite frustrating to the player who is winning.

Some players disconnect on purpose for 5—10 minutes during a difficult game to give themselves more time to analyze the complicated position. Then they log back on after they think they've found an optimum continuation. There is no way to prove who is disconnecting on purpose and who is doing it accidentally (and who simply has been cut off by their Internet service provider). After all, it's always possible that your opponent's three-year-old has unplugged the computer. You will never learn the real reason.

RUDENESS

Some players cannot live with themselves if they lose a game because they are not good enough, so they will use every excuse in the book, including accusing their opponents of cheating. Some players will resort to using foul language after a loss. Unfortunately, these horrible outbursts or false accusations are vented in the open for all to see, including children. Some servers have strict policies against this sort of behavior, but there will always be a few who slip through the cracks. So be prepared to deal with this problem if you decide to play Internet chess.

IMPERSONALITY

On most Internet chess servers, players are not required to use their real names. Players usually choose a handle, or nickname, they like, and unless the players choose to tell you who they really are, there is no way of knowing whom you are playing against. You could be facing a world champion playing anonymously, a beginner, or a cheater. You just have to guess. You may find your opponent to be especially chatty while others are so reticent they won't say a word—win, lose, or draw.

TECHNICAL DIFFICULTIES

When you play on the Internet, anything can happen. (But then if you've been using the Web for awhile this isn't news.) Sometimes, the server may crash. Sometimes, your own Internet service provider may boot you offline. Occasionally there is "lag" (slow transmission of the moves) due to router problems. Other times, your computer may freeze or your electricity may go out because of a bad storm. All these potential problems are usually beyond your control but nonetheless disrupt your game and cause a great deal of irritation. All you can do is hope that things will go smoothly on a day-to-day basis. However, expect the unexpected.

TECHNOLOGIES

Believe it or not, not everyone owns a computer, knows how to use one, or has access to the Internet. This is a bigger problem for the older generation. That is one of the reasons more players are not playing chess on the Internet. In some countries, of course, Internet access is not widespread or is far too expensive for most of the population.

The quality of computers can also come into play. For example, any player who has a powerful computer and a large monitor enjoys a great advantage over someone who is using a six-year-old computer with a 14-inch computer screen that flickers every few seconds.

Inferior technology can be a disadvantage when it comes to the mouse and modem, too. Imagine that you have to play a tennis game using an old wooden racket while your opponent has a sleek modern one. That would be quite unfair, wouldn't it? While that is a problem on the Internet, in over-the-board chess, both players use the same equipment.

LACK OF UNIFORM RULES AND POLICIES

Every server has its own rules and policies. No server has to follow any other server's rules. There is no overall international Internet chess federation that governs and monitors the activities or conduct of any server. Because of this lack of consistency, serious problems can sometimes arise.

For example, there was a recent case where players entered a big Internet chess tournament for the World Championship. In the middle of the tournament, some players were disqualified and expelled because the management felt that the players were cheating. However, no serious evidence was presented, no hearing was ever set, nor was there any process of appeal. Does anyone really know whether the players were guilty or innocent? No. In the meantime, the players' reputations were badly damaged. One of these players even took the organizer to court.

Most Internet chess servers recruit server administrators or server representatives who volunteer to help out. In some cases, these staff members (who can be as young as 14) use their positions and power to intimidate, harass, or abuse paying and nonpaying members. Because there is no federation or organization to appeal or complain to, the members have to suffer.

Don't expect these problems to change any time soon. In other words, play at your own risk.

PRIVACY

Privacy is an overall Internet problem, not only in the Internet chess arena. Most chess servers guarantee that the information you provide to them is secure and will not be revealed to the public. However, what these servers claim and what actually takes place are two different things. We have personally encountered instances where certain servers have disclosed information to the public even after having assured their members that their records were guaranteed to be confidential.

Some servers snoop and spy on the members illegally. Some servers even have the ability to read or observe private and personal chats between members. Of course, this is illegal and most servers claim they do not do such things. The question is—do you believe them?

But what can you do if your privacy is violated online? Who would you complain to? You can take the server to court but because many servers are so small, it is not even worth your time or money to go after them. Of course, you can try to mitigate the damage by limiting the information given to any chess server. However, unless you provide the information that is requested, you cannot get a playing membership. So it's a Catch-22 situation and a serious dilemma to think about if you sign on to one of these services as a member.

CAN INTERNET CHESS HELP ME?

We are true believers in Internet chess. It has many pluses and as you've just seen, it also has many minuses. However, the pluses outweigh the minuses in our view. If you are an avid chess lover, nothing beats Internet chess. Let us share with you some of the reasons we think Internet chess can help many people. Most of the chess players who play on the Internet are amateurs. By playing on the Internet, you can:

- Practice a lot more than playing over-the-board. With Internet chess, a chess player can play hundreds of games a day. With over-the-board chess, most players are lucky to play 50–75 games a year. You know the saying: "Practice makes perfect."

- Improve by playing stronger players. In over-the-board chess, it is hard for an amateur to get a chance to play against a chess expert or chess pro. The chance of being able to play a lot more games with players who are better than you improves dramatically with Internet chess.

- Improve by observing good players. With over-the-board chess, unless you are willing to travel to major tournament sites, it is almost impossible to have the opportunity to observe good players. With Internet chess, this is possible practically 24 hours a day, 7 days a week, 365 days a year.

- Take lessons from a chess pro for a much more reasonable price. To be able to take lessons with a chess grandmaster or a professional chess instructor/trainer in person can cost you from $60 to as much as $250 an hour. By contrast, the typical rate for chess lessons on the Internet is between $30 and $50 an hour. Some grandmasters charge as low as $20 an hour online.

- Access serious chess databases. Many servers offer a large chess database of games played on the server, chess puzzles, or even chess robots that can help you improve your game. These games and features can prove helpful to a chess player who is still getting acquainted with the game.

In our opinion, we strongly believe that Internet chess can help most players. You just have to do some comparisons of different sites and make your own informed decision.

SOME POPULAR CHESS SERVERS ON THE INTERNET

Below you will find a list and comparison of some of the more popular chess-playing servers on the Internet. In addition, there is also a general list of 14 other chess servers.

RATING

The criteria we used to rate the following sites were: cost, number of members, level of competition, server features, graphical interface, general environment, friendliness, ease of use, server activities, frequency and type of tournaments, chess information, variety of games (*variants chess*), direction, and privacy.

STRICTLY DEFINED

Variants chess refers to different forms of chess such as bughouse, crazyhouse, suicide chess, wild chess, Fischer random, and so on.

☺ ☺ ☺ ☺ ☺ = Exceptional

☺ ☺ ☺ ☺ = Very Good

☺ ☺ ☺ = Good

☺ ☺ = Average

☺ = Below Average

www.ChessClub.com

Rating: ☺ ☺ ☺ ☺

The Internet Chess Club is designed for players from novice to grandmaster. With over 25,000 paying members from all over the world, and over 125,000 games played per day, www.ChessClub.com is the longest-running and most vibrant chess community on the Internet.

The site's graphical interface is good and offers a lot of special features. The level of play is strong. The server size is large. Most of the time, over 1,000 players from all over the world are playing at once. But if you are looking for a cozy atmosphere with personal attention, this is not the place for you. If, on the other hand, you are looking for top-level Internet chess, you are at the right place.

Many of the world's top players play here. In fact, there are more titled players playing on this server than any other servers. You can play games and get a rating; watch grandmasters play while discussing the game; take lessons; play in tournaments; play in simultaneous exhibitions; try chess variants with names such as bughouse, crazyhouse, and atomic; play chess programs of all levels, and much more.

Membership fees: Membership fees are $49 a year for adults and half price for students.

Assessment: If you like the best competition and are willing to pay for it, this is it.

www.freechess.org

Rating: ☺ ☺ ☺

The freechess server is designed for players from novice to grandmaster. As its name suggests, the Free Internet Chess Server (FICS) is the world's largest free Internet chess server where you can play chess, observe games, talk to friends, obtain a rating, and rank yourself among other players from all over the world. This server is famous for variants chess. Most of the best variants chess players in the world play here.

The graphical interface is decent with a fair amount of features. The level of play is adequate. A significant number of players are playing at all times.

Membership fees: Free

Assessment: If you like free, you can't beat this server.

WWW.KASPAROVCHESS.COM

Rating: ☺ ☺ ☺

The KasparovChess server is designed for players from novice to grandmaster. Members of KasparovChess.com have access to all the interactive features, such as chat rooms and free daily newsletter message boards. In addition, they can obtain a rating in the Playing Zone.

The graphical interface of this server is poor and that's the main drawback. Otherwise, this server would have received a higher mark. The playing level and size are good. The contents of the site and chess news it offers are excellent.

Membership fees: There are two levels of membership:

- The basic membership is free but has some limitations, and members have to deal with annoying pop-up advertising.
- The upgraded membership is called the Champions Club. The Champions Club offers a lot more features, such as grandmaster chess lectures, simuls, and special courses with no pop-up advertising. It costs $59 per year. There are also private chess lessons and supplementary courses available for additional fees.

One of the main server administrators (as well as chess trainer and writing contributor on the server) worth noting is WGM Sophia Polgar, the middle of the three Polgar sisters. For private online lessons with Sophia, contact sofipol@netvision.net.il.

Assessment: For the chess contents, lessons, and various activities, this server is worth checking out.

WWW.CHESS.NET

Rating: ☺ ☺

The chess.net server is designed for players from novice to grandmaster. Whether you are looking for a social game or a competitive-rated game, there are always hundreds of players to choose from.

The graphical interface is decent but has had little improvement in recent years. The level of play is adequate, and the atmosphere is cozy. A decent amount of players from various countries participate. However, the management is weak, and there is a general lack of focus and direction. This used to be one of the better servers, but lately it has become just one of many.

Membership fees: There are two levels of memberships:

- The basic membership is free. However, there are restrictions and annoying advertising banners.
- If you want to have the use of all features and no banners, the upgrade Gold membership is $30 per year.

Assessment: This server would be okay if the Gold membership were free. To get the best bang for your buck, however, shop around.

www.USChessLive.com

Rating: ☺

The USChessLive server is designed for players from novice to grandmaster. It is one of the smallest serious servers, and had potential when it debuted. Now, very few titled players choose to play this site on a regular basis.

The graphical interface is good with decent features. The atmosphere is cozy. The level of play is just average. There are, however, some key weaknesses with this server:

- Even though many of the volunteers gave their heart and soul to make this server good, the senior management consists of computer programmers who are quite new to chess, management, business, or PR concepts. In general, the server suffers from a lack of direction and seriousness.
- It is very hard to play a game unless you can play during prime time, because the majority of the players are from the United States. And because there is hardly any strong competition, many of the better players move on to other servers.

Membership fees: There are two levels of membership for this relatively new Internet chess server:

- The basic membership is free. However, it limits the member to just 12 rated games per day and has very annoying advertising banners. It also basically isolates the members from the rest of the server activities, and the level of service is very poor.
- The Royal membership is designed for those users who want more from U.S. Chess Live and are willing to pay for it. The fees for the Royal membership are quite expensive at $59.95 per year for non-USCF members and $29.95 per year for USCF members. Youth and student Royal Membership fees are $29.95 per year for non-USCF members and $19.95 for USCF members.

Assessment: For the same money, there are much better choices unless this server puts in new management with experience and proper leadership. At this time, it is definitely not worth the money.

www.WorldChessNetwork.com

Rating: ☺ ☺ ☺

The WorldChessNetwork server is designed for players from novice to grandmaster. It is owned and operated by Master Games International, Inc., a corporation founded in 1997 by chess organizers, international grandmasters, and patrons of the game.

On the World Chess Network, you can play free chess, earn a rating, access your personal game history, and view games from around the world and more. High quality game sites require a download. The World Chess Network download is small (1 MB), and it takes just a few minutes.

This was the first chess server to offer "banter chess," in which two chess grandmasters play against each other while explaining their thoughts on each move to the audience—a great way to understand and learn chess.

The graphical interface is above average. The server activities for the Gold members are good. The server size and playing level are decent. The management is very professional and courteous.

Membership Fees: There are three levels of memberships:

- Regular (free): Limited features and only two rated games per day.
- Silver ($19.95 per year): Some limitations and 12 rated games per day.
- Gold ($49.95 per year or $79.95 for two years): Members receive the full benefits of the Red Carpet experience with more than two hundred events each month featuring many of the world's finest players.

Assessment: This server is definitely worth checking out. It is growing quite rapidly. The best deal is a two-year Gold membership.

www.VOGClub.com

Rating: ☺

The VOGClub is an online gaming club for chess and a few other classic games. Players can play rated or unrated games. Separate ratings are maintained for Bullet, Blitz, Standard, and Tournament play. Many tournaments, which are 100 percent automated, are run every day.

All rated games for all players are saved by the server and can be retrieved in PGN format at a later time. Large communities of players can have their own private rooms on VOG, which are not accessible by other players. The site is free, but some advanced features are available to Gold members only.

Membership Fees: Memberships start at $19.95 per year.

Assessment: This is a fun server but so far it lacks membership.

OTHER INTERNET CHESS SITES

There are also many other Internet chess servers. The following are some website addresses for these servers:

game.fide.com/chessgame

www.chess21.com

gameknot.com

www.instantchess.com

chessworld.net

www.playchess.de

www.ciudadfutura.com/superajedrez

www.ajedrezgratis.com

www.xadrezclube.com.br

www.freechess.de

www.vog.ru

www.pogo.com

www.caissa.com

www.itsyourturn.com

All in all, every server has its own strengths and weaknesses. In general, we think using the Internet will help improve your chess game, and you will have a lot of fun doing it.

HOW DO I SIGN UP AND WHAT DOES IT COST?

On all the Internet chess playing sites in the preceding list, you will find simple instructions explaining how to go about signing up. Even though we have tried to give you the most updated costs of membership, the servers may change their prices and polices.

The best thing to do is to log on, double check the prices, and follow the instructions. Once you create a handle and download and install the software, you are on your way to playing chess on the Internet.

For the upgrade membership on these Internet playing sites, most servers accept major credit cards. Most will also accept checks. All the information is easily accessible on their websites.

Now that you know many of the pros and cons regarding playing chess on the Internet, you can make informed decisions whether to play or not to play and which server makes the best match for your needs and experience. Enjoy!

Hour's Up!

1. True or False: On the Internet, it's possible to play up to 200 games a day.

2. True or False: A weekend tournament usually consists of four to six rounds of chess.

3. True or False: Almost no Internet chess sites allow you to take lessons from or play chess against a grandmaster.

4. True or False: Each chess server has its own regulations and standards.

5. Over-the-board play has an advantage over Internet chess in which area?

   a. You meet different kinds of people.

   b. You can play more games a year.

   c. You are judged under generally accepted rules.

   d. You can save money.

6. True or False: It's actually possible to play a world-famous champion over the Internet without knowing his or her identity.

7. Banter chess is

   a. A chat room feature on an Internet chess site.

   b. A game in which you and your opponent exchange information and gossip.

   c. An Internet game played by grandmasters who then comment on their moves.

8. True or False: It is possible on some Internet sites to get an official rating.

9. True or False: There is no governing authority for Internet chess sites.

10. True or False: It is relatively easy to determine when someone is cheating or has deliberately gone offline to gain more time for a move.

Part VI

What Else Do I Need to Know?

Hour 20

World Chess Champions: Past and Present

CHAPTER SUMMARY

LESSON PLAN:

This hour is about the game's most famous (and sometimes most eccentric) players.

In this hour you learn ...

- Who has won the international chess titles since the nineteenth century.
- Why chess champions achieve their success.
- What tactics the chess champions used to win.
- Why certain championship games have become classics.
- Why one chess tournament figured prominently in the history of Cold War politics between the United States and Soviet Union.

As you read the profiles of the world champions listed in this hour, you will notice some common themes: immersion in chess as a child, astonishing accomplishments at an early age, intense competitiveness, and dedication. Of course, there are always exceptions to the rule—chess champions whose first love wasn't chess at all but mathematics and law, or chess champions who seemed quite content to give up professional competition to go on to other pursuits. Although championships are usually sanctioned by FIDE, the principal international chess federation, there are other chess organizations with champions of their own. In addition, men and women compete separately for championships, a situation that some chess enthusiasts believe slights women. You'll have to judge for yourself.

UNOFFICIAL WORLD CHAMPIONS

The history of the world championship has always been one of the most fascinating topics for novice chess players. In this section, we look at famous unofficial champions.

- Up to 1824   Alexandre Louis Honoré Deschapelles—France. Alexandre abandoned chess for whist in 1824 when he was defeated by a rival named Louis Charles Mahé de La Bourdonnais.

- 1824–1840   Louis Charles Mahé de La Bourdonnais, France. Winner over Alexandre McDonnell (England) in 1834.

- 1840–1843 Pierre Charles Fournier de Saint-Amant—France. Winner over Howard Staunton in 1843 in London.

- 1843–1851 Howard Staunton, England. The illegitimate son of a British aristocrat, Staunton (which may not even be his real name) started his career as a Shakespearean actor. At the age of 28, shortly after he learned how to play chess, he joined the Old Westminster Chess Club in London, and a few years later, in 1841, he became editor of England's first successful chess magazine. In 1843 he lost a match to France's leading player, Saint-Amant, but won in a grudge match six months later. After a string of triumphant matches in England and France, he organized the world's first international chess tournament in 1851.

  - 1841–1843 Paris: H. Staunton 13—Saint-Amant 8. Staunton is the self-entitled "World Champion." He led off the match by scoring seven wins and one draw.

  - 1846, London: H. Staunton 15.5—B. Horwitz 8.5

- 1851–1858 Adolf Andersen, Prussia. Andersen won acclaim for his charismatic style, especially his aggressive kingside attacks which he executed with verve and audacity. He was known for his relentless drive to checkmate his opponents and the tactical capacity to pull it off. Many of the combinations he devised can still be found in chess anthologies today. He won the London Tournament in 1851 in which Staunton finished fourth.

  - 1851, London: (Round 1) A. Andersen 2.5—L. Kieseritzky .5

  - 1851, London: (Round 2) A. Andersen 4—J. Szen 2

  - 1851, London: (Round 3) A. Andersen 3—H. Staunton 1

  - 1851, London: (Final Match) A. Andersen 4.5—M. Wyvill 2.5

- 1858–1860 Paul Morphy—USA. Morphy's first loves were mathematics and law, but he achieved fame in the chess world after triumphing in the American Chess Congress of 1857. He then set out on a chess tour of Europe where he beat Andersen in 1858. However, he later came under attack from Howard Staunton who accused him of being an adventurer without any financial backing. Humiliated, Morphy returned to America where he tried—unsuccessfully—to build a law career. He suffered a nervous breakdown when a woman he was courting turned down his proposal for marriage on the grounds that she would never marry a "mere chess player." In spite of his sad ending, Morphy is credited with understanding far more about the game than his contemporaries did.

  - 1858, Paris: P. Morphy 8—A. Andersen 3

  - 1859, Paris: P. Morphy 7.5—A. Mongredien .5

He never played in Europe again and died delusional.

- 1860–1866   Adolf Andersen—Prussia. Winner of the big London Tournament in 1862.
  - 1861, London: A. Andersen 5—I. Kolisch 4
  - 1862   Winner of the big London Tournament, scored 12 points out of 13 games.
  - 1862, London: A. Andersen 4—L. Paulsen 4
- 1866–1886   Wilhelm Steinitz—Austria. Steinitz is known for his pioneering chess tactics that turned him into the first self-proclaimed world champion in 1866 when he defeated Andersen. He developed a reputation as a brilliant, if unsteady player, and held the championship until 1894 when he lost to Emanuel Lasker. He was one of the first chess players to have a major impact on the game through his writings.
  - 1866, London: W. Steinitz 8—A. Andersen 6, self-entitled "World Champion".
  - 1866, London: W. Steinitz 9.5—H. Bird 7.5
  - 1872, London: W. Steinitz 9—J. Zukertort 3
  - 1876, London: W. Steinitz 7—J. Blackburne 0

OFFICIAL FIDE WORLD CHAMPIONS

The following marks the beginning of the official world championship matches. Prior to this, people self proclaimed to be world champions when they beat their rivals in unofficial matches.

- 1866–1894   Wilhelm Steinitz—Austria
  - 1886, USA: W. Steinitz 12.5—Johann Zukertort (German) 7.5
  - 1889, La Havana: W. Steinitz 10.5—Mikhail Chigorin (Russia) 6.5
  - 1891, New York: W. Steinitz 10.5—Isidor Gunsberg (England, born Hungarian) 8.5
  - 1892, La Havana: W. Steinitz 12.5—Mikhail Chigorin (Russia) 10.5
- 1894–1921   Emanuel Lasker—Germany. Like many other chess players, Lasker was attracted to mathematics as a youth in Germany. After initial successes playing matches in London, Lasker traveled to the U.S. where he challenged—and beat—the aging champion Steinitz 10 games to 5. Lasker was to retain the world championship for an astonishing 27 years. In 1921, confronting the great Cuban player Jose Capablanca, he resigned, claiming ill health. In spite of his talent at chess, he never lost his interest in mathematics or philosophy.
  - 1894, New York, Philadelphia, and Montreal: E. Lasker 12—W. Steinitz 7
  - 1897, Moscow: E. Lasker 12.5—W. Steinitz 4.5
  - 1907, USA: E. Lasker 11.5—Frank James Marshall (USA) 3.5

- 1908, Dusseldorf and Munich: E. Lasker 10.5—S. Tarrasch (Germany) 5.5
- 1909, Paris: E. Lasker 8—David Janowski (France) 2
- 1910, Vienna and Berlin: E. Lasker 5—Karl Schlechter (Austria) 5. (Lasker keeps the title) 1910, Berlin: E. Lasker 9.5—David Janowski (France) 1.5

- 1921–1927   Jose Capablanca, Cuba. An undisputed genius, Capablanca was known for his intuitive grasp of the game, especially his astonishing capacity to play endgame positions that seemed next to impossible. He reigned as world champion, after defeating Lasker, until 1927. Bobby Fischer, who wrested the championship from him after a long period of Russian domination of the game, called Capablanca "possibly the greatest player in the entire history of the game."
  - 1921, La Havana: J.R. Capablanca 9—E. Lasker 5

- 1927–1935   Alexander Alekhine, France. After coming in third behind Lasker and Capablanca at a chess tournament held in St. Petersburg in 1914, Alekhine began to seriously consider a try at the championship himself. World War I interrupted his plans, and it wasn't until 1929 that he achieved his dream. His loss to Max Euwe of the Netherlands was partially due to his habit of drinking alcohol during the match in 1935. In the rematch (this time without imbibing), Alekhine regained the championship, becoming the first defeated champion to do so.
  - 1927, Buenos Aires: A. Alekhine 18.5—J. R. Capablanca 15.5
  - 1929, Germany and Holland: A. Alekhine 15.5—Efim Bogolioubov (Germany—born Russian) 9.5
  - 1934, Germany: A. Alekhine 15.5—Efim Bogolioubov 10.5

- 1935–1937   Max Euwe, Holland. Raised by chess-playing parents, Euwe always considered himself an amateur at the game. He held the championship for only two years. Nonetheless, the chess world heard from him again when, as president of FIDE, he acted as an arbitrator in the controversial Spassky-Fischer match in 1972.
  - 1935, Holland: M. Euwe 15.5—A. Alekhine 14.5

- 1937–1946: Alexander Alekhine, France. Alekhine regained his title after defeating Euwe in a rematch and held it until 1946.
  - 1937, Holland: A. Alekhine 15.5—M. Euwe 9.5

(1) Alexander Alekhine died before a championship against Mikhail Botvinnik could be organized. FIDE subsequently organized a tournament in 1948 in The Hague and Moscow. The field included Botvinnik, Smyslov, Reshevsky, Keres, and Euwe.

- 1948–1957   Mikhail Botvinnik, USSR. Trained as an electrical engineer, Botvinnik was the first Russian to hold the World Championship title after winning the 1948 tournament. He lost the title twice, only to regain it before finally going down to defeat in

1963. He was an ardent advocate of the game in the Soviet Union and although he never smoked, he would sometimes practice with heavy smokers so he would be able to play under adverse conditions.

- 1948, The Hague and Moscow: M. Botvinnik won the Candidate Tournament. Vasily Smyslov (USSR) 2, Paul Keres (USSR) 3, Samuel Reshevsky (USA) 4, Max Euwe (Holland) 5.

  - 1951, Moscow: M. Botvinnik 12—David Bronstein (USSR) 12. (Botvinnik keeps the title.)

  - 1954, Moscow: M. Botvinnik 12—Vassily Smyslov (USSR) 12. (Botvinnik keeps the title.)

- 1957–1958   Vasily Smyslov, USSR. Smyslov learned chess at the age of six from his father, but he actually aspired to a career as an opera singer. He only turned to chess as a career after failing an audition for the Bolshoi Opera. "I have always lived between chess and opera," he once said. He even sang to an audience in an interval in an intense match with Botvinnik.

  - 1957, Moscow: V. Smyslov 12.5—M. Botvinnik 9.5

- 1958–1960, Mikhail Botvinnik, USSR.

  - 1958, Moscow: M. Botvinnik 12.5—V. Smyslov 10.5

- 1960–1961, Mikhail Tal, USSR. The son of a physician, Tal became interested in chess when he saw the game played in his father's waiting room. But it wasn't until he was in his teens that he began to study the game seriously. Tal soon became so obsessed with the game that once, after undergoing surgery, he ran off to the chess club and had to be dragged back to his hospital bed. Tal was particularly known for his attacks, which often looked like madness, until the outcome became clear.

  - 1960, Moscow: M. Tal 12.5—M. Botvinnik 8.5

- 1961–1963, Mikhail Botvinnik, USSR

  - 1961, Moscow: M. Botvinnik 13—M. Tal 8

- 1963–1969   Tigran Petrosian, USSR. After his parents died when he was 16, Petrosian sought consolation in chess. He was known for being a very defensive player who would quietly consolidate his positions by controlling key squares. His style of play is considered less accessible than that of other champions.

  - 1963, Moscow: T. Petrosian 12.5—M. Botvinnik 9.5

  - 1966, Moscow: T. Petrosian 12.5—Boris Spassky (URSS) 11.5

- 1969–1972   Boris Spassky, USSR. Spassky learned chess as a boy in the Urals during World War II. After claiming the title from Petrosian, Spassky became one of the most popular modern champions because of his polite and affable manner. His defeat by America's Bobby Fischer in one of the most tumultuous matches ever fought against the background of US-Soviet rivalry ended 35 years of Soviet domination of the championship.

  - 1969, Moscow: B. Spassky 12.5—T. Petrosian 10.5

- 1972–1975   Robert (Bobby) Fischer, USA (2). Considered one of the greatest players of all time, Fischer once said, "All I want to do, ever, is play chess." Raised in Chicago, he learned chess at six, became the youngest Junior U.S. Champion at 13 and youngest Senior U.S. Champion at 14. In 1958, at 14, he became the youngest grandmaster in the history of the game. In 1972, in the historic match in Reykjavik, Iceland, he handed the Soviets a blistering defeat by beating Boris Spassky for the world title. But in 1975 he forfeited the title when he refused to play against Anatoly Karpov for the title under FIDE conditions. Fischer subsequently moved to Europe and then to Japan. For the last several years, he has been dogged by legal problems that have caused him to avoid returning to the United States.

  - 1972, Reykjavik: B. Fischer 12.5—B. Spassky 8.5

- 1975–1985   Anatoly Karpov, USSR. Karpov first learned chess moves at the age of four, and by the age of 15 he had become one of the youngest Soviet National Masters. Being uncomfortable about winning the championship as a result of Fischer's forfeit, he entered many competitive tournaments to prove that he deserved the championship. "To be a champion," he said, "requires being more than simply a strong player, one must be a strong human being as well." His victory in a match against Jan Timman of the Netherlands, while securing his hold on the FIDE championship, was undercut because his principal rival, fellow Russian Garry Kasparov, refused to play him under FIDE rules, choosing instead to play an independent match against Nigel Short of England.

  - 1975, with Fischer forfeiting, FIDE announced that Karpov was the new world champion

  - 1978, Baguio City: A. Karpov 16.5—Viktor Korchnoi (Stateless, Born Russian) 15.5

  - 1981, Merano: A. Karpov 11—Viktor Korchnoi (Switzerland, Born Russian) 7

  - 1984–1985, Moscow: A. Karpov 25—Garry Kasparov (URSS) 23. The match was suddenly interrupted by FIDE after 2 consecutive Kasparov wins.

- 1985–1993   Garry Kasparov, Russia (3). Kasparov learned chess from his father at seven, and by 12 he had become the USSR Junior Champion. Three years later he was a grandmaster. In 1984 he challenged Karpov for the championship; it was a long and brutal game—the longest ever title match in chess history, lasting six months—before the president of FIDE halted it. In the rematch in 1985, Kasparov won and became the then youngest world champion in the game's history at age 22. Breaking with FIDE in a dispute over rules, Kasparov founded the Professional Chess Association (PCA) and instituted his own matches, beginning with Nigel Short of England. Kasparov also achieved fame competing against nonhuman challengers, notably IBM's computer Deep Blue, a match that he won in 1985, and then in the late nineties, against a more powerful computer, Deeper Blue, a match that he lost. He remains the highest-rated player in chess.

- 1985, Moscow: G. Kasparov 13—A. Karpov 11
- 1986, London and Leningrad: G. Kasparov 12.5 A. Karpov 11.5
- 1987, Seville: G. Kasparov 12—A. Karpov 12. (G. Kasparov keeps the title.)
- 1990, New York and Lyon: G. Kasparov (Russia) 12.5—A. Karpov (URSS) 11.5

- 1993–1999, Anatoly Karpov, Russia (4)
  - 1993, Kasparov refused to play under FIDE jurisdiction
  - 1993, Holland and Djakarta: A Karpov 12.5—Jan Timman (Holland) 8.5
  - 1996, Elista: A. Karpov. 10.5—Gata Kamsky (USA, Born Russian) 7.5
  - 1998, Lausanne: A. Karpov 5—Viswanathan Anand (India) 3

- 1999–2000   Alexander Khalifman, Russia. Khalifman has been playing chess for many years; he is known for his openings and for his willingness to sacrifice material for long-term positional gains in exchange. Winner of numerous Russian and international tournaments, he established a school to train grandmasters in his native St. Petersburg.
  - 1999, Karpov refused to participate in FIDE's knockout tournament
  - 1999, Las Vegas, knockout tournament: A. Khalifman 3.5—Vladimir Akopian (Armenia) 2.5

- 2000–2002   Viswanathan Anand, India. Anand is the strongest chess player ever to come from India and is rated number three player in the world, just behind Kasparov. As a youth he had already achieved fame for his mastery of the game, which he could play at astonishing speed. He became grandmaster in 1987 after winning the World Junior Championship. His ability to grasp complex positions makes him a formidable opponent.
  - 2000, New Delhi and Tehran: Viswanathan Anand (India) 3.5—Alexei Shirov (Spain, born Russian) 0.5

- 2002–Present   Ruslan Ponomariov, Ukraine. Ponomariov aroused a great deal of skepticism when he announced his intention to become world champion as a boy, but he put many doubts to rest when he became grandmaster at 14. In January 2002, he gained the title, becoming the youngest champion in the history of the game.
  - Moscow: Ruslan Ponomariov (Ukraine) 4.5—Vassily Ivanchuk (Ukraine) 2.5

The numbers following numbers correspond to those in the preceding list.

(1) World Champion Alexander Alekhine died in 1946 while holding the World Champion Title.

(2) World Champion Robert Fischer refused to defend his title against Anatoly Karpov in 1975 unless FIDE met his conditions. FIDE refused and since Robert Fischer did not defend his title, the title was stripped from him.

(3) In 1993, World Champion Garry Kasparov and winner of FIDE qualification Nigel Short established the Professional Chess Association and played the World Championship Match for PCA-Title. Since Garry Kasparov did not play the match under FIDE jurisdiction he was stripped of his title.

(4) FIDE organized the alternative Karpov–Timman match in the same year. The winner of the match was Karpov and he was crowned FIDE World Champion once again.

PROFESSIONAL CHESS ASSOCIATION (PCA) WORLD CHAMPIONS

The PCA was founded by Garry Kasparov when he broke from FIDE in a dispute over FIDE rules. Its titles are not recognized by FIDE.

- 1993–2000 Garry Kasparov, Russia
  - 1993, London: G. Kasparov 12.5—Nigel Short (England) 7.5
  - 1995, New York: G. Kasparov 10.5—Viswanathan Anand (India) 7.5

BRAIN GAMES WORLD CHAMPIONS

Brain Games is another chess organization, based in England, that was formed by chess players who defected from FIDE. Its titles are not recognized by FIDE.

- 2000–Present   Vladimir Kramnik, Russia. Kramnik, from Tuapse, Russia, achieved his lifetime ambition by winning the World Chess Championship. He won games 2 and 10 and drew the rest to take the crown from Garry Kasparov at the Brain Games World Chess Championship in London. Kramnik made history as the first human being to win a match against Kasparov. It also is the first occasion in the World Championship history that the defending champion has failed to win a single game.
  - 2000, London: V. Kramnik 8.5—G. Kasparov (Russia) 6.5

FIDE Women's World Champions

Because women compete against other women for the championship, with somewhat different rules, their titles are listed separately from the male championships.

- 1927–1944: Vera Menchik, USSR, then Czech Republic, then England (1)
- 1950–1953: Lyudmila Rudenko, USSR
- 1953–1956: Yelizavyeta Bykova, USSR
- 1956–1958: Olga Rubtsova, USSR
- 1958–1962: Yelizavyeta Bykova, USSR
- 1962–1978: Nona Gaprindashvili, USSR
- 1978–1991: Maia Chiburdanidze, USSR then Georgia
- 1991–1996: Jun Xie, China
- 1996–1999: Zsuzsa (Susan) Polgar, Hungary (2)
- 1999–2001: Jun Xie, China
- 2001–Present: Chen Zhu, China (3)

The following numbers refer to the same numbers found in the preceding list.

(1) World Champion Vera Menchik held the Women's World Champion title until 1944 when she was killed with her sister Olga and their mother during a bombing raid.

(2) Zsuzsa Polgar was the first woman who earned the prestigious chess grandmaster title, a feat that very few women have accomplished. She was the number one ranked woman player in the world at the age of 15. She was and still is the highest rated women's world champion ever. After Zsuzsa Polgar won the World Championship Crown in 1996 by convincingly defeating former World Champion Maia Chiburdanidze (5.5–1.5) in the semifinal and the reigning World Champion Jun Xie (8.5–4.5), FIDE was unable to organize a rematch between her and former World Champion Jun Xie under acceptable conditions on a timely basis. When FIDE was finally able to arrange the rematch, Zsuzsa Polgar was unable to immediately defend her title due to the birth of her first son. FIDE illegally refused to grant Zsuzsa Polgar an extension and illegally stripped her of her World Champion title. World Champion Zsuzsa Polgar took FIDE to court and won. However, it was too late to return the World Champion title to her.

(3) World Champion Jun Xie declined to participate in the new FIDE Knockout World Championship. Chen Zhu, the sixth highest rated woman player in the world emerged as the new World Champion when she won the FIDE Knockout tournament in 2001.

GO TO ▶

For more information on international chess organizations, see Hour 1.

LEARNING FROM WORLD CHAMPIONS' GAMES

IM Donald Byrne—Robert Fischer (age 13) (One of Fischer's best and his most famous game)

New York, 1956

1. Ng1-f3 Ng8-f6	2. c2-c4 g7-g6	3. Nb1-c3 Bf8-g7
4. d2-d4 0-0	5. Bc1-f4 d7-d5	6. Qd1-b3 c7-c6
7. Ra1-d1 d5xc4	8. Qb3xc4 Nb8-d7	9. e2-e4 Nd7-b6
10. Qc4-c5 Bc8-g4	11. Bf4-g5 Nb6-a4	12. Qc5-a3 Na4xc3
13. b2xc3		

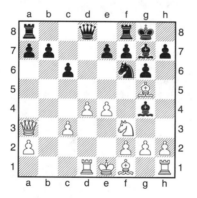

13... Nf6xe4	14. Bg5xe7 Qd8-b6	15. Bf1-c4 Ne4xc3
16. Be7-c5 Rf8-e8+	17. Ke1-f1 Bg4-e6	

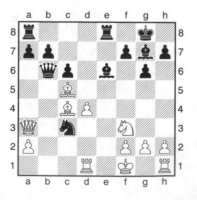

18. Bc5xb6 Be6xc4+	19. Kf1-g1 Nc3-e2+	20. Kg1-f1 Ne2xd4+
21. Kf1-g1 Nd4-e2+	22. Kg1-f1 Ne2-c3+	23. Kf1-g1 a7xb6
24. Qa3-b4 Ra8-a4	25. Qb4xb6 Nc3xd1	26. h2-h3 Ra4xa2
27. Kg1-h2 Nd1xf2	28. Rh1-e1 Re8xe1	29. Qb6-d8+ Bg7-f8
30. Nf3xe1 Bc4-d5	31. Ne1-f3 Nf2-e4	32. Qd8-b8 b7-b5
33. h3-h4 h7-h5	34. Nf3-e5 Kg8-g7	35. Kh2-g1 Bf8-c5+
36. Kg1-f1 Ne4-g3+	37. Kf1-e1 Bc5-b4+	38. Ke1-d1 Bd5-b3+
39. Kd1-c1 Ng3-e2+	40. Kc1-b1 Ne2-c3+	41. Kb1-c1 Ra2-c2#

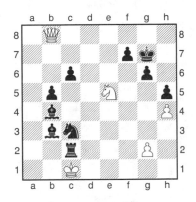

GM Anatoly Karpov—GM Valery Salov (A brilliant display by world champion Karpov)

Linares, 1993

1. d2-d4 Ng8-f6	2. c2-c4 e7-e6	3. Ng1-f3 b7-b6
4. g2-g3 Bc8-b7	5. Bf1-g2 Bf8-e7	6. Nb1-c3 Nf6-e4
7. Bc1-d2 Be7-f6	8. 0-0 0-0	9. Ra1-c1 c7-c5
10. d4-d5 e6xd5	11. c4xd5 Ne4xd2	12. Nf3xd2 d7-d6
13. Nd2-e4 Bf6-e7	14. f2-f4 Nb8-d7	15. g3-g4 a7-a6
16. a2-a4 Rf8-e8	17. g4-g5 Be7-f8	18. Kg1-h1 b6-b5
19. a4xb5 a6xb5	20. Nc3xb5 Qd8-b6	21. Nb5-c3 Qb6-b4
22. Qd1-d3 Nd7-b6	23. Qd3-g3 Kg8-h8	24. Rc1-d1 Nb6-c4
25. b2-b3 Nc4-b6	26. g5-g6	

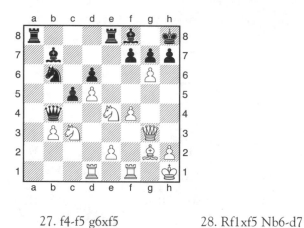

26... f7xg6	27. f4-f5 g6xf5	28. Rf1xf5 Nb6-d7
29. Rd1-f1 Nd7-e5	30. Rf5-f4 Qb4-b6	31. Ne4-g5 Ne5-g6
32. Ng5-f7+ Kh8-g8	33. Qg3xg6 Black resigns.	

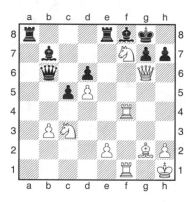

After 33... h7xg6 34. Rf4-h4 with the unavoidable mate next move with Rh4-h8#.

GM Garry Kasparov—GM Veselin Topalov (Considered by some to be the game of the decade)

Wijk aan Zee, 1999

1. e2-e4 d7-d6	2. d2-d4 Ng8-f6	3. Nb1-c3 g7-g6
4. Bc1-e3 Bf8-g7	5. Qd1-d2 c7-c6	6. f2-f3 b7-b5
7. Ng1-e2 Nb8-d7	8. Be3-h6 Bg7xh6	9. Qd2xh6 Bc8-b7
10. a2-a3 e7-e5	11. 0-0-0 Qd8-e7	12. Kc1-b1 a7-a6

13. Ne2-c1 0-0-0	14. Nc1-b3 e5xd4	15. Rd1xd4 c6-c5
16. Rd4-d1 Nd7-b6	17. g2-g3 Kc8-b8	18. Nb3-a5 Bb7-a8
19. Bf1-h3 d6-d5	20. Qh6-f4+ Kb8-a7	21. Rh1-e1 d5-d4
22. Nc3-d5 Nb6xd5	23. e4xd5 Qe7-d6	24. Rd1xd4 c5xd4
25. Re1-e7+		

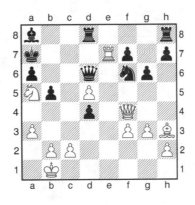

| 25... Ka7-b6 | 26. Qf4xd4+ Kb6xa5 | 27. b2-b4+ Ka5-a4 |
| 28. Qd4-c3 | | |

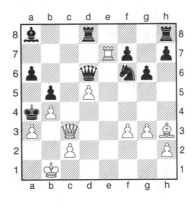

| 28... Qd6xd5 | 29. Re7-a7 Ba8-b7 | 30. Ra7xb7 Qd5-c4 |
| 31. Qc3xf6 Ka4xa3 | 32. Qf6xa6+ | |

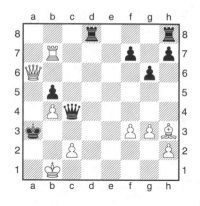

32... Ka3xb4	33. c2-c3+ Kb4xc3	34. Qa6-a1+ Kc3-d2
35. Qa1-b2+ Kd2-d1	36. Bh3-f1 Rd8-d2	37. Rb7-d7 Rd2xd7

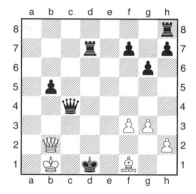

38. Bf1xc4 b5xc4	39. Qb2xh8 Rd7-d3	40. Qh8-a8 c4-c3
41. Qa8-a4+ Kd1-e1	42. f3-f4 f7-f5	43. Kb1-c1 Rd3-d2
44. Qa4-a7 Black resigns.		

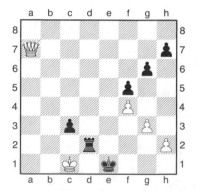

GM Vladimir Kramnik—GM Smbat Lputian (Illustration of Kramnik's strength)

Debrecen, 1992

1. d2-d4 e7-e6	2. c2-c4 Ng8-f6	3. Ng1-f3 d7-d5
4. Nb1-c3 Bf8-e7	5. Bc1-f4 0-0	6. e2-e3 c7-c6
7. Qd1-c2 Nb8-d7	8. h2-h3 a7-a6	9. Ra1-d1 h7-h6
10. a2-a3 d5xc4	11. Bf1xc4 Nf6-d5	12. 0-0 Nd5xf4
13. e3xf4 Qd8-c7	14. Nf3-e5 Nd7-f6	15. Bc4-a2 Bc8-d7
16. Ba2-b1 Bd7-e8	17. d4-d5	

17... Ra8-d8	18. Rf1-e1 Kg8-h8	19. d5xe6 Rd8xd1
20. Re1xd1 f7xe6	21. Nc3-e4 g7-g6	22. Ne4-c5 Be7xc5
23. Qc2xc5 Rf8-g8	24. Bb1-a2 Kh8-g7	25. Ba2xe6 Rg8-f8
26. Ne5-d7 Black resigns.		

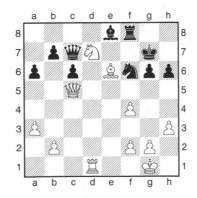

After 26… Nf6xd7   27. Rd1xd7+ Be8xd7   28. Qc5-e7+ Kg7-h8

29. Qe7xf8+ Kh8-h7   30. Qf8-g8#

GM Ruslan Ponomariov—GM Joe Gallagher (A dynamic and bold style of the young champion)

Biel, 2000

1. e2-e4 c7-c5   2. Ng1-f3 e7-e6   3. d2-d4 c5xd4

4. Nf3xd4 a7-a6   5. Nb1-c3 b7-b5   6. Bf1-d3 Bf8-c5

7. Nd4-b3 Bc5-e7   8. Qd1-g4 g7-g6   9. Qg4-e2 d7-d6

10. 0-0 b5-b4   11. Nc3-d1 Bc8-b7   12. a2-a3 Nb8-c6

13. Bc1-d2 b4xa3   14. Ra1xa3 Qd8-c8   15. Nd1-e3 Ng8-f6

16. Ne3-c4 Qc8-c7   17. Nc4-a5 Nc6-e5   18. Na5xb7 Ne5xd3

19. c2xd3 Qc7xb7   20. Nb3-a5 Qb7-d7   21. Ra3-b3 Ra8-c8

22. Na5-c4 Be7-d8   23. Bd2-h6

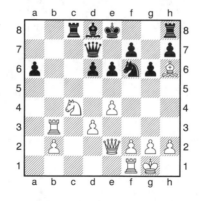

23… d6-d5   24. Nc4-b6 Bd8xb6   25. Rb3xb6 Qd7-a4

26. Qe2-f3 Nf6-d7   27. b2-b3 d5xe4   28. d3xe4 Qa4-a5

29. Rb6-b7 Qa5-h5   30. Qf3-f4 e6-e5   31. Qf4-d2 Nd7-c5

32. Rb7-a7 g6-g5   33. Qd2-d6 Black resigns.

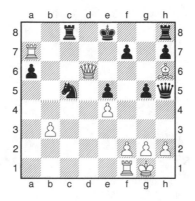

GM Zsuzsa Polgar—GM Anatoly Karpov (World Champion) (Quite a feat for a woman to defeat a male champion)

Blitz game, Roquebrune, 1992

1. d2-d4 Ng8-f6	2. c2-c4 e7-e6	3. Ng1-f3 b7-b6
4. g2-g3 Bc8-a6	5. b2-b3 Bf8-b4+	6. Bc1-d2 Bb4-e7
7. Bf1-g2 c7-c6	8. 0-0 d7-d5	9. Nf3-e5 Nf6-d7
10. Ne5xd7 Nb8xd7	11. Bd2-c3 0-0	12. Nb1-d2 f7-f5
13. Ra1-c1 Be7-a3	14. Rc1-b1 Ba3-d6	15. b3-b4 Qd8-c8
16. Qd1-b3 b6-b5	17. c4-c5 Bd6-c7	18. e2-e3 Qc8-e8
19. f2-f4 h7-h6	20. Nd2-f3 Kg8-h7	21. Kg1-f2 Nd7-f6
22. Nf3-e5 Bc7xe5	23. d4xe5 Nf6-g4+	24. Kf2-e2 Ng4xh2
25. Rf1-h1 Nh2-g4	26. Bg2-f3 Qe8-g6	27. Rh1-h4 Kh7-g8
28. Qb3-c2 Qg6-e8	29. Rb1-h1 Ba6-c8	30. Bf3xg4 f5xg4
31. Rh4xg4 Kg8-h8	32. Rg4-g6 Qe8-f7	33. g3-g4 Kh8-g8
34. Rh1xh6		

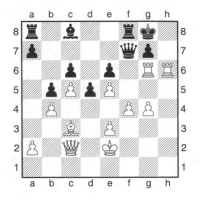

34... a7-a5   35. Rg6-g5 a5xb4   36. Qc2-h7#

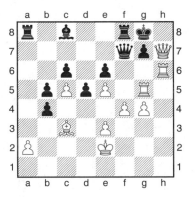

GM Nona Gaprindashvili (Women's World Champion)—GM Zsuzsa Polgar (A nice game by the future champion Zsuzsa)

Shanghai, 1992

1. d2-d4 d7-d5	2. c2-c4 d5xc4	3. Ng1-f3 Ng8-f6
4. Nb1-c3 c7-c6	5. e2-e4 b7-b5	6. e4-e5 Nf6-d5
7. a2-a4 Bc8-f5	8. Bf1-e2 b5-b4	9. Nf3-h4 b4xc3
10. Nh4xf5 e7-e6	11. Nf5-g3 c3xb2	12. Bc1xb2 Bf8-b4+
13. Ke1-f1 c4-c3	14. Bb2-c1 0-0	15. Ng3-e4 Nb8-d7
16. Be2-d3 f7-f5	17. e5xf6 Nd7xf6	18. Ne4-g5 Qd8-d6

19. Qd1-c2 h7-h6   20. h2-h4 h6xg5   21. h4xg5 Nf6-g4

22. Bd3-h7+ Kg8-f7   23. Qc2-e4 Ng4xf2   24. Kf1xf2 Kf7-e7+

25. Kf2-e2 Qd6-g3 White resigns.

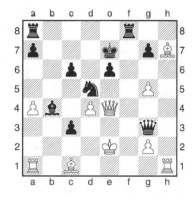

After 26. Rh1-f1 Rf8xf1   27. Ke2xf1 Ra8-f8+   28. Kf1-g1 Bb4-d6 Black wins.

GM Zsuzsa Polgar—GM Vasily Smyslov (World Champion) (Another male champion became a victim of Zsuzsa Polgar)

Wien, 1993

In this position, it seems that black poses a very strong threat of mating white with Qh4xh2+. White, however, found an incredible combination to save the mate and won the game.

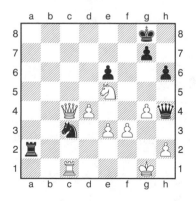

39. Qc4xa2 Nc3xa2   40. Rc1-c8+ Kg8-h7   41. Rc8-h8+ Kh7xh8

42. Ne5-g6+

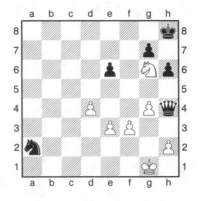

42... Kh8-h7   43. Ng6xh4

This is a lost position for black as white is two pawns ahead. Black resigns shortly.

GM Zsuzsa Polgar—GM Maia Chiburdanidze (Women's World Champion) (The game that earned Zsuzsa the right to challenge for the world title)

St. Petersburg, 1995, World Championship Semi-Final

1. d2-d4 Ng8-f6	2. c2-c4 g7-g6	3. Nb1-c3 Bf8-g7
4. e2-e4 d7-d6	5. f2-f4 0-0	6. Ng1-f3 Nb8-a6
7. Bf1-d3 Bc8-g4	8. 0-0 Nf6-d7	9. Bc1-e3 e7-e5
10. f4xe5 c7-c5	11. d4-d5 Nd7xe5	12. Bd3-e2 Ne5xf3+
13. Be2xf3 Bg4xf3	14. Qd1xf3 Qd8-e7	15. Be3-f4 Na6-c7
16. Qf3-g3 Ra8-d8	17. Kg1-h1 Bg7-d4	18. Ra1-e1 f7-f6
19. Nc3-e2 Bd4-e5	20. Ne2-g1 a7-a6	21. Ng1-f3 Be5xf4
22. Qg3xf4 b7-b5	23. b2-b3 Rd8-b8	24. b3-b4 c5xb4
25. c4-c5		

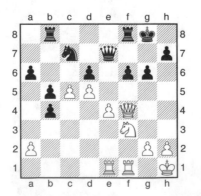

25... Rb8-d8	26. Nf3-d4 d6xc5	27. Nd4-c6 Qe7-d7
28. Nc6xd8 Qd7xd8	29. Re1-c1 c5-c4	30. d5-d6 Nc7-e6
31. Qf4-d2 Qd8-d7	32. Qd2xb4 Ne6-g5	33. Qb4-c5 Rf8-e8
34. Rc1-e1 Re8-e6	35. e4-e5 f6-f5	36. a2-a4 Ng5-f7
37. a4xb5 a6xb5	38. Qc5-c7 Qd7xc7	39. d6xc7 Re6-c6
40. e5-e6 Rc6xc7	41. e6-e7 Nf7-d6	42. e7-e8Q+ Nd6xe8
43. Re1xe8+ Kg8-f7	44. Re8-b8 c4-c3	45. Kh1-g1 Black resigns.

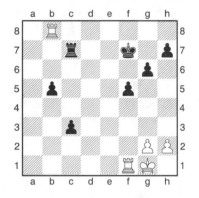

GM Zsuzsa Polgar—GM Jun Xie (Defending Women's World Champion) (The game that gave Zsuzsa her fourth world championship title)

Jaen, 1996

World Championship Final (final game to capture the ultimate world champion title)

1. d2-d4 Ng8-f6	2. Ng1-f3 g7-g6	3. c2-c4 Bf8-g7
4. g2-g3 0-0	5. Bf1-g2 d7-d5	6. c4xd5 Nf6xd5
7. 0-0 Nb8-c6	8. e2-e4 Nd5-b6	9. d4-d5 Nc6-a5
10. Qd1-e1 Na5-c4	11. Nb1-c3 e7-e6	12. b2-b3 Qd8-f6
13. b3xc4 Qf6xc3	14. Qe1xc3 Bg7xc3	15. Ra1-b1 Bc3-g7
16. Bc1-f4 c7-c6	17. d5xc6 b7xc6	18. Bf4-d6 Rf8-e8
19. c4-c5 Nb6-c4	20. e4-e5 Bc8-a6	21. Rf1-c1 Re8-c8
22. Bg2-f1		

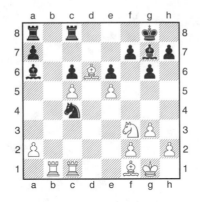

22... Nc4xe5   23. Nf3xe5 Ba6xf1   24. Kg1xf1 Black resigns.

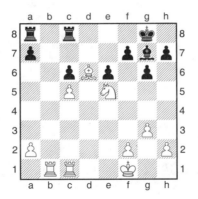

HOUR'S UP!

1. The most controversial chess match of modern times took place in what country?

   a. Iceland

   b. England

   c. France

   d. Italy

2. That match took place between which two players?

   a. Spassky and Kasparov

   b. Fischer and Anand

   c. Fisher and Spassky

   d. Fisher and Euwe

3. True or False: FIDE, Brain Games, and the Professional Chess Association are all recognized chess organizations.

4. True or False: Bobby Fischer is the current world chess champion.

5. The Soviets dominated chess by producing champions for how many years?

   a. Twenty

   b. Over thirty

   c. Over forty

   d. Fifteen

6. The current overall FIDE chess champion is

   a. Ukrainian

   b. American

   c. English

   d. German

7. Who made the statement "I have always lived between chess and opera"?

   a. Vasily Smyslov

   b. Garry Kasparov

   c. Bobby Fischer

   d. Emanuel Lasker

8. Who made the statement "To be a champion requires being more than simply a strong player, one must be a strong human being as well"?

   a. Boris Spassky

   b. Anatoly Karpov

   c. Bobby Fischer

   d. Alexander Khalifman

9. One of these chess players was rebuffed by a woman he proposed to because she refused to marry a "mere chess player." Who was it?

   a. Howard Staunton

   b. Paul Morphy

   c. Adolf Anderson

   d. Jose Capablanca

10. Which one of these chess players did Bobby Fischer call "possibly the greatest chess player of all time."

    a. Howard Staunton

    b. Boris Spassky

    c. Jose Capablanca

    d. Himself

HOUR 21

A Step-by-Step Analysis of an Essential Chess Game

CHAPTER SUMMARY

LESSON PLAN:

Assess your skills as we analyze a classic game step by step from opening all the way to checkmate.

In this hour you learn …

- How to analyze a classic game.
- More on the importance of piece development.
- More on the importance of castling.
- What to do if you are behind or ahead in developing your pieces.

By now we hope that you have a good idea how to develop your pieces and pursue a strategic plan that allows you to do so as quickly as possible, protect your king, and exploit the mistakes and weaknesses of your opponent. After you assess your skills by reviewing this classic game, we review the reasons one side won and why a number of unfortunate blunders caused the other side to lose.

FOLLOWING AND ANALYZING A MODEL GAME

Paul Morphy was an unofficial American world champion from 1858 to 1860. Count Isouard and the Duke of Brunswick (team of two against Morphy) were amateur players. Think about what your own moves would have been as you follow this game.

Paul Morphy—Count Isouard and the Duke of Brunswick

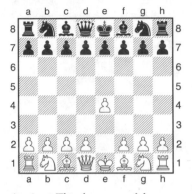

*1. **e2-e4** This shows one of the most popular first moves for white. The idea is to occupy the center square e4 while controlling the other center square d5. In addition, white also opens the diagonal f1-a6 for the bishop on f1.*

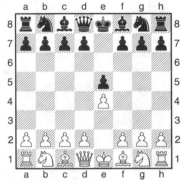

*1... **e7-e5** Black does the same as white, controlling d4 and occupying e5, while opening up the f8-a3 diagonal for the bishop on f8.*

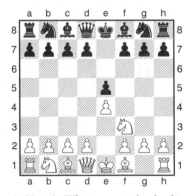

*2. **Ng1-f3** White starts to develop his pieces. The knight on f3 controls d4 while attacking the black e5 pawn.*

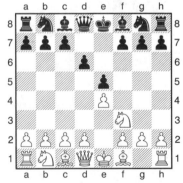

*2... **d7-d6** This is the Philidor Defense. Black is defending the e5 pawn while opening up the h3-c8 diagonal for the bishop on c8.*

STRICTLY DEFINED

The Philidor Defense was named after the player Francois-Andre Danican Philidor (1726–1795), who was the best chess player of his time.

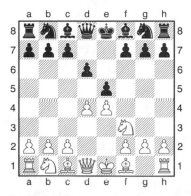

3. **d2-d4** *This aggressive move controls d4 while attacking the e5 pawn, clearing the c1-h6 diagonal for the bishop on c1.*

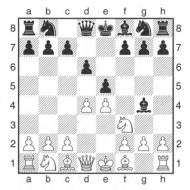

3... **Bc8-g4** *Rather than directly defending the e5 pawn, black decided to attack the white knight on f3, pinning it and also relieving some of the threats against the black e5 pawn. This move, however, is a small mistake, as it will become clear.*

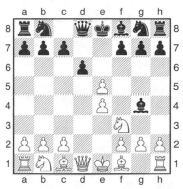

4. **d4xe5** *White immediately captures the e5 pawn.*

If black captures back with 4... d6xe5, white will play 5. Qd1xd8+. Black would then have no choice but to capture back the queen by Ke8xd8 and would no longer be able to castle. Then white would capture the pawn on e5 with d6. Nf3xe5. At that point, white would have a solid advantage.

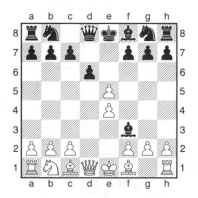

4... **Bg4xf3** *Because taking back the pawn on e5 with d6xe5 is not a very good option, black decides to capture the knight on f3, alleviating some pressure on the e5 pawn.*

There are a few reasons why taking the knight on f3 is not a good trade: For one thing, the black bishop had to move twice—the first time from c8 to g4 and then again from g4 to f3. In the meantime, the white knight only made one move to f3. That gave white one move in development advantage. Second, bishops are usually more preferred than knights in a position like this.

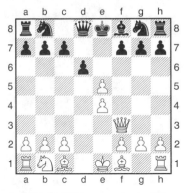

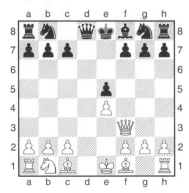

5. **Qd1xf3** *White captures the bishop with the queen and not the pawn on g2 because white does not want to have double pawns (two pawns from the same player doubling up on the same file)—something usually to avoid in chess. In addition, the queen on f3 can potentially represent a threat to black on f7 at a later time.*

5... **d6xe5** *Black captures back the pawn.*

Now the game seems to be quiet, uneventful, and harmless, but in the eyes of a chess master, black is in serious trouble. You will soon see how white can take advantage of it by developing a deadly attack.

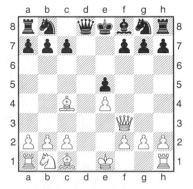

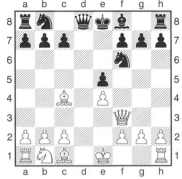

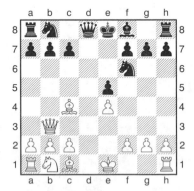

6. **Bf1-c4** *This is the first wave of attack. By developing the bishop on f1 to c4, white threatens to check-mate black on the next move with 7. Qf3xf7.*

6... **Ng8-f6** *Black does not realize the danger yet. Therefore, black develops the knight normally while stopping the queen from capturing the pawn on f7. A better move for black would have been to defend the f7 pawn with 6... Qd8-d7.*

7. **Qf3-b3** *This is the second wave of attack. When black stopped the threat on f7, white immediately shifted the queen to b3, creating a double attack on b7 and f7. Black cannot possibly defend both weaknesses.*

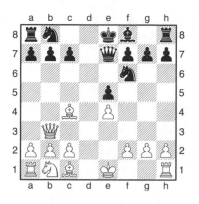

*7... **Qd8-e7** Black is forced to give up either the pawn on b7 or f7. Black decides to defend the pawn on f7.*

If white plays 8. Qb3xb7, white wins a free pawn. However, black will then play 8... Qe7-b4+, forcing white to exchange queens. There is a serious problem for black with this move: by placing the queen on e7, black closes up the a3-f8 diagonal for the bishop on f8. And if the bishop cannot get out, the king cannot castle.

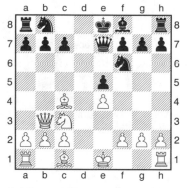

8. **Nb1-c3** *White's position is dominating. White does not want black to be let off the hook by allowing the queen exchange with Qe7-b4+, which could drag out the game. 8. Nb1-c3 blocks the check. This move reminds us that sometimes it is better to develop your pieces than to go after a pawn.*

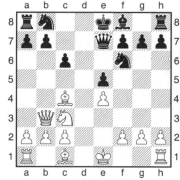

8... **c7-c6** *Black allows the queen on e7 to protect the b7 pawn.*

GO TO ▶

For more information on the pin go to Hour 14.

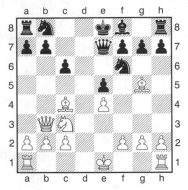

9. **Bc1-g5** *White develops the last minor piece. This move also pins the black knight on f6. White is in total control while black is still having a hard time getting the pieces out.*

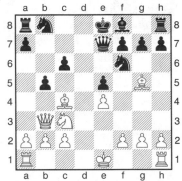

9... **b7-b5** *Black wants to open up some space by pushing back the white bishop on c4. If white moves the bishop back, black will then play Nb8-d7, slowing white's development of its pieces. However, black did not anticipate white's response.*

JUST A MINUTE

If your king is still in the middle during the early or middle part of the game, try not to open files and diagonals because the king can get into serious trouble.

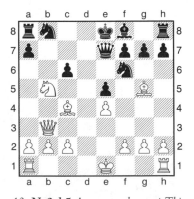

10. **Nc3xb5** *A very good move! This is the beginning of a series of beautiful sacrifices.*

What white wants to do is simple. The black king is vulnerable because it is not yet castled. Not all of black's pieces are developed. Therefore, white wants to open up the position to expose the black king.

PROCEED WITH CAUTION

If you are ahead in development, open up the files and diagonals so your pieces can do damage. If you are behind in development, try not to open things up to allow yourself time to get your pieces out. This brings us back to a very important point in the opening: Develop your pieces as soon as possible.

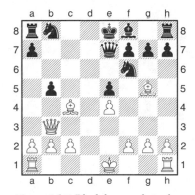

*10... **c6xb5** Black has no choice but to capture the knight and hope that white does not make all the best moves.*

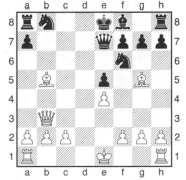

*11. **Bc4xb5+** The bishop on b5 is checking the black king. As you can see, black's kingside is blocked. The bishop on f8 and the rook on h8 cannot get out. In the meantime, black's queenside has opened up, leaving the king exposed.*

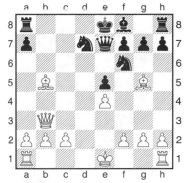

*11... **Nb8-d7** Black develops the knight and defends the check at the same time, hoping to shield the king to some degree.*

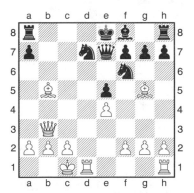

*12. **0-0-0** Not only is white getting his king to safety, he is also putting the rook on d1—an opened file—thereby putting more pressure on the black knight on d7. White does not give black a moment to recuperate.*

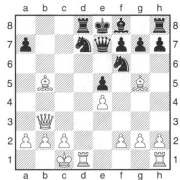

*12... **Ra8-d8** Black is providing protection for the black knight on d7.*

Had black made the following moves instead of 12... Ra8-d8, the following would have occurred.

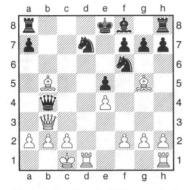

Black plays 12... Qe7-b4 instead of 12... Ra8-d8, trying to exchange the queen.

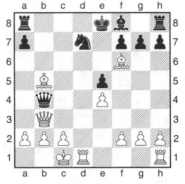

13. Bg5xf6 White is capturing the knight on f6 and attacking the other knight on d7.

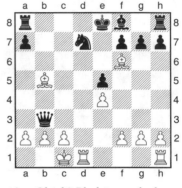

13... Qb4xb3 Black is completely lost.

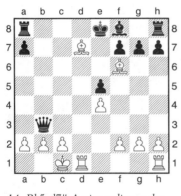

14. Bb5xd7# A nice ending to the game!

Instead, however, the game progresses as follows.

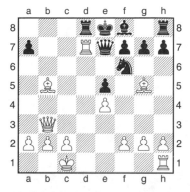

13. Rd1xd7 *Another spectacular move, continuing the attack! Once again, white is taking advantage of the fact that black cannot use the bishop on f8 and the rook on h8. In addition, the black knight on f6 is also useless because it is pinned. Black is in complete disarray.*

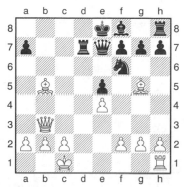

13... Rd8xd7 *This is practically a forced move because black cannot capture the white rook with anything else.*

Black has four useless pieces: The bishop on f8 and the rook on h8 are stuck, and the knight on f6 and the rook on d7 are pinned. This is an example of what not to do. Once again, the key lesson here is: Develop your pieces and castle as soon as possible.

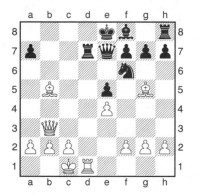

14. Rh1-d1 *Now that the knight on d7 is gone, black's position is even weaker. So what does white want to do now? The answer is simple: Continue the attack! The most obvious target is the black rook on d7, because it is pinned and completely helpless.*

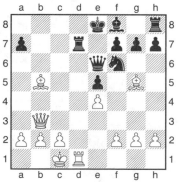

14... Qe7-e6 *Finally, black is moving his queen out of the a3-f8 diagonal so that the bishop on f8 can get out. Unfortunately, it is too little too late for black.*

15. Bb5xd7+ *White does not give black time to get the bishop out and castle. He mounts another direct attack.*

15... **Nf6xd7** *If black captures the bishop with the queen, white will play 16. Qb3-b8+, forcing black to play 16... Ke8-e7. Then white will follow up with 17. Qb8xe5+.*

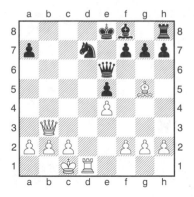

Now black has two choices:

- If black plays 17... Qd7-e6, white will checkmate black in two with 18. Qe5-c7+ Ke7-e8 and 19. Rd1-d8#.

- If black plays 17... Ke7-d8, white will play 18. Bg5xf6+ g7xf6   19. Qe5xf6+ Kd8-c7 20. Rd1xd7+ Kc7xd7   21. Qf6xh8. This would give white a huge material advantage.

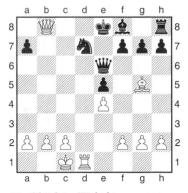

16. **Qb3-b8+** *With this amazing move, white is sacrificing the queen for checkmate. Once again white is reinforcing its attack, not allowing black to regroup.*

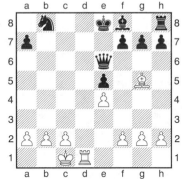

16... **Nd7xb8** *Taking the queen is black's only legal move.*

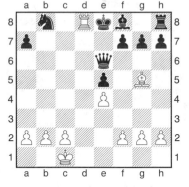

17. **Rd1-d8#** *A beautiful finish to a game!*

DRAWING LESSONS FROM THE GAME

What have we learned here from the black side?

- Black's tragic mistake was not to develop all the pieces immediately.
- Black's second tragic mistake was leaving the king exposed to serious danger by not castling.
- It is critically important to get all the pieces out and get the king to safety as soon as possible. Because black failed to do either one, he was punished severely!

GO TO ▷
To refresh your memory about the key rules of success, see Hour 7.

What have we learned from the white side?

- White followed the key rules of chess by developing all pieces immediately.
- In addition, when white realized that black's lack of development was a serious problem, white kept the pressure on, not allowing black to recuperate.
- White refused to take a free pawn on move eight so that he could continue his development faster and bring all his forces into the massive attack.

HOUR'S UP!

1. True or False: Unrelenting pressure by white is one of the major reasons that black lost.
2. At the end of the game, black had only one legal move left in which it captured a piece. Which piece was it?
   a. Rook
   b. Knight
   c. Queen
   d. Bishop
3. True or false: Black was unable to castle because white would not allow it to get its bishop out.
4. If you are ahead in development, you want to
   a. Open up your ranks and files.
   b. Open up your ranks and diagonals.
   c. Open up your files and diagonals.
   d. Not open up your files or ranks to protect your king.

5. If you are behind in development, you want to
   a. Not open up your files and diagonals.
   b. Open up your files and diagonals.
   c. Not open up your ranks and files.
6. True or False: Black castled too late in the game.
7. True or False: During the end of the game, white was willing to sacrifice a queen for checkmate.
8. True or False: White was targeting black's weak f7 pawn in the opening.
9. True or False: At one point in the middlegame, black had four useless pieces.
10. True or False: The opening moves by white and black were symmetrical.

HOUR 22

Miniatures: Lessons from Four Classic Games

CHAPTER SUMMARY

LESSON PLAN:

In this hour, we analyze four of the most famous brilliant chess miniatures step by step.

In this hour you learn ...

- How three chess masters secured checkmates with quick dispatch.
- How to perform a Legall's mate.
- How to perform a French Defense.
- How to perform a Scotch Gambit.
- How to perform a Belgrade Gambit.

Miniatures are games that take place in a brief period of time. One of the miniatures we examine in this hour took place in the middle of the nineteenth century, another in the early twentieth century, and the most recent in 1940. But no matter when they were played, each of these games has important lessons to teach us about strategy. You will see how even proficient chess players can make mistakes, fail to see or plan ahead, or misconstrue their opponent's intentions. By the same token, you will see how the winners were able to exploit mistakes and blunders while simultaneously pursuing a well thought-out plan that inexorably led them to victory.

GAME 1

This game was played by two of the most famous chess players—Reti and Tartakower—in the early 1900s.

Reti—Tartakower

Vienna, 1910

1. e2-e4 c7-c6

This opening is called the Caro-Kann Defense, a solid opening for black, and was named after British player Horatio Caro (1862–1920) and Viennese player Marcus Kann (1820–1886).

2. d2-d4 d7-d5   3. Nb1-c3 d5xe4
4. Nc3xe4 Ng8-f6

5. Qd1-d3

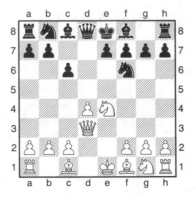

This is not the best move. Normally, you try to avoid bringing out the queen too early in the game. A better move would have been 5. Ne4xf6+.

5... e7-e5

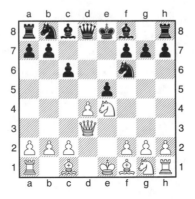

This is not a very good move by black because it unnecessarily weakens the black king. Two better choices would have been either 5... Nf6xe4 to trade off the strong active white knight in the center or 5... Nb8-d7 to give reinforcement to the knight on f6.

If black plays 5... Bc8-f5, pinning the white knight on e4, it would be a blunder because white can create a discovery attack with 6. Ne4xf6+, winning the black bishop on f5.

6. **d4xe5 Qd8-a5+**

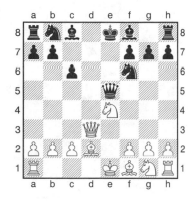

7. **Bc1-d2 Qa5xe5**

Black thinks he has just made a good move by pinning the white knight on e4.

8. **0-0-0**

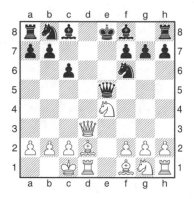

White, on the other hand, simply ignores the pin by castling, sacrificing the knight. Actually, white is setting up a devious trap.

8... **Nf6xe4**

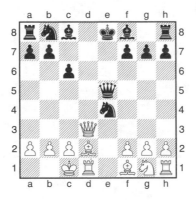

Black unsuspectingly takes the bait. If black would have played 8... Qe5xe4, white could pin the queen by playing 9. Rd1-e1, winning the black queen as a result.

9. **Qd3-d8+!!**

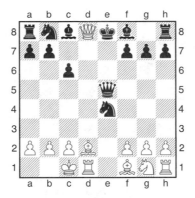

GO TO ▷
For a list of notation symbols and their meanings, see Hour 9.

White has just unleashed an absolutely brilliant checkmate combination.

9... **Ke8xd8**

Black has no choice but to capture the white queen.

10. **Bd2-g5+!!**

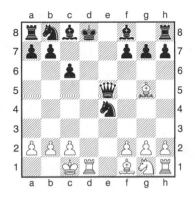

Double check! Now black has only two choices. If black plays 10... Kd8-c7, white will play 11. Bg5-d8#. If black plays 10... Kd8-e8, white will play 11. Rd1-d8#. There is no way out of this forced checkmate. A brilliant checkmate combination!

10... Black resigns because there is no defense to this mate threat.

GAME 2

Now let's take a look at a second famous game that dates back to the middle of the nineteenth century.

Falkbear—Amateur

1847

1. e2-e4 e7-e5   2. Ng1-f3 Nb8-c6   3. d2-d4

This opening is called the Scotch Gambit.

3... e5xd4   4. Bf1-c4 d7-d6   5. c2-c3 d4xc3   6. Nb1xc3

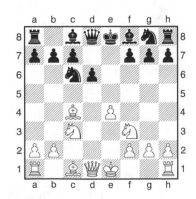

So far, everything seems to be normal. White sacrifices a pawn on move 5 to gain a development advantage.

6... Bc8-g4?

This is not a good move because it allows white to play 7. Qd1-b3, creating a double attack on black's b7 and f7 pawns. A better move for black would have been 6… Ng8-f6.

7. 0-0?

White fails to take advantage of black's weaknesses. 7.Qd1-b3 would have been much better.

7... Nc6-e5??

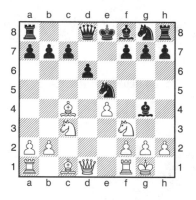

Black has just made a horrible blunder. Black thinks that because his bishop on g4 is pinning the white knight on f3, he can put more pressure on this knight. However, black does not foresee what he has set himself up for.

8. Nf3xe5!!

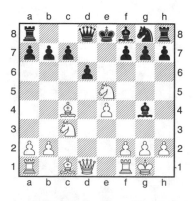

A brilliant move! White makes a discovery attack sacrifice move by giving up his queen! If black plays 8… d6xe5, white wins the black bishop with 9. Qd1xg4.

8... Bg4xd1

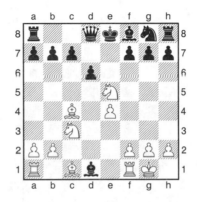

Black decides to accept white's queen sacrifice.

9. Bc4xf7+!

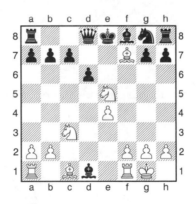

White starts his mating combination. 9. Ne5xf7. Forking the queen and rook would be a horrible blunder because white has already given up his own queen.

9... Ke8-e7

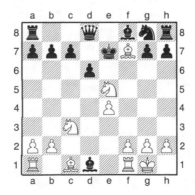

Black has only one legal move.

10. **Nc3-d5#**. This is called the Legall's mate. A beautiful sacrifice to achieve the mate!

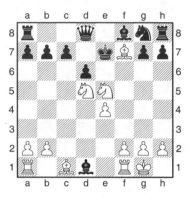

FYI Legall's mate was named after a player, Legall, sometime in the mid-1700s. His first name is unknown.

Game 3

Now let's turn to yet another famous game—this one from 1940.

Foltys—Mogila

1940

1. **e2-e4 e7-e6**

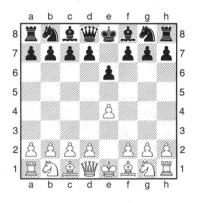

This opening is called the French Defense, so named when a team from Paris used it successfully to defeat London in a correspondence match sometime in the 1800s.

2. d2-d4 d7-d5   **3. Nb1-d2 Ng8-f6**   **4. Bf1-d3 c7-c5**

5. e4-e5 Nf6-d7   **6. c2-c3 Nb8-c6**   **7. Ng1-e2 Bf8-e7**

8. Nd2-f3 0-0   **9. Ne2-f4 b7-b6**

A better move for black here would have been 9… Rf8-e8 and then 10… Nd7-f8 in order to defend the h7 pawn. We will soon see why defending the h7 pawn is so important.

10. h2-h4

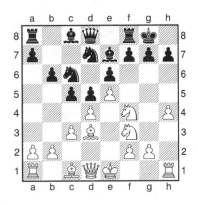

White is planning a mating attack on the kingside. In the next few moves, we will see white's full plan on how to achieve this mating attack.

10… Rf8-e8

This move is a little too late. A better choice now is 10… h7-h6, which would move the h7 pawn away from the direct attack of the white bishop on d3.

11. Bd3xh7+!

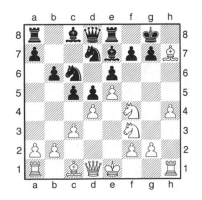

White is sacrificing his bishop to start a kingside mating attack.

11... Kg8xh7

If black moves his king away to f8 or h8, he simply loses a pawn without any compensation. Therefore, black decides to accept white's bishop sacrifice and make white prove that his mating attack works.

12. Nf3-g5+!

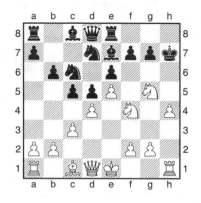

The second move of the mating attack.

12... Kh7-g8

If black takes the white knight with 12... Be7xg5, white would play 13. h4xg5+ discovered check, opening the deadly h file and following it up by 14. Qd1-h5 with a mating threat of 15. Qh5-h8#. If 12... Kh7-h8, white would reply with 13. Ng5xf7+, forking and winning the queen.

13. Qd1-h5!

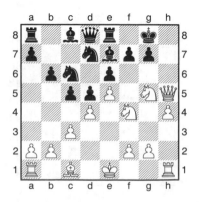

White threatens checkmate with 14. Qh5-h7+ Kg8-f8 15. Qh7-h8#.

13... Be7xg5

Black has no choice but to get rid of the dangerous g5 knight to avoid checkmate.

14. h4xg5!

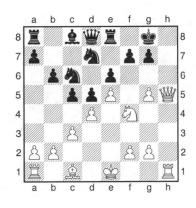

White captures back the bishop while opening up the deadly h file to continue the mating attack. Now white is threatening checkmate with 15. Qh5-h8#.

14... Kg8-f8

The black king is trying to escape from the 15. Qh5-h8# threat.

15. Qh5-h8+

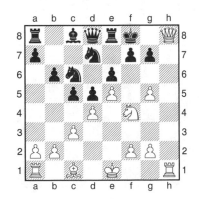

White is still relentlessly pursuing the black king.

15... Kf8-e7

The black king has only one legal square to move to.

16. Nf4-g6+!!

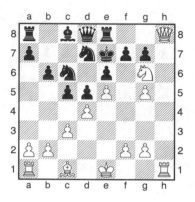

Another brilliant sacrifice: the final blow to black's defense. White is continuing to pursue a checkmate.

16... f7xg6

Once again, black's only legal move.

17. Qh8xg7#

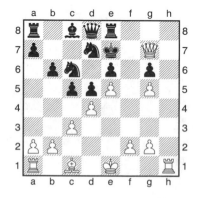

Finishing off the black king with checkmate! A beautiful mating attack!

GAME 4

Blumenfeld—Amateur

1903

1. e2-e4 e7-e5   2. Ng1-f3 Nb8-c6   3. Nb1-c3 g7-g6

4. d2-d4 e5xd4   5. Nc3-d5

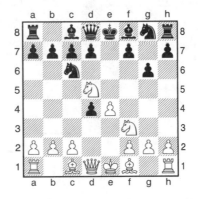

This is called the Belgrade Gambit (so named after it was used by Yugoslavian master Nikola Karaklajic). Another option would be 5. Nf3xd4.

5... **Bf8-g7**

6. **Bc1-g5 Ng8-e7?**

A bad move! Black would be better off with 6... Nc6-e7 or 6... f7-f6.

7. **Nf3xd4! Bg7xd4**

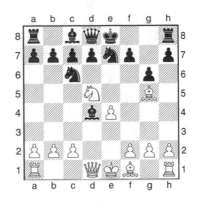

White was threatening 8. Nd4xc6, with the threat of winning the black knight on e7 on the next move. If black takes the knight on d4 with 7... Nc6xd4, white would respond with 8. Bg5xe7, winning the black queen.

8. **Qd1xd4!!**

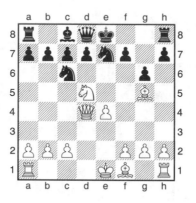

White is sacrificing his queen to create a mating attack.

8... **Nc6xd4**

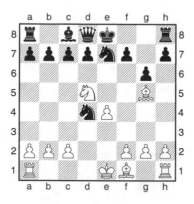

White is attacking the black rook on h8. White is also threatening to put his knight on the f6 square. Black's position is now in shambles because it has too many weaknesses. He chooses to capture the white queen.

9. **Nd5-f6+**

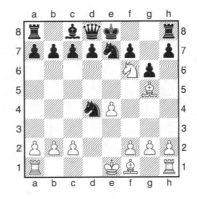

White pursues the mating attack.

9... **Ke8-f8**

Black has only one legal move

10. **Bg5-h6#**

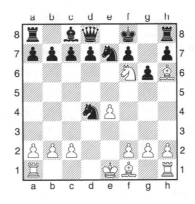

White finishes off black with a nice checkmate!

HOUR'S UP!

1. True or False: In the first game, white gave a double check right before he checkmated.

2. In the second example, white won with a

   a. Simple mate

   b. Back Rank mate

   c. Legall's mate

   d. Smothered mate

3. With move 11 in the third game, white sacrificed a

   a. Queen

   b. Rook

   c. Bishop

   d. Knight

4. In the fourth (last) game, white checkmated by using the

   a. Queen and rook

   b. Bishop and knight

   c. 2 bishops

   d. 2 knights

5. True or False: In the second game, white used the Belgrade Gambit.

6. True or False: In the third game, white sacrificed first a bishop and then a knight.

7. True or False: In the third game, both sides castled to put their kings to safety.

8. True or False: White won in all four of the preceding games.

9. In move 8 of the fourth game, white sacrificed a

   a. Queen

   b. Rook

   c. Bishop

   d. Knight

10. True or False: It is important to watch out for traps even early in the game.

HOUR 23

Improving Your Basic Endgame Knowledge

CHAPTER SUMMARY

LESSON PLAN:

In this hour you test what you've learned and improve on some essential endgame knowledge.

In this hour you learn ...

- How well you can mate with one and two rooks.
- How well you can mate with a rook and a minor piece.
- How well you can mate with two minor pieces.
- How well you can mate with a queen.
- How well you can promote a pawn to various pieces.

This is your chance to put what you've learned so far to the test. We present you with 32 exercises using pieces individually and in combination. Can you exploit an opponent's weakness? Escape a trap? Make the best use of the material you have? Try these yourself first, and then check the answers in Appendix E.

ROOK EXERCISES

The exercises in this section are presented to help you develop your skills at using your rooks.

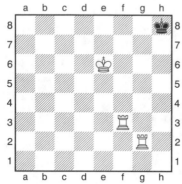

Exercise 1. White to move and mate in one. In this position, white isolated the black king to the h file. How does white checkmate the black king?

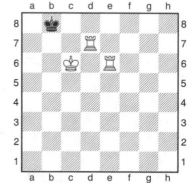

Exercise 2. White to move and mate in one. In this position, white pushed the black king to the eighth rank. How can black be mated in the next move?

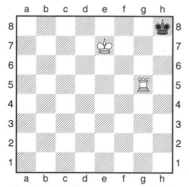

Exercise 3. White to move and mate in two. In this position, the black king is stuck in the corner. How do the white king and rook work together to create a mate in two moves?

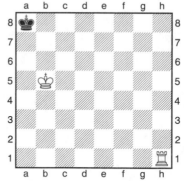

Exercise 4. White to move and mate in two. In this position, white wants to block the black king in the corner in order to achieve a mate. How does white do this in two moves?

KNIGHT WITH ROOK EXERCISES

The exercises in this section are presented to help you develop your skills at using knights and rooks together.

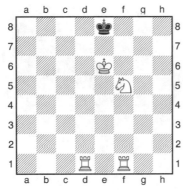

Exercise 5. White to move and mate in one. White has a substantial material advantage and can mate black in the next move. Can you find this mating move?

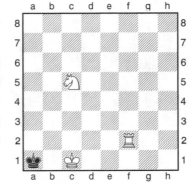

Exercise 6. White to move and mate in one. The black king is trapped in the a1 corner. How can white checkmate black in one move?

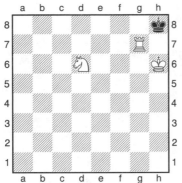

Exercise 7. White to move and mate in one. The white rook and king isolated the black king on h8. Now, white is ready to checkmate black in one move. Do you see this move?

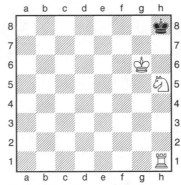

Exercise 8. White to move and mate in one. The white rook and knight can work together to mate the black king in the next move. Can you find the mate?

ROOK AND BISHOP EXERCISES

The exercises in this section are presented to help you develop your skills at using your rooks and bishops together.

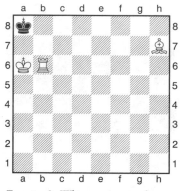

Exercise 9. White to move and mate in one. The white king and rook have trapped the black king in the corner. Because the king is stuck, white can mate black in the next move and avoid a stalemate. Can you find this move?

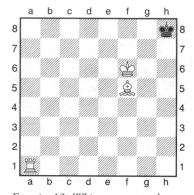

Exercise 10. White to move and mate in one. In this position, the black king is stuck on the eighth rank. How can white checkmate black in the next move?

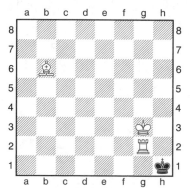

Exercise 11. White to move and mate in one. In this position, the black king is in danger of being stalemated. White can mate black two different ways in the next move and avoid stalemate. Can you find the mate?

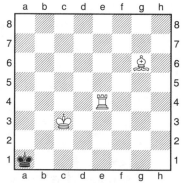

Exercise 12. White to move and mate in one. In this position, the black king is cornered. However, the king can escape to squares b1 and a2. How can white eliminate both squares and mate black in one move?

BISHOP AND KNIGHT EXERCISES

The exercises in this section are presented to help you develop your skills at using your bishops and knights together.

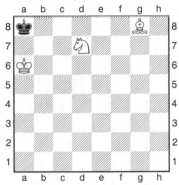

Exercise 13. White to move and mate in one. The white king and knight are blocking the black king from getting out of the a8 corner. White can mate black in the next move.

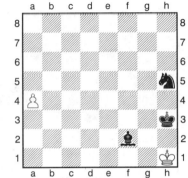

Exercise 14. Black to move and mate in one. The black king and bishop have successfully trapped the white king. But black has to be careful not to stalemate white. Can you find a mate in one for black?

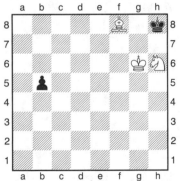

Exercise 15. White to move and mate in one. The white king and knight have successfully cornered the black king and can mate in one move. Can you find the mate?

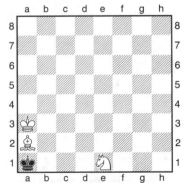

Exercise 16. White to move and mate in one. The white bishop and the white king trapped the black king on a1. How can white checkmate black next move?

BISHOP EXERCISES

The exercises in this section are presented to help you develop your skills at using your bishops.

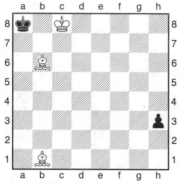

Exercise 17. White to move and mate in one. The best way to mate a king is to trap the king in the corner. White has done that successfully. How can white checkmate black next move?

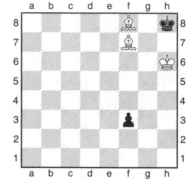

Exercise 18. White to move and mate in one. The same thing happened in this position. The black king is stuck in the corner. Can you find the mate in one move for white?

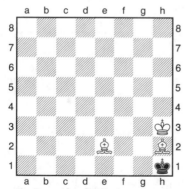

Exercise 19. White to move and mate in one, but white is also in danger of a stalemate. Can you find the checkmate?

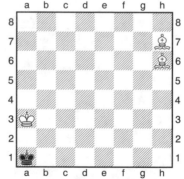

Exercise 20. White to move and mate in one. The two white bishops are beautifully set up to mate black. How can white mate black in one move?

QUEEN EXERCISES

This section provides exercised designed to help you make better use of your queen.

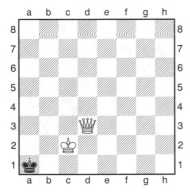

Exercise 21. White to move and mate in one. White is up a queen and has two ways of checkmating black next move. Can you find either checkmate?

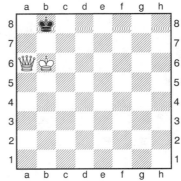

Exercise 22. White to move and mate in one. White has a winning material advantage. How can white utilize this advantage and checkmate black next move?

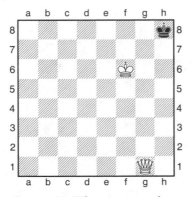

Exercise 23. White to move and mate in one. The white king and queen have successfully forced the black king in the corner. Find the checkmate in one for white!

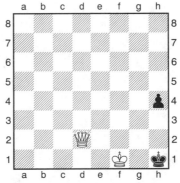

Exercise 24. White to move and mate in one. White has a queen advantage versus a pawn. In addition, the black king is trapped in the corner. Can you find a checkmate in one for white?

PAWN EXERCISES

This section provides exercised designed to help you make better use of your pawns.

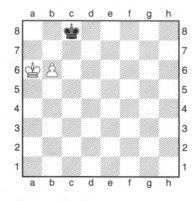

Exercise 25. White to move and win. White has a chance to win the game by promoting the pawn. However, the right move will allow white to promote, and the wrong move will result in a draw. What is the correct move?

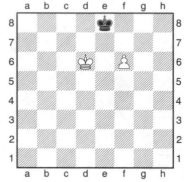

Exercise 26. White to move and win. White can win with the pawn promotion. How can the white king assist the white pawn to promote and win the game?

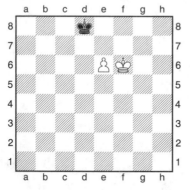

Exercise 27. White to move and win. The only way white can win is by promoting the pawn. How can the white king help the pawn be promoted and thus win the game?

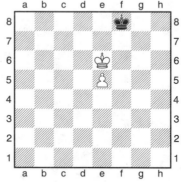

Exercise 28. White to move and win. White is up a pawn and can win the game if the pawn can be promoted. How can white force the promotion and win the game?

VARIOUS PAWN EXERCISES

In this section you see that the pawn does not necessarily have to be promoted to a queen to win.

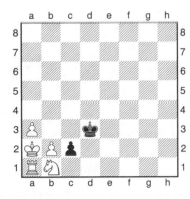

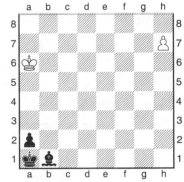

Exercise 29. Black to move and mate in one. Black is down by a lot of material. However, black has a chance to checkmate white right now. How does black checkmate white?

Exercise 30. White to move and mate in one. White is down by a bishop but has a chance to mate black next move. How can white win?

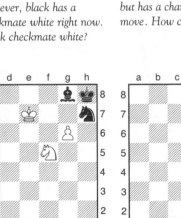

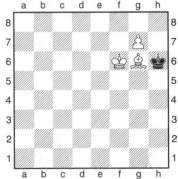

Exercise 31. White to move and mate in one. The black king is not in a good place in the corner. Because of this, white has the opportunity to checkmate black immediately. Can you find this checkmate?

Exercise 32. White to move and mate in one. The black king is trapped on h6. White can take advantage of this opportunity to checkmate black next move. How is it done?

HOUR'S UP!

1. True or False: You can never checkmate when you are giving a discovered check.

2. True or False: In a pawn endgame, in order to promote your pawn, it is vital to get control of the promotion square.

3. In most of the above exercises, where did the king get checkmated?

   a. Center

   b. Corner

   c. On the e file

   d. On the third rank

4. True or False: It is better to capture one of the opponent's pieces than to give checkmate.

5. True or False: In the endgame, you often have to be careful to avoid stalemate.

6. True or False: In some positions, you can have several ways to checkmate.

7. True or False: Two rooks are able to checkmate a lone king without the help of the king.

8. True or False: You should always promote your pawns to a queen.

9. True or False: In pawn endgames, your goal is to get your pawn promoted.

10. In the very last exercise (32), white promoted his pawn to a

    a. Queen

    b. Rook

    c. Bishop

    d. Knight

Hour 24

Reviewing What I Have Learned

Testing yourself on what's been discussed in the preceding hours will help you master the concepts of the game and will serve you in good stead in every game you play—with a friend or a professional player, whether it's over-the-board, on the Internet, or even against a computer. After you've tried your hand at them, you can find the solutions in Appendix E.

CHAPTER SUMMARY

LESSON PLAN:

In this hour you have the chance to test what you've learned and review some basic principles.

In this hour you learn ...

- How well you've learned chess tactics.
- How well you know how to open.
- How well you know how to develop your pieces.
- What fundamental principles to keep in mind when you play.

Test 1

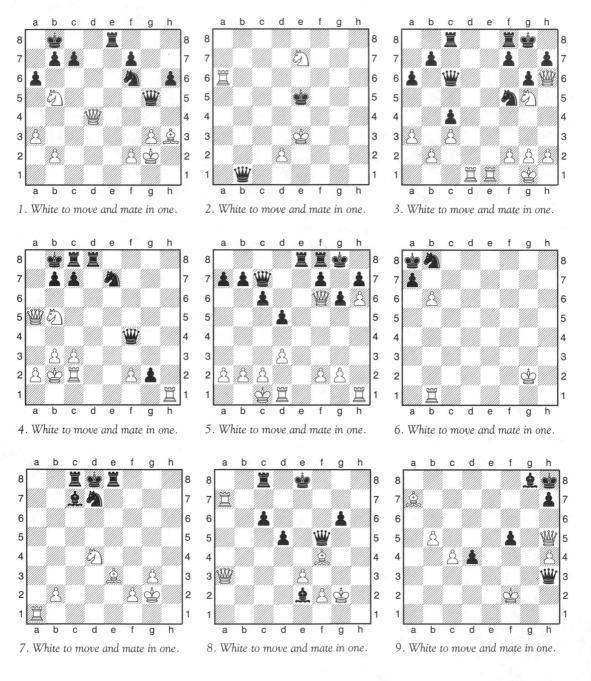

1. White to move and mate in one.

2. White to move and mate in one.

3. White to move and mate in one.

4. White to move and mate in one.

5. White to move and mate in one.

6. White to move and mate in one.

7. White to move and mate in one.

8. White to move and mate in one.

9. White to move and mate in one.

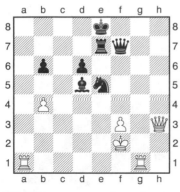

10. *White to move and mate in one.*

11. *White to move and mate in one.*

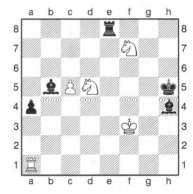

12. *White to move and mate in one.*

Test 2

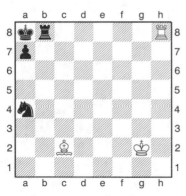

1. White to move and mate in one.

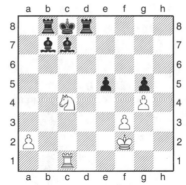

2. White to move and mate in one.

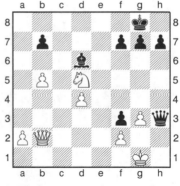

3. Black to move and mate in one.

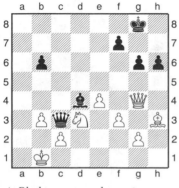

4. Black to move and mate in one.

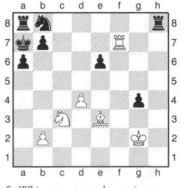

5. White to move and mate in one.

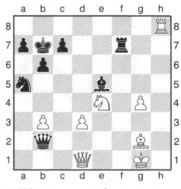

6. White to move and mate in one.

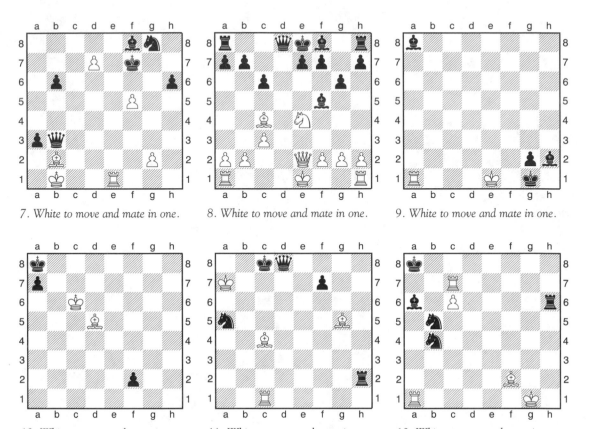

7. White to move and mate in one.

8. White to move and mate in one.

9. White to move and mate in one.

10. White to move and mate in one.

11. White to move and mate in one.

12. White to move and mate in one.

TEST 3

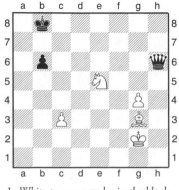

1. White to move and win the black queen.

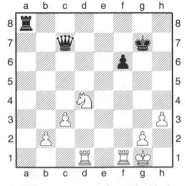

2. White to move and win the black queen.

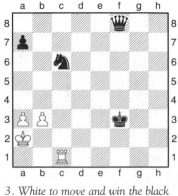

3. White to move and win the black queen.

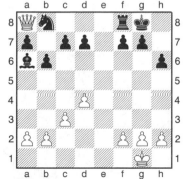

4. *White to move and win the black queen.*

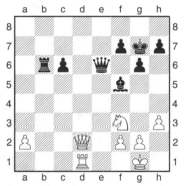

5. *Black to move and trap the white queen.*

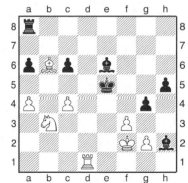

6. *White to move and win the black bishop.*

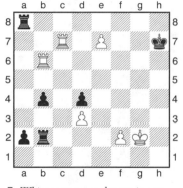

7. *White to move and mate in one.*

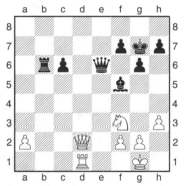

8. *White to move and win the black rook.*

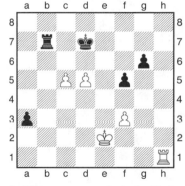

9. *White to move and win the black rook.*

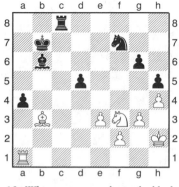

10. *White to move and win the black knight.*

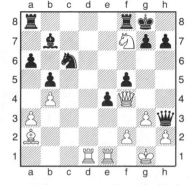

11. *White to move and win the black queen.*

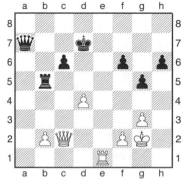

12. *White to move and win the black queen.*

Test 4

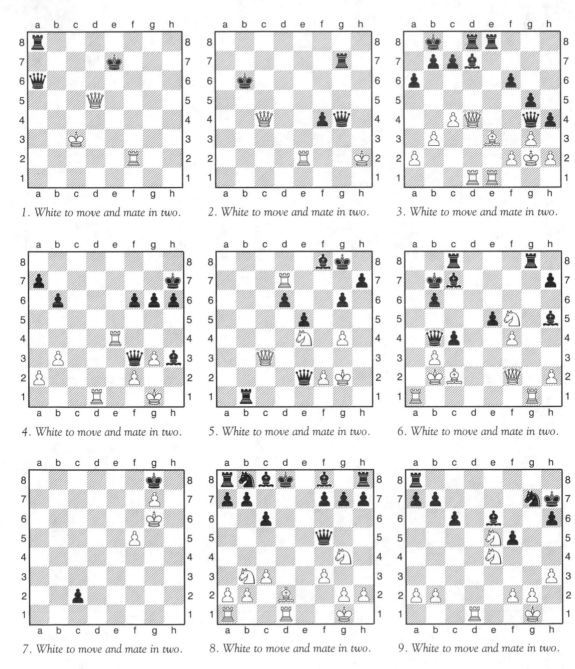

1. White to move and mate in two.

2. White to move and mate in two.

3. White to move and mate in two.

4. White to move and mate in two.

5. White to move and mate in two.

6. White to move and mate in two.

7. White to move and mate in two.

8. White to move and mate in two.

9. White to move and mate in two.

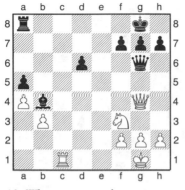

10. White to move and mate in two.

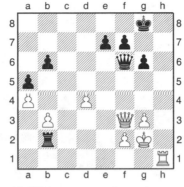

11. White to move and mate in two.

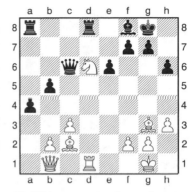

12. White to move and mate in two.

TEST 5

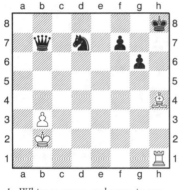

1. White to move and mate in two.

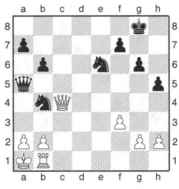

2. Black to move and mate in two.

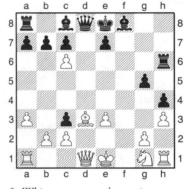

3. White to move and mate in two.

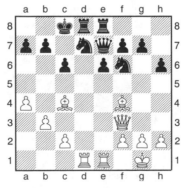

4. Black to move and mate in two.

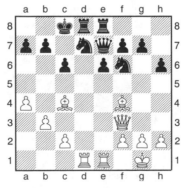

5. White to move and mate in two.

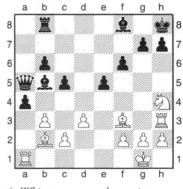

6. White to move and mate in two.

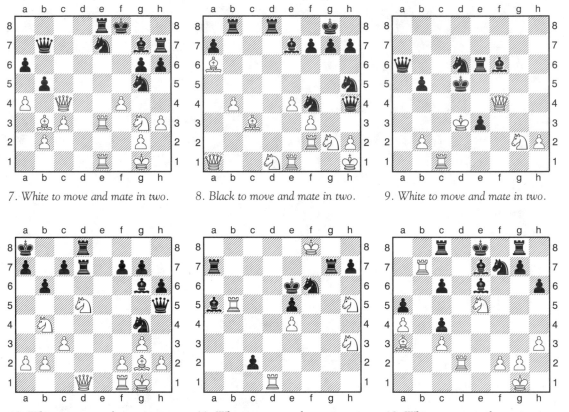

7. *White to move and mate in two.*

8. *Black to move and mate in two.*

9. *White to move and mate in two.*

10. *White to move and mate in two.*

11. *White to move and mate in two.*

12. *White to move and mate in two.*

HOW TO MAXIMIZE EVERYTHING I KNOW

Now that we're near the end of our final lesson, it may be useful to review some of the basic ideas that we've been emphasizing throughout the book.

Follow the opening principles:

- Control the center.
- Develop your pieces ASAP.
- Castle early to keep the king safe.
- Try not to move the same piece twice (unless it is necessary) before developing the rest of the pieces.
- Don't bring your queen out too early.

Keep practicing your tactics by solving all the puzzles in this book. It will make you sharp. And practice as much as you can by joining a local chess club or an Internet server.

How to Have Fun Playing Chess

Chess is not a solitary activity. So if you're the type who enjoys friendly competition, chess offers you the chance to make new friends with every game you play. When you travel, visit the local chess clubs in that area. If you don't have the opportunity to travel, you can still make friends of all ages from all over the world through Internet play.

If you are not the competitive type, however, you can still have great fun in chess by exploring the artistic—and aesthetic—aspect of the game. Any number of chess books are available that feature some of the most beautiful games ever played. When a game is played perfectly, it is like music to your ears.

Now Go Get Them

Let's be realistic. No one can win every game. So don't get discouraged if you lose. Learn from your mistakes and get better after every game. Good luck, have fun—and welcome to our world of chess!

Hour's Up!

1. True or False: Black always makes the first move in chess.
2. Which piece is the most powerful and most valuable in chess?
   a. Rook
   b. Knight
   c. Queen
   d. Bishop
3. The rook is worth more in points than
   a. Two bishops
   b. One queen
   c. Four pawns
   d. One bishop and one knight
4. The body that governs chess internationally is called
   a. FIFA
   b. FIDE
   c. USCF
   d. IOC

5. True or False: The center squares are e4, d4, e5, and d5.

6. True or False: It is best to keep your king safe by castling ASAP.

7. True or False: It is better to checkmate your opponent than to stalemate your opponent.

8. True or False: The bishop moves diagonally.

9. True or False: You cannot castle while you are in check.

10. True or False: The pawn can be promoted to a queen when it gets to the eighth rank.

APPENDIX A
Glossary

advantage   A player is said to have an advantage when his position is better than his opponent's. An advantage can be strategic or material.

algebraic notation   The most popular system to record chess moves, sometimes known as coordinate notation. The files are identified alphabetically, ranks numerically, and each square is uniquely named by its file and rank number, in that order.

analysis   A detailed examination of the variations that could possibly arise in a chess position.

annotation   Comments on one or more moves of a game.

attack   An active threat. To make an aggressive move, or series of moves, often intended to threaten the capture of an opponent's piece or to checkmate.

blunder   A bad move. Some blunders are obvious to all players. Other blunders may only be recognized by very experienced players.

capturing   The taking of an opponent's piece by moving your piece to a square occupied by the opponent's piece and removing it from play.

castle   A special move intended to protect the king behind a row of pawns and place the rook in the center. When castling is played, the king and the rook move simultaneously (counting together as one move) along the back rank. This move can be made only once in the game. It is normal to castle in the opening phase of the game. Castle is also another name for the rook.

center   The geographical center of the board, whose most important squares are e4, e5, d4, and d5. The e and d files are referred to as the center files.

check   A check occurs when a player attacks an opponent's king. Whenever check takes place, the player will announce "check" to his opponent so that he is made aware of the threat.

checkmate   An attack against an opponent's king from which no escape or defense is possible. When checkmate occurs, the opponent is forced to resign and the game is over.

connected pawns   A pawn that can guard or be guarded by another pawn on an adjoining file. This term is generally used in the plural to define a group of two or more such pawns.

control   To dominate a particular situation or area of the board. A player can control diagonals, an open file, a sector of the board, or even a single square.

counterattack   When a player who has come under attack launches an attack of his own rather than defending against the opponent's attack.

critical position/move   A pivotal move or position which may decide the fate of the game.

defense   A move or sequence of moves by a player intended to stop an opponent's attack.

develop   To bring a piece into play. Moving pieces from the squares they occupy at the beginning of the game to positions—usually in the center—where they can be more effective and have more mobility.

discovered attack   Also known as discovery, a discovered attack occurs when one piece moves and uncovers an attack by a piece behind it. It is extremely powerful because both pieces can create an attack at the same time. Most commonly it involves a check or a capture, often leading to gain of material or sometimes even to checkmate.

draw   A tied game in which neither side wins. In formal matches, a half point is awarded to each player in a drawn game.

en passant   A French phrase which literally means "in passing." A pawn is said to be en passant when, on its first move, it advances two squares and lands beside an enemy pawn. In this event the enemy pawn is allowed to take the pawn as if it had only advanced one square. For example, black has a pawn on his fifth rank (say d4) and white, taking advantage of the facility to move a pawn two squares forward on its first move, moves (say) e2-e4, black can capture this pawn—but only on the very next move—placing the capturing pawn on e3.

endgame   The last of the three phases of a chess game, usually characterized by a scarcity of pieces on the board.

equality   A chess game is considered equal when neither side has an advantage or when the players' advantages, while different, put them on an equal footing.

FIDE   The French acronym for the Fédération Internationale des Échecs—the International Chess Federation—the official organization governing chess tournament play, which grants such titles as grandmaster and international master.

file   The vertical columns of the chessboard, designated using algebraic notation by a letter, beginning with a file, b file, and so on.

forced move   A move in which there is no legal or reasonable alternative.

fork   A tactic in which on one move, a piece attacks two of its enemy's pieces at the same time.

gambit   An often risky tactic in a chess opening in which a player voluntarily sacrifices material (usually a pawn) to gain positional or developmental superiority over his opponent.

GM   Short for grandmaster.

grandmaster   The highest title awarded by FIDE for outstanding international play based on ratings and performances. These ratings are earned by acquiring a certain number of points cumulatively amassed from victories (as well as draws) in officially designated matches. Once a player is awarded grandmaster, he or she remains one regardless of how the player performs in the future.

IM   Short form for international master.

initiative   A player has an initiative in a game when he is able to threaten an opponent in such a way as to force him to react.

international master   A chess ranking just below grandmaster, awarded by FIDE.

insufficient material   A situation when both players lack enough pieces to mate their opponent, leading to a draw.

kingside   This refers to the half of the board where the king is positioned—the e, f, g, and h files.

legal move   A move that is allowed by chess regulations. If a player cannot make any legal moves and a king is not in check, then a game is considered stalemated, resulting in a draw.

major pieces   The queen and the rooks because they have more power than the other (minor) pieces.

master A title given to players who achieve a United States Chess Federation (USCF) rating of 2200 or more.

mate A slang term for checkmate.

middlegame The second of three phases of a chess game, characterized by a great deal of strategizing and maneuvering.

miniature A game that takes place in a brief period of time.

minor pieces The bishops and knights are considered minor pieces because they are not as powerful as the queen or rooks (major pieces).

mobility Refers to the freedom of movement of each piece. If a player has an advantage in space, that means his pieces have greater mobility than his opponent's.

occupy A piece is said to occupy the square that it rests on. A queen or rook that controls a rank or file is said to occupy that file or rank, while a bishop is said to occupy a diagonal.

open file A vertical column of a chessboard that is unobstructed by pawns of either side.

opening The first of three phases of a chess game, usually constituting the first 10 to 15 moves in which a player castles and develops his pieces. There are several classic openings that chess students and experts alike study as guidance for their own games.

opening repertoire A set of openings that a player is prepared to play in advance of the game to give him an advantage.

openings A specific sequence of moves played by some of the best chess players over the last few hundred years or more that have proven effective in establishing the initiative in a game. There are over 1,000 recorded opening variations.

open position A position in which there are open files, usually resulting from the exchange of several pawns.

passed pawn A pawn that cannot be blocked from reaching its last rank by opposing pawns, thus putting it in a position to queen.

pin A pin is a tactical element in which by attacking one piece you are indirectly attacking a piece behind it. That makes the second piece vulnerable to capture if your opponent moves the first piece under attack (the pinned piece) out of the way. A pin is only valuable if the piece being indirectly attacked is the king or a more valuable piece than the attacking piece (the pinning piece).

plan A strategy that a player applies over the short or long term to reach an objective—to gain control over the center or checkmate an opposing king, for instance. Optimally, a player makes his moves based on a plan.

point count   A system which assigns value to each piece, making it possible for a player to decide whether to sacrifice or exchange a particular piece, depending on what can be obtained in exchange (material or positional advantage, for example.) In this system, the king is worth 0 points (because it is infinitely valuable and cannot be exchanged for any other piece), the queen = 9 points, the rook = 5 points, the bishop = 3 points, the knight = 3 points, and the pawn = 1 point.

promotion   This occurs when a pawn has reached its last rank and can be traded for a queen, bishop, knight, or rook of the same color.

queenside   The half of the board where the queen is positioned and which takes up the a, b, c, and d files.

rank   The eight horizontal rows of a chessboard that in algebraic notation are designated by a number (1-8).

rating   A number awarded by an official chess organization that indicates the strength of a player—the higher the number, the stronger the player.

resign   To surrender the game because of a hopeless position, often indicated by gently tipping over the king or saying the words, "I resign."

sacrifice   The act of giving up material for positional advantage. Sometimes sacrifices may only be temporary because the material loss can be quickly recovered.

skewer   The skewer is a tactical element that consists of an attack on an opponent's valuable piece that forces it to move. In the process, it leaves behind another piece that is vulnerable to capture.

stalemate   A stalemate occurs when one player has no legal moves to make, the king is not in check, and it is the player's turn to move. In this case the game is declared a draw.

strategy   The reasoning underlying a move, a series of moves, a plan, or even an idea.

tactic(s)   A move or series of moves that take advantage of short-term opportunities.

time control   A set number of moves that must be played in a certain amount of time.

trap   A move or series of moves that tricks an opponent into making a mistake or blunder.

zugzwang   A German word for a position in which whoever has the obligation to move will have no choice but to worsen his or her position. Unlike in other games where a player can say, "I pass," a chess player has to move.

APPENDIX B

Learning from Software and Playing Against a Chess Computer

You've probably read about how Garry Kasparov, top-ranked chess player in the world, lost a game to an IBM computer called Deeper Blue in the late '90s. But while computers make for powerful opponents, they also make for equally powerful teaching tools. In this appendix, you find out how you can learn about and play chess from a wide variety of software programs and test your skills against programs that not only feature games, but offer opportunities to analyze your moves (and mistakes) so that you can improve your play. Obviously, not every one of these programs is going to be right for you. Some programs are more appropriate for beginners, and others will be of interest only after you have more experience. No doubt many of these programs will undergo revisions and new ones will be coming onto the market. But the information in this hour will give you an idea where to start and what kind of adventures await you when you do.

How Can Chess Software Help Me?

Computer chess software can help all chess players, including the top chess professionals. There is software available that can teach you openings, middlegames, and endgames. There is also software that can help your tactical or positional skills. With the strength of today's chess software, it's as if you have a chess grandmaster or a chess professional sitting next to you, helping you—and best of all, he's ready to help you anytime you wish.

Even for the most sophisticated chess software, the cost is relatively reasonable, starting as low as $25. Most of these programs cost somewhere around $30–$60.

One of the most elaborate chess software packages on the market is ChessBase, a personal, stand-alone chess database that has become the standard throughout the world. Many people use ChessBase, whether it's the world champion or the amateur next door. It is the program of choice for players who love the game and want to know more about it.

With ChessBase, you can do the following:

- Enter moves, annotate and save games—including variations, text commentary, spoken comments, embedded pictures, soundtracks, and video sequences—and analyze positions with GM-strength modules Fritz and Crafty (both included).

- Retrieve games according to openings, players, and tournaments; generate tournament cross tables and full graphic statistics of players or openings; merge games on-the-fly into an opening tree; and generate a player's dossier containing all available information from the database.

- Find the new move in a game with one mouse click; generate a comprehensive openings report with main and critical lines, plans, and most important games; search for material distribution, positions, and maneuvers; and search for mates and stalemates.

- Classify games according to self-defined middle and endgame criteria, print games in superb DTP quality with diagrams and multiple columns, and much, much more.

The only thing that the software does not do is cook dinner for you. Maybe one day soon that will happen, too.

In addition, there are chess databases of more than two million games available for just a little more than $100. There are also many sources on the Internet where you can download up-to-date games for free.

With the available software on the market today, we believe any player who is serious about becoming a decent chess player can do so.

What Chess Software Is Right for Me?

Everyone has a different preference when it comes to chess training and playing software. Most of them, we believe, can help you. The following are some of the more popular training software, database management, and playing programs.

CHESSBASE 8.0

ChessBase is a personal, stand-alone chess database that has become the standard throughout the world. New features include:

- An explorer-style database browser
- Easy and direct access to the comprehensive ChessBase online database
- Freely configurable board and list window, new table notation for openings repertoire, and virtual sorting of database lists
- Optimal integration of the ChessBase analysis engine
- New 300% larger players' encyclopedia
- Print preview
- Automatic e-mail transmission of positions, games, or databases
- Management of team championships
- Intelligent search variations
- Improved search speed

(Source: www.chessbase.com)

MEGA DATABASE 2002

This annotated database contains more than 2 million games from the years 1530 to 2001 in the highest ChessBase quality standard. Of these, 45,000 games contain commentary from top players, with ChessBase opening classification and more than 54,000 key positions, direct access to players, tournaments, middlegame themes, and endgames.

(Source: www.chessbase.com)

CHESSBASE OPENING ENCYCLOPEDIA 2002

The ChessBase Opening Encyclopedia features the complete coverage of all opening sectors, offering an optimal start opening training. Many well-known specialists have made contributions in their field of expertise, such as Anand, Bareev, Dautov, Yusupov, Kasparov, Korchnoi, Nunn, and Ribli. For each of the 500 opening sectors, according to ECO standard, there is at least one opening survey, so the database is the ideal tool for building a complete opening repertoire.

(Source: www.chessbase.com)

FRITZ ENDGAME TURBO

(Nalimov Tablebases) The Fritz Endgame Turbo contains four database CDs with Nalimov tablebases. With the help of the Endgame Turbo, endgames with five or less pieces will be played dramatically better, because the programs can use the Endgame Turbo in their search.

System requirements: The Endgame Turbo works together with Fritz6, Nimzo7.32, Junior6, Hiarcs7.32, and as an analysis engine in ChessBase 7.0.

(Source: www.chessbase.com)

ENDGAME STUDY DATABASE 2000

Harold van der Heiden of the Netherlands is one of the most renowned connoisseurs of endgame studies of our day. His unique collection now contains more than 58,000 famous studies.

(Source: www.chessbase.com)

THE ABC OF ENDGAMES

Realizing the necessity of making yourself familiar with endgames, you will soon be confronted with a problem: where to start and where to finish? There is an abundance (maybe an overabundance) of material, and in reference books like the *Cheron* or *Averbahk*, the real basic endings are hard to find among the many exceptional positions.

But who tells you what information is crucial for all chess players and what constitutes only specialized knowledge for professionals? The answer is: the "ABC of Endgames." With a total number of 176 treated endgames, the material on the CD is definitely manageable. In addition, the 29 examples offered for study are considered indispensable.

These examples include classics such as "Lucena-positions," and "impotent couple" as well as practical hints for the surprisingly frequent endgame "rook + bishop vs. rock" situation. All these standard examples are including in ABC's small survey. And for those of you wishing to deepen your knowledge even further, you can access database texts with the relevant type of endgame, examples of which you can immediately call up.

(Source: www.chessbase.com)

CHESS ASSISTANT 6 (CA6)

Chess Assistant 6 is a tool for analyzing games (your own or games played by others), managing chess games and databases, playing chess on the Internet, viewing electronic texts in Chess Assistant format, playing chess against the computer, or publishing on the Internet.

(Source: http://store.convekta.com)

Chess Opening 2001

Detailed theoretical material covers all the 500 ECO indices (Staff of GMs and IMs contributing). It contains a database of 500,000 games played by the world's top players with records compiled up to January 1, 2001.

Chess Opening 2001 allows the player to perform searches, move along the Tree of positions, annotate games, print games and comments, and so on.

(Source: http://store.convekta.com)

Encyclopedia of Middlegame, Vol. I

Encyclopedia of Middlegame, Vol. I is a program designed by GM Alexander Kalinin to help students understand the ideas and strategies behind typical middlegame positions according to the openings they originate from. This program is intended for stronger players. Having no analogues among chess programs, Middlegame contains detailed material on two courses: typical structures of middlegame and playing technique for the most popular openings. Training material contains more than 600 examples and is subdivided into themes according to typical methods and ideas of playing.

(Source: http://store.convekta.com)

Encyclopedia of Middlegame II

Encyclopedia of Middlegame II is a program written by GM Alexander Kalinin. A CD contains a course titled Typical Plans and Methods in the Most Popular Openings.

The following openings are viewed:

- Sicilian Defense (Dragon, Najdorf, Paulsen variations)
- Ruy Lopez (Open variation, Exchanged Variation)
- King's Gambit
- Italian game
- Evans Gambit
- Pirc-Ufimtsev
- Alekhine's Defense
- Nimzo-Indian Defense
- Queen's-Indian Defense
- Queen's Gambit
- Modern Benoni

The program is not another Middlegame, Vol. I version but a completely new program based on different material.

(Source: http://store.convekta.com)

CHESS TACTICS FOR BEGINNERS

This program is based on a bestseller by the experienced coach Sergey Ivashchenko. It is intended for beginners, both children and adults. Exercises are arranged in five courses according to their increasing difficulty. Each course contains exercises for practice and test. The program includes positions from practical games, endgame studies, and training examples.

(Source: http://store.convekta.com)

STRATEGY 2.0

Designed by GM Alexander Kalinin to teach students strategy and positional play, Strategy 2.0 is a significantly expanded version of the original Strategy, containing not only more exercises but also many new lessons not present in the first edition.

This chess program presents 1800 instructive positions with 18 of the most important strategic themes such as the following:

- Advantage in development
- Advantage in space
- Attack on the king
- Attack on the queenside
- Weak squares
- Pawn structure
- Open files and diagonals
- Central squares
- Position of pieces
- Exchange
- Positional sacrifice
- Preventive tactics
- Isolated queen's pawn
- Hanging pawns
- The rule of two weaknesses

- Planning defense
- Counterattack

(Source: http://store.convekta.com)

MORE

There are many more database management and training software packages available, but the list we've provided here should be a good start.

As for chess playing software, you can pick any of the ones listed above in the chess playing software section of your local computer software store. All of the software is quite strong and can probably defeat 99 percent of human chess players.

HOW MUCH DOES IT COST?

The price of computer software changes quite rapidly. For the most current information or prices, there are many websites that you can check out. Here are some examples of a few popular sites. You can also check your local yellow pages.

ChessBase News: www.chessbase.com

Chess Express: www.chessexpress.com

ChessBase USA: www.chessbaseusa.com

Convekta Chess Store: store.convekta.com/shop_model.asp

The London Chess Centre: www.chesscenter.com

ChessCafe.com: www.chesscafe.com

Chess 4 Less: www.chess4less.com

U.S. Chess Online: www.shopuschess.org

Your Move Chess & Games: www.chessusa.com

DIFFERENT TYPES OF CHESS PLAYING SOFTWARE

With Pocket Fritz you can play chess on your Pocket PC anywhere and anytime you like, you can take a quick look at opening variations on your way to a tournament, or check out the most recent games of your opponent.

Pocket Fritz is the chess master in your shirt pocket. It may be small in size, but its playing strength is gigantic. It even managed to obtain a draw in the match against the world class

GMs Michael Adams and Peter Leko at the Chess Classic in Mainz 2001. Its performance rating was ELO 2505.

However, if you really set your mind to it, you can still beat Pocket Fritz. In case you make a terrible blunder, the built-in coach will help you. You can pick up the latest tactical lessons from the Internet and solve the problems on your way to work or school.

Pocket Fritz can do much more. For example, it will analyze games with you and save them in a database. What's more, if you connect your Pocket PC to the Internet (for example, through a cell phone), you have full access to the giant ChessBase Online Database, which contains almost two million games. Pocket Fritz will show you if the current position has ever occurred before and which moves were played.

(Source: www.chessbase.com)

Fritz 7

Fritz 7 is more than just a chess program; it is the key to a new world of chess. Fritz 7 connects you with chess enthusiasts in New York, London, Bombay, Sidney, or with your pal down the street. Visit the Fritz server where everyday is chess club day, all over the world, from morning to evening, or in the middle of the night.

With Fritz 7 and a normal Internet connection, you are exactly two clicks away from our chess server Playchess.com. It's a no-fuss connection. You can immediately start a blitz game, play a tournament, or simply watch and chat. You will also find the latest chess news, live coverage of international tournaments, and online training sessions. This is a new world of chess. You owe it to yourself.

(Source: www.chessbase.com)

HIARCS 8

The program HIARCS, written by Mark Uniacke of England, has been one of the world's top programs ever since it won the microcomputer world chess championship in 1993. HIARCS stands for "Higher Intelligence Auto Response Chess System." And indeed the distinguishing feature is that the author, like no other, uses a maximum of chess knowledge to increase the playing strength of his program.

The new version of HIARCS has been improved and enhanced in a number of areas, especially in its search algorithms and the implementation of concrete chess knowledge. The search tree has been further optimized and results in an increase in search depth of up to three ply in the middlegame. The maximum search depth is now 62 ply! This leads to substantially increased tactical power while at the same time the program maintains its active positional playing style.

Chess knowledge has always been the program's main strength. The improved search algorithms made it possible to implement even more advanced positional functions, especially in the areas of "typical pawn structures" and "dynamic evaluation of the center." HIARCS 8 evaluates important factors like weak squares, king's safety, piece exchanges, initiative, and king attack much more reliably than the predecessor versions.

(Source: www.chessbase.com)

SHREDDER 6

Shredder is the work of Stefan Meyer-Kahlen and has a history of very impressive results in computer chess tournaments. It has earned five official world championship titles.

Shredder comes with two separated interfaces. First, there is the full Fritz 7 GUI, including the latest "Playchess" server software that allows you to play against people all over the world. On the same CD-ROM, you also get Stefan Meyer-Kahlen's own Shredder user platform.

A tournament book optimized for the Shredder playing style, written by Sandro Necci is available, as well as complete tablebases for three- and four-piece endings. The Shredder engine runs under both interfaces with equal strength, and it can handle one or more processors (SMP). Under the Shredder GUI, you also have the Universal Chess Interface (UCI) and Winboard protocols that allow you to install a large number of professional and amateur engines.

Shredder also has a unique "Triple Brain" function, which allows you to run two engines in parallel, while a third module decides which analysis is better in the current situation. The Endgame Oracle gives you analytical tools that were never before available for all three, four, five and—theoretically—six piece endings.

Owners of Pocket Fritz will be interested in the option that allows you to convert Shredder opening books into Pocket Fritz readable format. Shredder also supports the intelligent electronic PC board made by DGT and TASC of Holland.

(Source: www.chessbase.com)

CHESSTIGER 14.0

Christoph Théron's ChessTiger is the shooting star among the chess engines. It has gained enormously in strength over the past few years as its impressive victories in several international tournaments have demonstrated—the Open Championship of Spain 1998 as well as the French Open Championships 1999 and 2000.

In autumn of 1999, ChessTiger entered the ranking list of chess programs (SSDF) and immediately topped the list. Apart from ChessTiger 14.0, the CD also contains GambitTiger 2.0.

GambitTiger is a particularly aggressive special version of ChessTiger that mercilessly applies its additional knowledge to attack the king. That's why GambitTiger often chooses moves that other programs would never play. Yet the success of this unconventional way of playing speaks for itself. In autumn of 2000, GambitTiger won the Dutch Open Championship by a long shot.

Recently GambitTiger showed its claws in the Linares of chess programs and came in second behind DeepFritz. In contrast to their direct predecessors, ChessTiger 14.0 and GambitTiger also take advantage of the endgame databases (tablebases) and support multivariation mode.

(Source: www.chessbase.com)

Junior 7.0

Junior7, written by Amir Ban and Shay Bushinsky from Israel, is the reigning Computer Chess World Champion—a title it won in Maastricht in August 2001, 8/9 (no loss)—two full points ahead of all its competition.

Junior's unique style is very human-like, often preferring positional advantages to material. Junior's first debut in the world of computer chess was in the 1995 world championships where it surprisingly shared third place together with Frenchchess and the Deep Blue proto-type. Two years later, Junior won the World Micro Computer Championship title held in Paris, November 1997.

In August 2000, its parallel version known as Deep Junior took part in the Super-GM tournament at Dortmund and went on to score 50 percent—a performance of 2703 ELO, beating among others super grandmaster Peter Leko of Hungary. This was the greatest achievement of a computer program in official chess tournament history. Among its notable tournament wins are Cadaqués 2000 and the Internet Computer Chess Championship 2002.

Experts all over the world are impressed by the ruthless attacking style of Junior. IM Hannu Wegner writes: "The latest version of Junior has clearly made tremendous progress in tactics and especially in the execution of brilliant kingside attacks." Garry Kasparov, the world's number one chess player, has often praised Junior as a valuable tool for analysis and selected to use it during one of his most important title matches.

(Source: www.chessbase.com)

Deep Junior 7.0—for Two or More Processors

Deep Junior 7.0 is the multiprocessor-capable version of Junior7 that will run on computers with one, two, or more processors. With more processors, it calculates much faster than on a single processor and plays stronger.

Nimzo 8

Nimzo is one of the world's top programs and has won a number of computer chess tournaments. It's now available in an improved version.

Highlights include a strongly improved engine, about 50 ELO points above the previous version, and an openings book extended and up to the latest theory. It allows you to play blindfold chess and offers endgame tablebases in RAM. In fact, Nimzo8 is the first program to keep tablebases in its memory so that they can be used in a quiescence search. Programming language is Che ++.

(Source: www.chessbase.com)

PocketGrandmaster

PocketGrandmaster is a fully featured and extremely strong chess-playing program for Pocket PCs running Pocket PC 2002/Windows CE.

PocketGrandmaster boasts a fully configurable board and simple yet far-reaching functions that allow it to work with game databases. The program enables game replay, includes a chess clock, offers an analysis mode for tutoring and problem solving, and even provides hints to help improve your game play!

PocketGrandmaster allows you to select among a variety of preconfigured levels, allows the creation of new, user-defined levels, and offers different playing modes for both tournament and blitz games.

PocketGrandmaster features an extremely strong chess engine and plays interesting and often aggressive chess. The engine is a successor of GromitChess, which finished 4th in the World Microcomputer Chess Championships 2001, winning the title of the 18th World Microcomputer Amateur Chess Champion.

(Source: www.pocketgrandmaster.com/english/index.html)

Chessmaster 8000

Selling over four million copies and winning numerous awards would be enough for most software programs, but since its launch over a decade ago, the Chessmaster series has remained the most dominant franchise in the history of chess software.

Chessmaster pioneered the use of Natural Language Advice, so that players could get tips for moves through simple vocal cues from the computer in easy-to-understand English.

This year's launch features:

- A revamped chess engine. It is the most powerful chess engine available on a personal computer, playing at grandmaster level at its top strength.
- Stunning new chess sets in new 16-bit graphics.
- An entire endgame course by International Master Josh Waitzkin. Using examples drawn from Josh's own tournament games, it's the equivalent of several books on the subject—and a lot more fun besides!
- Exclusive "Match the Masters" feature by noted chess author and teacher Bruce Pandolfini.
- An improved interface with new animated cursors.
- New Natural Language Advice specially aimed at kids.

(Source: www.chessmaster.com)

REBEL

Rebel is one of the strongest and most complete chess programs in the world. Rebel is famous for its playing strength but especially for its deep positional understanding. Therefore, the quality of the returned analysis is high and mostly reliable, factors that make Rebel flexible enough to play against humans as well as against other computer opponents.

Rebel, however, is not a chess product with bells and whistles that you turn off once you have seen them. Rebel is intended for the serious and professional chess player who wants the best. Rebel is known for being very user friendly, so much so that you hardly need the manual.

For first-time users, Rebel is easy to understand. It is famous for its build-in database with dazzling possibilities. Every version of Rebel is always released with a big opening book with the latest opening theory.

Rebel has many analysis options that allow you to review and assess your own (or grandmaster) games or favorite positions. Rebel will show you the places in games where mistakes were made. It also is known for many unique, extra, and useful features not found in other chess software.

(Source: www.rebel.nl)

WEBSITES FOR OTHER CHESS PLAYING PROGRAMS/SOFTWARE

KnightCap: samba.anu.edu.au/KnightCap

GromitChess: home.t-online.de/home/hobblefrank

Skaki Chess: home.att.net/~glazarou/skaki.htm

UruChess: www.puntadeleste.to/uruchess

Pharaon: www.fzibi.com/pharaon.htm

DarkThought: supertech.lcs.mit.edu/~heinz/dt

Steffen's Chess Page: www.jakob.at/steffen/hossa.html

Green Light Chess: www.7sun.com/chess

Power Chess 98: gamespot.com/gamespot/filters/products/0,11114,89745,00.html

GNU Project: www.gnu.org/software/chess/chess.html

Exchess: home.earthlink.net/~econerd/EXchess.html

ARK Angles: www.arkangles.com

Amyan Chess Program: www.geocities.com/zodiamoon/amyan

Omid's Computer Chess Website: www.cs.biu.ac.il/~davoudo

ChessPartner: www.lokasoft.nl/uk

GAMBIT-SOFT: www.gambitsoft.de

Purple Software: www.purplesoft.com

Comet: members.aol.com/utuerke/comet

International Computer Chess Association: http://www.cs.unimaas.nl/ICCA

APPENDIX C

Increasing Your Skills: Chess Books and Magazines

In this section, you can find out what books are most suited for your needs, skills, and experience in playing chess. Some of the books we've included in our recommended list are meant for beginners; others are intended for seasoned players who are interested in certain aspects of the game such as openings or middlegames. Some of these books are of special interest for those of you who want to know more about the history of the game and lives of the legendary chess champions. There are books here, too, that can serve as guides, taking you back to some of the groundbreaking games that are now considered classics. In addition, we've included a section—with a list of relevant websites—devoted to the most popular chess magazines and columnists who will be able to keep you up-to-date on the latest developments in the game.

WHAT CHESS BOOKS SHOULD YOU READ?

There are thousands of chess books out there. It is hard to know what is good and what is not. The following is a list of books we think can be helpful to your chess development.

Alexander Alekhine's Best Games by Alexander Alekhine and John Nunn. "Alekhine's games and writings inspired me from an early age," writes Garry Kasparov in the foreword to this book. "I fell in love with the rich complexity of his ideas at the chessboard. I hope readers of this book will feel similarly inspired by Alekhine's masterpieces."

Alexander Alekhine captivated the chess world with his dazzling combinative play. His genius has been a strong influence on every great player since, none more so than World Champion Garry Kasparov. This book contains a selection of the very best of Alekhine's annotations of his own games.

My Best Games of Chess by Vishy Anand. Crystal-clear explanations of grandmaster tactics and strategies from which players of all abilities can learn. Anand annotates the finest and most interesting games from his career. In this expanded edition by the official FIDE World Champion, he describes his best games and brings his career right up to date.

This book features Anand's detailed and entertaining commentaries of 57 of his best games, culminating with the victory over Alexi Shirov that clinched the FIDE World Championship. Anand's renowned ability to penetrate to the heart of complex positions comes over supremely well in his notes, which will amply repay careful study.

The book is full of flowing attacking masterpieces explained logically step-by-step, practical hints from a world champion, and puzzle positions to test your skill.

One Hundred Selected Games by Mikhail Botvinnik. The 100 outstanding games in this volume were chosen by Mikhail Botvinnik as the best games he played before becoming a world champion in 1948. They cover the period from his first big tournament to the International Tournament at Groningen in 1946.

Capablanca: A Compendium of Games, Notes, Articles, Correspondence, Illustrations, and Other Rare Archival Materials on the Cuban Chess Genius Jose Raul Capablanca, 1888–1942.

Although there are many books about the legendary Capablanca, most are concentrated on his main tournament and match games and have delved little into his life.

This volume—less a biography than a compilation of documents and data—repairs that imbalance by presenting a substantial amount of neglected (and fascinating) material. His letters, articles, notes, and games—nothing by or about Capablanca is unimportant.

The production values are great, and 26 historic photos are included. The documentation is accurate and authoritative; this book is essential for fans of Capablanca and all chess devotees.

Chess Fundamentals by José Capablanca. José Capablanca's classic instructional manual "Chess Fundamentals" first appeared in 1921, the year he defeated Emanuel Lasker for the world championship title. This handbook is packed with timeless advice on different aspects of practical play and illustrated by Capablanca's own games.

Logical Chess: Move by Move by Irving Chernev. One of the true chess classics; Chernev analyzes games move by move, while the reader absorbs the foundations of good chess play.

Modern Chess Openings, Fourteenth Edition, by Nick De Firmian. Why is *Modern Chess Openings* called "the chess player's bible"? Because since it was first published over a half-century ago, it has been one of the most trusted books in the chess world. It is considered among the world's most current and comprehensive one-volume reference works on chess openings, and it has been completely revised to reflect the changes and advances made in chess over the past eight years, including major tournament matches and published theoretical works.

The revision analyzes and evaluates current popular opening variations. Nick DeFirmian is one of America's leading grandmasters and a United States Chess Champion.

Judgment and Planning in Chess by Max Euwe. *Judgment and Planning in Chess* focuses on that crucial point in the chess game—eight or so moves into the game—where the opening development breaks off and the middlegame begins. This is precisely the part of the game that falls between opening books and middlegame books.

Dr. Euwe, one of the world's chess champions, studies a number of orthodox openings and positions from the point where the opening stage has come to an end. He describes the characteristics of the position reached, shows why one or the other side stands a better chance of winning, and gives a practical demonstration of the means by which the game can be brought to its logical conclusion.

"Written with all the expository power for which the ex-champion is famous," said the Times Literary Supplement. This well-known book is regarded as one of the standard manuals for developing players.

The Middlegame—Book I by Max Euwe and G. Kramer. Max Euwe was World Chess Champion in the 1930s, and he collaborated with International Master Kramer to write this great treatise on how to play chess middlegames. Book I of the series covers pawn formations and static features of the game of chess. Thousands of satisfied customers have made this one of the most popular books on chess middlegames. Completely re-edited and translated to algebraic notation in this 1994 edition.

Grandmaster Max Euwe, a Dutchman, became world champion of chess in the 1930s by defeating the great Alexander Alekhine. He later authored several famous books on chess with G. Kramer and later in his life was a beloved and greatly respected gentleman and scholar in the chess community.

The Middlegame—Book II by Max Euwe and G. Kramer. Book II of the series covers the dynamic features of the game of chess. This book also contains a fascinating section on the playing styles of the world's strongest players at the time of its first publication, as well as some interesting insights on the psychological aspects of the game of chess.

My 60 Memorable Games by Bobby Fischer. A collection of Bobby Fischer's best games, with his own annotations. Fischer was one of the all-time great players, but he is also very controversial. If you are a fan of Bobby Fischer, you will like this book. If you are not, you might have another opinion.

Bobby Fischer by Lou Hays. The book offers possibly the largest collection of games by one of the strongest players of all time. Special emphasis is given to his classic openings.

Kramnik: My Life and Games by Vladimir Kramnik. Kramnik annotates his best games and talks about himself, beginning with his unusual childhood. The book is illustrated and includes some photographs previously unpublished. This is the first book by Kramnik or about Kramnik.

How Karpov Wins by Edmar Mednis. From 1975 to 1985, Anatoly Karpov reigned as world champion of chess. He is a tough, deliberate player who seldom makes bad moves. But until the publication of this book, little was known about Karpov himself or his style of playing chess. It remained for International Grandmaster Edmar Mednis to analyze Karpov's style of play and to reveal something of the Russian champion's life and personality.

How to Play Good Opening Moves by Edmar Mednis. The reader learns how to select good moves based on three primary principles of opening moves.

My System: 21st Century Edition by Aron Nimzowitsch. Aron Nimzowitsch was one of the world's strongest chess grandmasters in the early part of the twentieth century. This is the all-time chess classic of Aron Nimzowitsch, now revised in 1991 to offer algebraic notation and updated so that it's readily comprehensible in English. It is one of the three or four best-selling chess books of all time with over 400 diagrams.

Chess Praxis by Aron Nimzowitsch & Ken Artz. This book is Grandmaster Aron Nimzowitsch's companion volume to *My System: 21st Century Edition*. This is one of the best-selling and classic chess books of all time. This book provides the fullest exposition of Nimzowitch's new analysis and theories; it is considered one of the dozen most important books ever written about chess.

Nunn's Chess Openings edited by John Nunn. *Nunn's Chess Openings* is the chess-player's new bible. This single volume covers all chess openings in detail. Garry Kasparov once said that a good book about openings should be written by a team of experts. This is that book. Four players, all known as outstanding experts in their fields, have contributed to this volume.

Understanding Chess Move by Move by John Nunn. John Nunn is one of the most highly regarded chess writers in the world. He has carefully selected 30 modern games to help the reader understand the most important aspects of chess and to illustrate modern chess principles in action.

Virtually every move is explained using words that everyone can understand. Jargon is avoided as much as possible. Almost all the examples are taken from the 1990s and show how key ideas are handled by the grandmasters of today.

The emphasis of this book is on general principles that readers will be able to use in their own games, and detailed analysis is only given where it is necessary. Each game contains many lessons, but to help guide the reader, the thirty games are grouped thematically into those highlighting openings, middlegames, and endgames.

Chess—5,334 Problems, Combinations & Games by Laszlo Polgar. A re-creation of chess tactics as they were taught to the Polgar sisters—Zsuzsa, Zsofia, and Judit—the most successful family of chess. (Zsuzsa won the Women's World Champion in 1996 and she was the first woman to earn the prestigious grandmaster title in 1992; Zsofia achieved one of the best ever results in an international tournament with a rating of over 2900 when she won in Rome; Judit is currently the number one-ranked woman player in the world and among the top 20 in the world overall.)

Chess Middlegames—77 Types in 4158 Positions by Laszlo Polgar. A re-creation of chess middlegames taught by the Polgar sisters.

Chess Endgames—171 Types in 4560 Positions by Laszlo Polgar. A re-creation of chess endgames taught by the Polgar sisters, the most successful family of chess.

The Complete Chess Player by Fred Reinfeld. A very good book that can help you understand chess better. It is written professionally and is quite easy to understand. The authors provide several examples with detailed explanations of the moves. Fred Reinfeld is an accomplished chess author with many classic books under his belt. His style is unique and his ability to make things easy to understand make him one of the better chess authors.

The Seven Deadly Chess Sins by Jonathan Rowson. Everyone loses chess games occasionally, but all too often we lose a game because of moves that, deep down, we knew were flawed. Why do we commit these chessboard sins? Are they the result of general misconceptions about chess and how it should be played? And how can we recognize the warning signs better?

In this thought-provoking and entertaining book, Jonathan Rowson investigates, in his inimitable style, the main reasons why chess-players sometimes go horribly astray, focusing on the underlying psychological pitfalls: thinking (unnecessary or erroneous); blinking (missing opportunities, lack of resolution); wanting (too much concern with the result of the game); materialism (lack of attention to nonmaterial factors); egoism (insufficient awareness of the opponent and his ideas); perfectionism (running short of time, trying too hard); looseness ("losing the plot", drifting, poor concentration).

Playing Winning Chess (Winning Chess Series) by Yasser Seirawan and Jeremy Silman. This is the first of a four-part series by International Grandmaster Yasser Seirawan that is addressed to the chess novice. He explains the game's development and basics of play, sharing stories of some of the wild and wonderful characters from chess history and the author's own experiences.

Playing Winning Chess offers a valuable introduction to chess—the moves, strategies, and philosophy of the game. The book teaches the Seirawan method: force, time, space, and pawn structure. The book contains dozens of instructive examples, question-and-answer sections, psychological hints, and sample games to teach players to strategize and play aggressively while having fun. Personal anecdotes make this especially readable:

Winning Chess Tactics by Yasser Seirawan and Jeremy Silman. This is the second in Seirawan's four volumes, taking the reader from the very basics of chess through appreciation of advanced play. This book is a fascinating and enlightening introduction to the details of chess from two internationally recognized players.

Chess players can now put the tactics of the world's chess legends to work for them, such as the double attack, the pin, the skewer, and more in every game. International Grand Master Yasser Seirawan and International Master Jeremy Silman teach players how to plan their strategy for the game from the very first move, think ahead through every obstruction their opponent will throw their way, and position themselves for effective combination and an endgame they've always dreamed of. Tacticians will enjoy the copious chessboard illustrations.

Winning Chess Strategies (Winning Chess Series) by Yasser Seirawan & Jeremy Silman. This is the third book in the series by International Grandmaster Yasser Seirawan, with Jeremy Silman. In chess, there is a class of moves that are appropriate for a given situation. Chess experts all tend to make the same type of move presented with the same set of circumstances, although variation in the actual moves is to be expected. Although no one move is best in any given situation, the authors argue what type of move to use is crucial. As most chess players know, learning strategy is key before progressing to the details of tactics.

Winning Chess Openings (Winning Chess Series) by Yasser Seirawan. The two greatest challenges for beginning chess players are not only to survive the opening phase, but also to choose appropriate attack and defense formations in the process. This book shows readers how to do both with either white or black pieces—a unique concept in chess books. Readers learn how to build a safe house for a king; eliminate losses of 10 moves or fewer;

and utilize elements such as time, force, space, and pawn structure. This book instructs readers how to develop an understanding of opening principles that can be applied to every game—and best of all, they won't have to memorize hundreds of opening lines to do it!

Winning Chess Endings (Winning Chess Series) by Yasser Seirawan. This book offers a good introduction to the moves, strategies, and philosophy of chess endings. The author uses his storytelling skills and technical knowledge to describe exactly when winning positions occurred in famous matches. His objective is for readers to develop an understanding of endgames that can be applied to any game they play.

Winning Chess Brilliancies (Winning Chess Series) by Yasser Seirawan. This book by International Grand Master Yasser Seirawan provides a move-by-move account of the best chess games of the last 25 years by the world's most formidable chess players. Seirawan serves as guide of these remarkable and historical chess games, providing insights and explanations of game play. Readers learn about dazzling chess combinations, devious strategies, and the occasionally ruthless blows that world champions inflict on their opponents—and inadvertently on themselves! The author makes these controversial games both entertaining and easy to understand.

The Amateur's Mind: Turning Chess Misconceptions into Chess Mastery by Jeremy Silman. Silman's method is based on understanding the imbalances inherent in every position. He analyzes seven different elements of the game: (1) material (2) minor pieces (3) pawn structure (4) files and weak squares (5) space (6) development and (7) initiative. An important contribution to a chess player's thinking about middlegames.

How to Reassess Your Chess Expanded, Third Edition, by Jeremy Silman. American IM Jeremy Silman has established himself as one of the premier instructional chess writers in the world today. One of his most popular books, it offers a complete step-by-step course designed to improve all phases of your game. Silman makes instructional strategies seem clear and logical.

Reassess Your Chess Workbook: How to Master Chess Imbalances by Jeremy Silman. Responding to mail from readers of his previous books, the author has created this workbook to enable players to test themselves and their levels of understanding of the game.

Part 1 looks at his system and considers some modern chess thinking techniques, Part 2 presents problems, and Part 3 offers solutions, in opening, middlegame, and endgame. Silman presents more than 100 problems to test.

The Small Encyclopedia of Chess Openings (Chess Informant). Chess Informant collects all chess openings in one book of more than 500 pages. Expand your opening repertoire with one of the most trusted publishers in chess literature.

Smyslov's 125 Selected Games by Vasily Smyslov. One hundred twenty-five of the most incredible annotated games you will ever see. This is a classic work by World Champion Vasily Smyslov. You can learn so much in so many areas from this book: openings, middlegames, tactics, endgames, and so on. In addition to being one of the best chess players of all time, this book puts Smyslov over the top as a chess author as well.

Grandmaster Secrets Endings by Andy Soltis. Most endgame books are difficult and boring for the majority of tournament players. Most of the books are not very helpful either. Soltis' book, however, is a rare exception, mixing instruction and entertainment. The layout shows a great deal of care, the many drawings are absolutely wonderful, and the actual print is easy on the eyes.

The subtitle of this book is "Everything you need to know about the endgame." Grandmaster Soltis did a good job in realizing this promise. This is one of the better endgame books ever written for the amateur chess player.

The Life and Games of Mikhail Tal by Mikhail Tal. A collection of great games by one of the most dynamic world champions ever. This is an autobiography with brilliantly annotated games and many photographs.

What makes Mikhail Tal's style so different from that of other top grandmasters shines through in this book. Tal's personality and unique thinking process makes this book a very good read.

The Game of Chess by Seigbart Tarrasch. A famous chess manual for 75 years, now re-edited for the modern chess player. Dr. Tarrasch was one of the original five grandmasters and one of the world's strongest players in the late nineteenth century. This manual teaches chess from the novice level to Class A/expert strength players. It fully covers tactics, endings, and opening play. Tarrasch's works have been revered and recommended by chess masters for generations.

USCF's Official Rules of Chess Rulebook, Fourth Edition. Complete rules of the chess game for both USCF and FIDE. A must-have book for every tournament player.

The Genius of Paul Morphy by Chris Ward. The brilliant American chess master Paul Morphy (1837-1884) had a dazzling gift for attacking play that is admired to the present day. Author Chris Ward undertakes a fascinating examination of Morphy's games and style of play, providing a revealing insight into how Morphy was able to dominate his contemporaries.

FERRETING OUT THE BEST CHESS MAGAZINES AND CHESS COLUMNS

The official chess magazine for the United States Chess Federation is *Chess Life*. It is probably the best-selling chess magazine in the U.S. *Chess Life* contains news, information, game analysis, chess training columns, tournament schedules, and many other chess-related items.

Regular members of the United States Chess Federation receive *Chess Life* at the beginning of every month, 12 times a year. If you are not a member, you can buy *Chess Life* in a bookstore like Barnes and Noble. For more information about *Chess Life*, visit www.uschess.org.

The United States Chess Federation also publishes the magazine *School Mates* for junior members. *School Mates* is sent to junior members quarterly. For more information about *School Mates*, visit www.uschess.org.

The Week in Chess is probably the best online chess source. Mark Crowther publishes it. The web site is http://www.chesscenter.com/twic/twic.html. It is definitely worth a look.

There are also many other informative chess magazines and sources available (both in print and online), in many different languages.

ONLINE CHESS MAGAZINES AND NEWSPAPERS

The following are some popular and useful chess information websites:

ChessWise: www.chesswise.com

New In Chess: www.newinchess.com

Chess columns by GM Robert Byrne: www.nytimes.com/diversions/chess

ChessCafe: www.chesscafe.com

SmartChess: www.smartchess.com/SmartChessOnline/default.htm

Chess Doctor: www.chessdoctor.com

Chess Mail: www.chessmail.com

London Chess Center: www.chess.co.uk/mag.html

British Chess Federation: www.bcf.ndirect.co.uk/chessmoves/index.html

Correspondence Chess: ccn.correspondencechess.com

Chess Publishing: www.chesspublishing.com

Washington Post chess column by GM Lubomir Kavalek: www.washingtonpost.com/wp-dyn/style/columns/chess

Mind Sports Worldwide: www.msoworld.com/mindzine/news/chess/chess.html

Chess World Magazine: www.fs2000.org/cwm

Kasparov Chess: www.kasparov.com

Ajedrez Integral: ajedrez.w3.to

Europe Echecs: www.europe-echecs.com

British Chess Magazine: www.bcmchess.co.uk

Chess Then and Now: www.psymon.com/chess

APPENDIX D

Chess Information and Resources

You can explore the world of chess through the Internet. We have compiled an exciting and fairly comprehensive list of organizations, academic institutions, and websites, all dedicated to chess. You can find school programs and tournaments especially intended to enhance academic excellence through chess. Many of these programs, by the way, serve disadvantaged kids. And if there isn't a chess club or organization near you, not to worry. All you need is an Internet connection, and you can access a cornucopia of chess information, find like-minded chess players by e-mail, and deepen your understanding of the game. Did you know that several colleges and universities in the U.S. offer chess scholarships, some worth thousands of dollars? And if you have any doubts as to how widespread chess is in the world, take a look at the list of national chess club websites—from Andorra and Argentina to Vietnam and Yugoslavia. However much their cultures or politics may differ, they have one thing in common: chess.

NATIONAL CHESS WEBSITES, RESOURCES, AND CHESS INFORMATION

ZSUZSA POLGAR'S OFFICIAL SITE

www.polgarchess.com or www.SusanPolgar.com

Official website of the Women's World Chess Champion Zsuzsa Polgar.

THE OFFICIAL SITE OF THE UNITED STATES CHESS FEDERATION

www.uschess.org

With the USCF memberships, you will receive

- An official membership card.
- The opportunity to earn a national rating!
- The opportunity to play correspondence chess by e-mail or regular mail.
- Big discounts on the best official chess equipment.

Memberships:

Adult Memberships:

- Full regular adult membership: $40, 1 Year, *Chess Life* (12 issues)
- 2-year full regular adult membership: $75, 2 Year, *Chess Life* (24 issues)
- 3-year full regular adult membership: $109, 3 Years, *Chess Life* (36 issues)
- Trial membership: $25, 6 months, *Chess Life* (6 issues) (new members only)
- Sustaining membership: $95, 1 Year, *Chess Life* (12 issues)
- Life membership: $850, *Chess Life* (12 issues/year)
- Internet regular membership: $32, No *Chess Life*

Scholastic/Youth Memberships:

- Scholastic membership: age 14 and under, $13, 1 year, *School Mates* (4 issues)
- 2-year Scholastic membership: age 14 and under, $25, 2 years, *School Mates* (8 issues)
- 3-year scholastic membership: age 14 and under, $36, 3 years, *School Mates* (12 issues)
- Youth membership: age 19 and under, $20, 1 year, *Chess Life* (12 issues)
- 2-year youth membership: age 19 and under, $38, 2 years, *Chess Life* (24 issues)
- 3-year youth membership: age 19 and under, $55, 3 years, *Chess Life* (36 issues)

Senior Memberships: Age 65 Plus:

- Senior membership: age 65 and older, $30, 1 year, *Chess Life* (12 issues)
- 2-year senior membership: age 65 and older, $56, 2 years, *Chess Life* (24 issues)
- 3-year senior membership: age 65 and older, $82, 3 years, *Chess Life* (36 issues)
- Senior life membership: age 65 and older, $425, *Chess Life* (12 issues/year)

For more information regarding USCF memberships, visit the official website of the USCF: http://www.uschess.org. Once you are there, click the "join" icon.

You can expect to receive your membership card within two weeks; your first issue of *Chess Life* in approximately six weeks (when you receive your first issue of *SchoolMates* depends on when you are ordering, as this publication is published every quarter). You can call the Membership department at the USCF: 1-845-562-8350, ext. 169 or e-mail: membership@uschess.org

THE NATIONAL SCHOLASTIC CHESS FOUNDATION (NSCF)

www.nscfchess.org
E-mail: nscf@nscfchess.org

NSCF is a not-for-profit foundation organized for educational purposes. Its teaching and tournament activities are conducted primarily in the New York City–Westchester County–Lower Connecticut area. The Foundation's objective is to provide a national forum for discussing chess teaching techniques for children. The NSCF promotes the study of chess as an educational tool in curricular classes and enrichment programs for elementary, middle, and high schools. Special emphasis is placed on using chess to assist children who come from socioeconomic backgrounds.

THE GREAT KNIGHTS CHESS CLUB

www.greatknights.org
E-mail: info@GreatKnights.org

The Great Knights
5507-10 Nesconset Highway #171
Mt. Sinai, NY 11766

Ira Leibowitz: (631) 928-1100

The Great Knights Chess Club is a not-for-profit corporation with about 200 members, dedicated for the advancement of children in Long Island in Grades K–12. Its ChessPLUS Program offers exposure to places and ideas that the children may not encounter in the course of their daily activities.

AMERICA'S FOUNDATION FOR CHESS

www.af4c.org

720 N. 35th Street
Seattle, WA 98103
Tel: (206) 675-0490

The Foundation describes its mission as one of strengthening the minds and character of young people by advancing chess in our schools and culture.

Its goals are:

- Bringing chess to children to develop strong critical thinking and interpersonal skills
- Increasing public awareness of the value of chess in our social fabric in order to reinforce the message that chess is fun and exciting
- Establishing the educational benefits of chess

America's Foundation for Chess annually hosts the U. S. Chess Championships and is developing a program to bring chess into the regular school curriculum in elementary and middle school grades.

CHESS PROMOTIONS, INC.

E-mail: BeatrizMarinello@aol.com
Tel: (917) 553-4522

This private organization currently runs chess programs in the following places:

- Horace Mann School Chess Program—New York City.
- New Castle Chess Program—Chappaqua, NY. The program includes teaching chess as part of the curriculum in two elementary schools and running an after-school chess program and monthly chess tournaments.
- Kids' Base Chess Program—Scarsdale, NY. The program includes an after-school chess program and Chess Tournaments.
- Yonkers Chess Program—Yonkers, NY. This program is impacting mostly inner-city children. Classes and tournaments at the Yonkers Police Athletic League are available at no cost for the children.

THE AMERICAN CHESS SCHOOL

E-mail: amchess@amchess.org

www.amchess.org

The American Chess School is best known for its Castle Chess Camp, USA Junior Chess Olympics, research on the educational benefits of chess, and workshops. The American Chess School organizes and operates chess camps, tournaments, scholastic chess clubs, leagues, exhibitions, workshops, classes, chess research, and other chess events.

Your Move Chess & Games

E-mail: icd@icdchess.com

www.ChessUSA.com

21 Walt Whitman Road
Huntington Station, NY 11746
Tel: 1-800-645-4710

ChessUSA boasts that it is America's largest chess store and that its website is the most visited chess shopping website on the Internet. It offers over 3,000 different items and the largest and widest selection of chess equipment. The store also hosts the Computer-Chess Club and the Chess Thinker's Forum on its website, which is used by over 18,000 members.

Chess City Magazine

www.chesscity.com

This magazine is dedicated to the amateur player. It has a huge range of instructional materials, opening analysis, book excerpts, photos, and historical documents. Articles feature anecdotes, politics, gossip, and inside coverage of major chess events dating back over two decades. Opening gambits and unorthodox openings get special attention.

Chess City offers a special section on chess technology, including Open Source web technology from the Caxton Project. Everything on the site is free.

The Southern California Chess Federation (SCCF)

E-mail: randallhough@yahoo.com

www.geocities.com/Colosseum/Field/8184

P.O. Box 205
Monterey Park, CA 91754

Tel: (626) 282-7412

SCCF is devoted to creating more opportunities for tournament chess play, and to promoting chess generally. The Federation publishes *Rank & File* magazine six times a year. Dues are $12/year, $7.50 for juniors under 19.

CHESS DIGEST

www.chessdigest.com

Chess Digest began as a hobby magazine business in 1962 in Dallas, Texas. Although it no longer publishes magazines, Chess Digest, Inc. has grown into a major chess book publisher and supplier with over 2,000 different chess titles from both the U.S. and Europe. Chess Digest, Inc. is still a family owned and operated business.

THE U.S. CHESS CENTER

www.chessctr.org

1501 M Street, NW
Washington, D.C. 20005

(202) 857-4922

The U.S. Chess Center teaches chess to children, especially those from the inner city, as a means of improving their academic and social skills. The Center offers a wide range of classes and activities, including tournaments for children and adults, and also has a small gift shop that sells chess equipment and books. The Center staff teaches chess at schools during the school day, runs after-school chess clubs, and offers classes at its headquarters in downtown Washington.

CONTINENTAL CHESS

www.chesstour.com

Continental Chess has organized tournaments throughout the U.S. since the 1960s. The tournaments are open to players of all ages, from grandmasters to beginners. Most tournaments include sections in which less experienced players play only each other. This is not a membership organization, although it is affiliated with the U.S. Chess Federation. Participants in its events are awarded USCF ratings and can obtain USCF membership as well. Future events are planned in California, Colorado, Connecticut, Florida, Illinois, Iowa, Massachusetts, Nevada, New York, Ohio, Pennsylvania, Vermont, and Washington D.C. Information about tournaments, dates, and locations can be found at www.ChessCalendar.com. There is no fee to observe any tournament.

FRED WILSON'S CHESS BOOKS

E-mail: fred@fredwilsonchess.com

www.fredwilsonchess.com

80 East 11th Street
New York, New York 10003
(212) 533-6381
Hours: Monday through Saturday 12–7

Fred Wilson's is a specialty bookstore, dealing mostly in out-of-print chess literature and periodicals. Children's chess classes are available through the store, and the store sponsors a chess camp at the Friends Seminary.

MARSHALL CHESS CLUB

www.marshallchessclub.org

23 West 10th Street
New York, NY 10011
(212) 477-3716
A not-for-profit membership club.

Membership Rates:

- NYC Resident: $275/year or $160 for 6 months
- Scholastic/Junior (Under 20): $105/year
- Trial Membership: $80 for 3 months
- Patron Membership: $500/year
- Senior (annual only): $160/year
- National Master $150
- FIDE Master $100
- International Master $50
- Nonresident (living over 50 miles away): $140/year or $80/6 months
- Associate (Living greater than 250 miles away): $80
- Student (full-time; under 26 years old): $140/year or $80/6 months

UNITED STATES BRAILLE CHESS ASSOCIATION

www.crisscrosstech.com/usbca

NEWS AND VIEWS ABOUT THE U.S. CHESS FEDERATION AND AMERICAN CHESS

www.chessnews.org

COLLEGES OFFERING CHESS SCHOLARSHIPS

Florida:

- Harriet L. Wilkes Honors College of Florida Atlantic University ($500 yearly scholarship).

Louisiana:

- Louisiana State University in Baton Rouge.

Maryland:

- The University of Maryland at Baltimore offers three types of four-year chess scholarships.

Mississippi:

- Ole Miss in Oxford offers two $500 scholarships for the top girl and top boy winners of the Dexter Visits the 2nd Tiger Scholastic Chess Tournament.
- Mississippi State University in Starkville offers two $500 scholarships for the top boy and girl chess players at the Mississippi State Chess Championships for 2002 and 2003.
- Jackson State University in Jackson offers two $500 scholarships for the top boy and girl chess players at the Mississippi State Chess Championships for 2002 and 2003. And yes, they get to choose their college!

Oklahoma:

- Rose State College in Oklahoma.

Rhode Island:

- Rhode Island College.

Tennessee:

- Tennessee Technical University (4 years valued at $12,000).

Texas:

- University of Texas—Dallas Academic Excellence Scholarship—waiver of all tuition and mandatory fees plus $1000 per year toward housing for each of 4 years. Scholarship will be upgraded if student has an excellent academic record. Approximate value $18,000+.

  www.utdallas.edu/orgs/chess
- Texas A&M University—Kingsville Housing Scholarship—this is a four-year scholarship and is valued at $7,500.

- University of Texas—Brownsville President's Chess Scholarship—UTB will offer two four-year scholarships to top students in South Texas. These scholarships will include tuition, books, and fees with a value of over $10,000 each.

- Southwest Texas State University. San Marcos Optimist International Scholarship— $1,000.

- Del Mar College President's Chess Scholarship—A two-year scholarship to include tuition, books, and fees with a value of over $4,000 for a student within the local five-county area.

- Incarnate Word Academy, Corpus Christi President's Award—one semester scholarship for a boy or girl entering sixth through eighth grade for the 2002–2003 school year with a value of $2,500.

(Source: www.USChess.org)

INTERNATIONAL CHESS WEBSITES

INTERNATIONAL CHESS CORRESPONDENCE FEDERATION

www.iccf.com

The International Chess Correspondence Federation (ICCF) is the official worldwide organization for correspondence chess, played by post and other forms of transmission (for example, fax and e-mail). ICCF provides a wide variety of tournaments and services. Its mission is to "organize, develop, and promote the study and practice of international correspondence chess … to enhance friendship and harmony amongst the peoples of the world, according to our motto 'Amici Sumus' (we are friends)."

WORLD CORRESPONDENCE CHESS FEDERATION

http://www.ewccf.com/

The World Correspondence Chess Federation (WCCF) offers opportunities to find other e-mail chess players and a variety of chess events and tournaments via e-mail. Use of the site is free.

WORLD BLITZ CHESS ASSOCIATION

http://hometown.aol.com/wbcablitz/main.html

Compare your ability with Kasparov, Dlugy, Browne, Anand, Timman, Karpov, Seirawan, Ehlvest, Korchnoi, and many others …. You will receive an official International Blitz Rating.

A subscription to *Blitz Chess*, the only magazine in the world covering blitz chess, is available through the site, which features in-depth coverage of major events and even chess humor. Affiliates may hold rated events and receive free listings for their events in the magazine.

MARK CROWTHER'S WEEKLY NEWS COLUMN

www.chesscenter.com/twic/twic.html

Mark Crowther's weekly news column on international chess tournaments includes many game scores and is one of the best websites for worldwide chess information.

OTHER INTERNATIONAL CHESS WEBSITES

Andorra Chess Federation
http://www.feva.ad

Local Argentine Chess Federation
www.ajedrezbsas.org.ar

Armenian Chess Federation
www.armchess.am

Australian Chess Federation
www.auschess.org.au

Austrian Chess Federation
www.chess.at

Chess Federation of the Republic
Bashkortostan (West Russian republic)
chess.ufanet.ru

Barbados Chess Federation
barbados.org/chess

Belgium Chess Federation
www.ping.be/dwarrelwind/kbsb

Belgrade Chess Federation
www.beochess.org.yu

Bermuda Chess Association
www.bermuda.bm/chess

Brazilian Chess Federation
www.cbx.org.br

British Chess Federation
www.bcf.org.uk/index.html

British Columbia Chess Federation
www.chess.bc.ca/index.html

British Federation for Correspondence Chess
www.echess.org.uk

Brunei Chess Federation
www.bruneichess.com

Bulgarian Chess Federation
www.chessbg.com

Canadian Correspondence Chess
Association
correspondencechess.com/ccca/index.htm

Chess Federation of Canada
www.chess.ca

Colombian Chess News
www.gimnasio-moderno.edu.co/ajedrezgm/indexaj.htm

Croatian Chess Federation
www.crochess.com

Chess Federation of Northern Cyprus
www.feva.ad

Czech Chess Federation
www.chess.cz

Danish Chess Federation
www.dsu.dk

Estonian Chess Federation
www.maleliit.ee

European Chess Union
www.eurochess.org

The Faroese Chess Federation
www.faroechess.com

French Chess Federation
www.echecs.asso.fr

Central Chess Federation of Finland
www.kolumbus.fi/shakkiliitto

German Chess Federation
www.schachbund.de

Georgian Chess Federation
www.gcf.org.ge

Hungarian Chess Federation
www.chess.hu

Chess Federation of Islamic Republic of Iran
www.iranchess.com

Official Website of the Irish Chess Union
homepage.eircom.net/~acad

Italian Chess Federation
www.infcom.it/fsi

Jamaican Chess Federation
www.jamaicachess.com

Japan Chess Federation
jca-chess.com

Korea Chess Club
www.koreachess.org

Chess Federation of Liechtenstein
www.supra.net/schach

Lithuanian Chess Federation
www.chess.lt

Homepage of the Luxembourg Chess Club
www.gambit.lu

Macau Chess Association
www.unitel.net/chessmacau

Malta Chess Federation
www.kemmunet.net.mt/chessmalta

Mexican Chess Federation
www.galeon.com/fenamac

Netherlands Chess Federation
www.schaakbond.nl

New Zealand Chess Federation
ourworld.compuserve.com/homepages/
nzchess

Chess Federation of Paraguay
www.quanta.com.py/feparaj/index.htm

Portugal Chess Association
www.apmx.pt

Friends of the National Chess Federation
of the Philippines
www.philippinechess.com

Portugal Chess Federation
www.fpx.pt

Scottish Chess Federation
www.scottishchess.com

Scottish Correspondence Chess
Association
www.users.globalnet.co.uk/~scca

Slovak Chess Federation
www.chess.sk

Chess Federation of Slovenia
www.sah-zveza.si/index.asp

Chess South Africa
www.ccza.com/Chessa/index.htm

Swiss Chess Federation
www.schachbund.ch

Tasmanian Chess Federation
www.tased.edu.au/tasonline/taschess

Turkish Chess Federation
www.tsf.org.tr

Chess in Vietnam
www.vietnamchess.com

Yugoslavia Chess Federation
www.geocities.com/yugchessfed/
YUGhomepage.html

APPENDIX E

Exercise Answers for Hours 15, 23, and 24

This appendix contains the answers to the exercises in Hours 15, 23, and 24. But before you look here, try to work out the solutions yourself!

HOUR 15

1. 1. Qd2xh6#
2. 1. Ra6xh6#
3. 1. Ra1xa6#
4. 1. Qf1xa6#
5. 1. Ne5-f7+ fork, wins the black queen on d6
6. 1. f2-f4 forks the black queen on e5 and the rook on g5
7. 1. Bg4-e6+ fork, checking the king and attacking the queen on d5
8. 1. Re2-e8+ fork, checking the king and attacking the queen on d8
9. 1. Bc2-e4 skewer, winning the rook on a8
10. 1. Rc1-d1 skewer, winning the rook on d8
11. 1. Qg3-c3+ skewer, winning the queen on h8
12. 1. Ra2-d2+ skewer, winning the rook on d8
13. 1. Ba4-e8+ discovered check, winning the queen on g6
14. 1. Ne3-c4+ discovered check, winning the queen on a5
15. 1. a5xb6#

16. 1. Rd4-d6+ discovered check, winning the queen on c6

17. 1. Rh8-h7 putting black in zugzwang   1... Kh5-h4   2. Rh7xh6#

18. 1. Kd7-c8 putting black in zugzwang   1... Na8-c7   2. Kc8xc7 Ka7-a8   3. Kc7xb6 with a winning advantage for white

19. 1. Rg3-f3 Kh2-h1   2. Rf3-h3#

20. 1.Kb3-a3 Kb1-a1   2. Rc3-c1# (or 1. Rc3-c2 Kb1-a1   2. Rc2-c1#)

Hour 23

1. 1. Rf3-h3#

2. 1. Re6-e8#

3. 1. Ke7-f7# Kh8-h7   2. Rg5-h5#

4. 1. Kb5-b6 Ka8-b8   2. Rh1-h8#

5. 1. Nf5-g7#

6. 1. Nc5-b3#

7. 1. Nd6-f7#

8. 1. Nh5-f6#

9. 1. Bh7-e4#

10. 1. Ra1-a8#

11. 1. Rg2-g1# (or 1. Rg2-h2#)

12. 1. Re4-a4#

13. 1. Bg8-d5#

14. 1... Nh5-g3#

15. 1. Bf8-g7#

16. 1. Ne1-c2#

17. 1. Bb1-e4#

18. 1. Bf8-g7#

19. 1. Be2-f3#

20. 1. Bh6-g7#

21. 1. Qd3-a3# or Qd3-a6#

22. 1. Qa6-b7#

23. 1. Qg1-g7#

24. 1. Qd2-g2#

25. 1. Ka6-a7 followed by 2. b6-b7 3. b7-b8(Q)

26. 1. Kd6-e6 Ke8-f8 2. f6-f7 Kf8-g7 3. Ke6-e7 followed by 4. f7-f8(Q)

27. 1. Kf6-f7 followed by 2. e6-e7 3. e7-e8(Q)

28. 1. Ke6-d7 followed by 2. e5-e6 3. e6-e7 4. e7-e8(Q)

29. 1... c2-c1(N)#

30. 1. h7-h8(B)# (or 1.h7-h8(Q)#)

31. 1. g6-g7#

32. 1. g7-g8(N)#

HOUR 24

TEST 1

1. 1. Qd4-a7#

2. 1. d2-d4#

3. 1. Qh6xh7#

4. 1. Qa5-a7#

5. 1. Qf6-g7#

6. 1. b6-b7#

7. 1. Nd4-c6#

8. 1. Qa3-e7#

9. 1. Ba7xd4#

10. 1. Qh3-c8#

11. 1. Ra4-g4#

12. 1. Nd5-f4#

TEST 2

1. 1. Bc2-e4#

2. 1. Nc4-b6#

3. 1... Qh3-g2#

4. 1... Qc3-a1#

5. 1. d4-d5#

6. 1. Ne4-c5#

7. 1. d7-d8(N)#

8. 1. Ne4-f6#

9. 1. Ke1-e2#

10. 1. Kc6-c7#

11. 1. Bc4-e6#

12. 1. Rc7-c8#

Test 3

1. 1. Ne5-f7+

2. 1. Nd4-e6+

3. 1. Rc1-f1+

4. 1. Bd4-c5+

5. 1... Nb8-c6

6. 1. Bb6-c7+

7. 1. e7-e8(Q) or (R)#

8. 1. Qd2-d4+

9. 1. c5-c6+

10. 1. Bb3xd5+

11. 1. Nf7-g5+

12. 1. Qc2-h7+

Test 4

1. 1. Rf2-f7+ Ke7-e8   2. Qd5-d7#

2. 1. Re2-b2+ Kb6-a7   2. Qc4-a2# (or 2. Qc4-a4#)

3. 1. Qd4-a7+ Kb8-c8   2. Qa7-a8#

4. 1. Re4-e7+ Kh7-h8   2. Rd1-d8#

5. 1. Ne4-f6+ Kg8-h8   2. Rd7xh7#

6. 1. Bc2-e4+ Kb7-b8   2. Ra1-a8#

7. 1. f5-f6 c2-c1(Q)   2. f6-f7#

8. 1. Bd2-g5+ Kd8-e8   2. Rd1-d8# (if 1... Kd8-c7   2. Bg5-d8#)

9. 1. Ne4-f6+ Kh7-h8   2. Ne5-g6#

10. 1. Rc1-c8+ Ra8xc8   2. Qg4xc8# (or 1. Qg4-c8+ Ra8xc8   2. Rc1xc8#)

11. 1. Qf3-a8+ Kg8-g7   2. Qa8-h8#

12. 1. Bc2-h7+ Kg8-h8   2. Nd6xf7#

TEST 5

1. 1. Bh4-f6+ Kh8-g8   2. Rh1-h8#

2. 1... Qa5xa2+   2. Qc4xa2 Nb4-c2#

3. 1. Qd1-h5+ Rh6xh5   2. Bd3-g6#

4. 1... Nf5-g3+   2. h2xg3 Re5-h5#

5. 1. Qf3xc6+ b7xc6   2. Bc4-a6#

6. 1. Nh4-g6+ Kh8-g8   2. Bf3-d5#

7. 1. Qc4-g8+ Ne7xg8   2. Re3xe8#

8. 1... Nh5-g3+   2. Kh1-g1 Nf4-h3#

9. 1. Qf4-e5+ Kd5xe5   2. Rc1-c5# (If 1... Bf6xe5 2. Ng2xe3# If 1... Re6xe5   2. Ng2-f4#)

10. 1. Nd5xb6+ Ka8-b8   2. Nb4-a6#

11. 1. Nh3-f4+ e5xf4   2. Nh5xf4# (or 1. Nh5-f4+ e5xf4   2. Nh3xf4#)

12. 1. Rb7xe7+ Ke8-f8   2. Ne5-g6#

APPENDIX F
Quiz Answers

Hour 1

1. True
2. False
3. False
4. True
5. True

6. False
7. True
8. False
9. True
10. True

Hour 2

1. True
2. b
3. True
4. True
5. a

6. a
7. c
8. True
9. a
10. False

Hour 3

1. a
2. c
3. True
4. True
5. True

6. True
7. c
8. a
9. True
10. False

Hour 4

1. a
2. c
3. True
4. b
5. True

6. d
7. d
8. b
9. True
10. c

Hour 5

1.	False	6.	True
2.	True	7.	False
3.	a	8.	True
4.	d	9.	True
5.	c	10.	a

Hour 6

1.	c	6.	True
2.	c	7.	c
3.	a	8.	b
4.	a	9.	True
5.	c	10.	d

Hour 7

1.	b	6.	c
2.	True	7.	c
3.	d	8.	True
4.	True	9.	True
5.	True	10.	False

Hour 8

1.	True	6.	True
2.	True	7.	False
3.	True	8.	c
4.	c	9.	a
5.	a	10.	d

Hour 9

1. False
2. False
3. True
4. d
5. True

6. d
7. b
8. False
9. True
10. True

Hour 10

1. False
2. a
3. True
4. False
5. c

6. b
7. d
8. True
9. a
10. True

Hour 11

1. True
2. False
3. True
4. c
5. d

6. True
7. False
8. b
9. a
10. True

Hour 12

1. False
2. True
3. False
4. False
5. c

6. d
7. d
8. True
9. True
10. False

HOUR 13

1. False
2. True
3. c
4. False
5. True
6. True
7. True
8. False
9. False
10. c

HOUR 14

1. True
2. a
3. b
4. b
5. c
6. True
7. True
8. False
9. True
10. d

HOUR 15

1. True
2. a
3. c
4. d
5. d
6. False
7. True
8. False
9. False
10. a

HOUR 16

1. False
2. c
3. False
4. True
5. b
6. a
7. d
8. c
9. False
10. True

HOUR 17

1. True	6. b
2. True	7. d
3. False	8. False
4. a	9. False
5. d	10. b

HOUR 18

1. True	6. True
2. True	7. False
3. a	8. True
4. b	9. True
5. True	10. a

HOUR 19

1. True	6. True
2. True	7. c
3. False	8. True
4. True	9. True
5. c	10. True

HOUR 20

1. a	6. a
2. c	7. a
3. True	8. b
4. False	9. b
5. b	10. c

Hour 21

1. True
2. c
3. True
4. c
5. a
6. False
7. True
8. True
9. True
10. True

Hour 22

1. True
2. c
3. c
4. b
5. False
6. True
7. False
8. True
9. a
10. True

Hour 23

1. False
2. True
3. b
4. False
5. True
6. True
7. True
8. False
9. True
10. d

Hour 24

1. False
2. c
3. c
4. b
5. True
6. True
7. True
8. True
9. True
10. True

Index

U

V

W - X - Y - Z